Cover design by Sheri McDonald

Book design by Sheri McDonald

Sheri McDonald, Lifelike Dolls Magazine
Visit the Lifelike Dolls website at www.LIfelikeDollsMag.com

Printed in the United States of America

First Printing: November 2010

ISBN #: 978-0-557-63985-4

Lifelike Dolls Magazine focuses on artist dolls made and collected around the world. In each issue, tutorials are found for creating or improving various types of artist dolls.

This book is a compilation of tutorials and patterns found in Lifelike Dolls Magazine in 2009 and 2010.

DOLL TUTORIALS

REBORN DOLL TUTORIALS

Page

TUTORIALS FOR SCULPTED DOLLS

Page

MISCELLANEOUS DOLL TUTORIALS

Page

PATTERNS

KNITTED PATTERNS

Page

CROCHET PATTERNS

Page

SEWING PROJECTS

Page

OTHER

Page

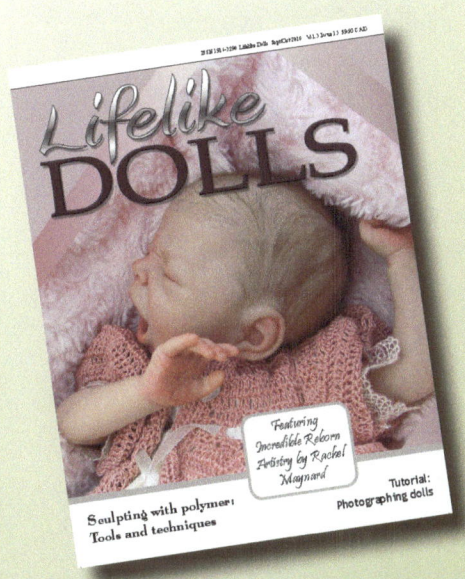

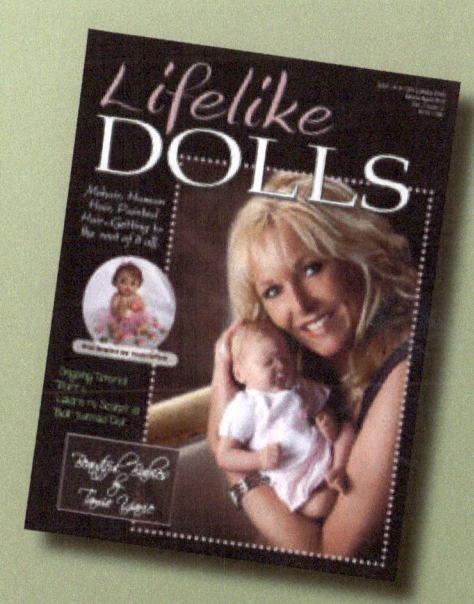

Rooting Lashes on an Open Eye Doll

1

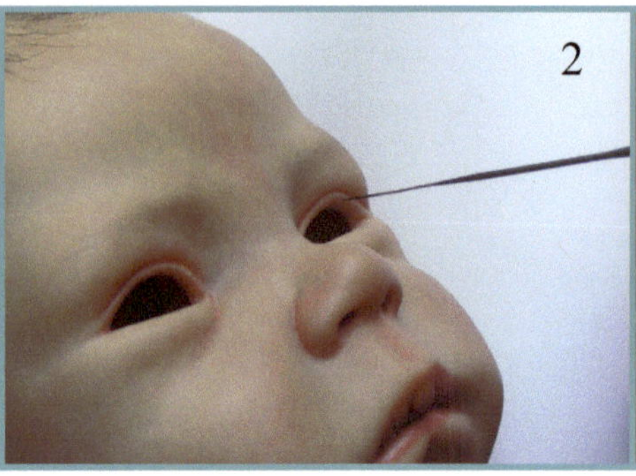
2

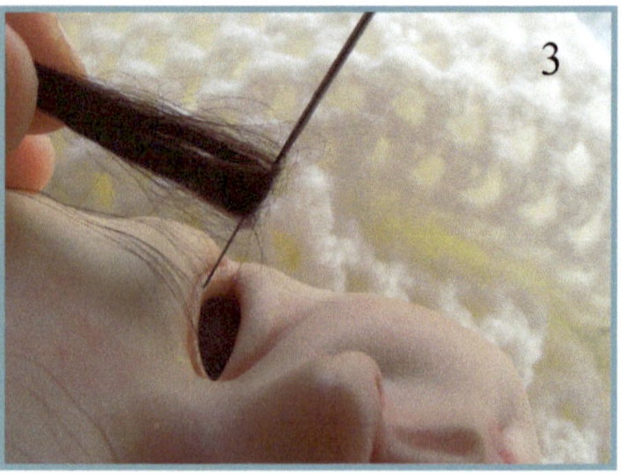
3

Before you start to root your lashes make sure that you have cut the back of the eye sockets ready for inserting the eyes.

1. Take a lock of mohair in your chosen colours and fold it in half to make a loop. (see pic 1)
2. You need to push the hair into the vinyl in the outer edge of the lid. Have a look at baby photos to get an idea of where they should sit. If you push the needle in a roughly 90degrees to the eyelid you should get nicely placed lashes. (See pic 2)
3. Put your needle through the loop of hair and get the tip of your needle into place on your eyelid, then drop the loop of hair down towards the tip of the needle and push the needle through the vinyl. (see pic 3 and 4)
4. Each hair will double over into 2 lashes, so its best to make sure you're using fine mohair so that the lashes don't look too thick. If you accidentally root too many hairs, use some tweezers to pull out the extra hairs. (see pic 5)
5. Continue to root across the eyelid, if you want thicker lashes then root close together, and for more wispy lashes root further apart. (see pic 6)
6. Once you have finished rooting your lashes, dampen your finger with water and slick the hair up against the forehead. (see pic 7)

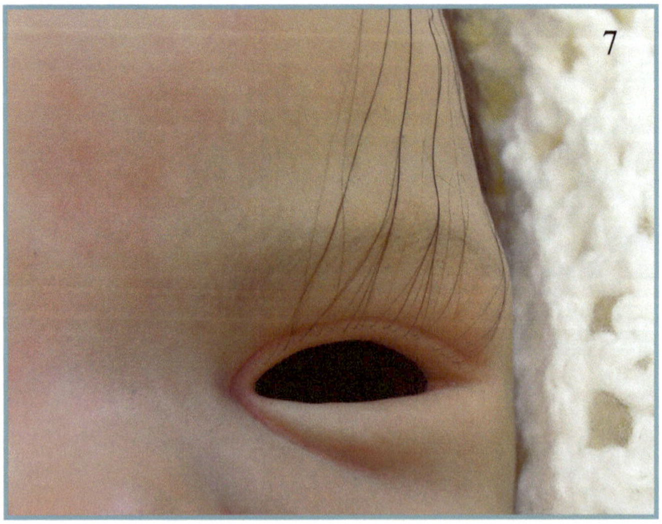
7

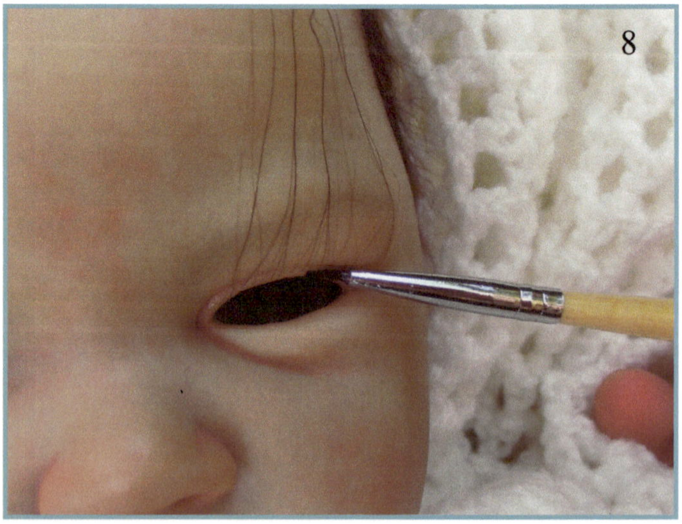
8

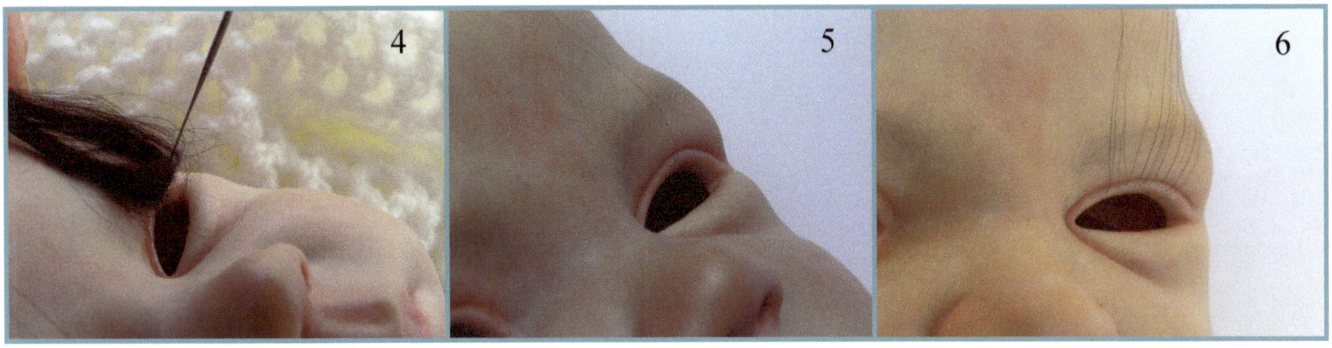

7. Take a small amount of PVA glue (E600 is too thick for lashes) and using a small paint brush glue the lashes to the back of the eye lid. You can do this through the front of the eye or by going in through the neck ring, whichever you find easier. I usually put the glue in from the front and then use my finger to smear it around the eye socket to make sure all the hairs have been covered.
8. Whilst waiting for the glue to dry and while the hair is still slicked to the forehead, you can use a tiny amount of paper glaze (baby tears) across the underside of the eyelid, if you spread it so that it just touches the rooted ends of the lashes, it will help keep the lashes in a lovely position. (see pic 8)
9. Once the glue has had time to dry, and the hair that was slicked upwards has also dried, its time to insert you chosen eyes.
10. After inserting the eyes it's time to trim the lashes. I use spring scissors which are usually used for fly fishing, because the tips of the scissors are so tiny I am able to trim each hair individually making the lashes look wispy and realistic. You should find that because the hair was dampened and pulled upwards your lashes should be set so that they stay upwards. (see pic 9 and 10)

by Rachel Maynard, Precious Little Babies
www.preciouslittlebabies.co.uk

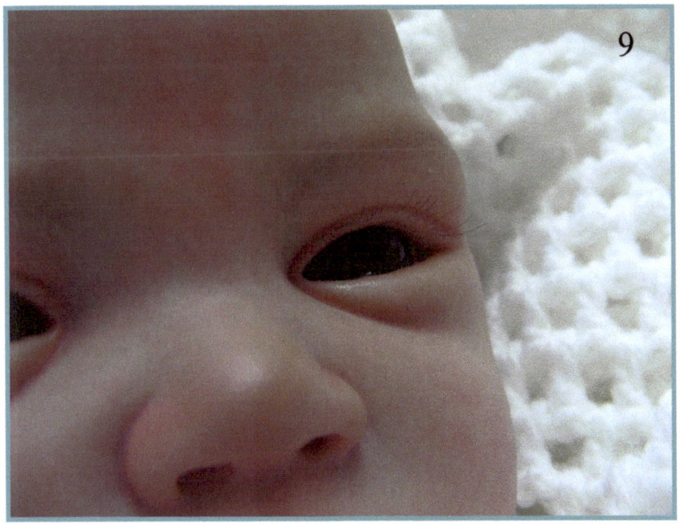

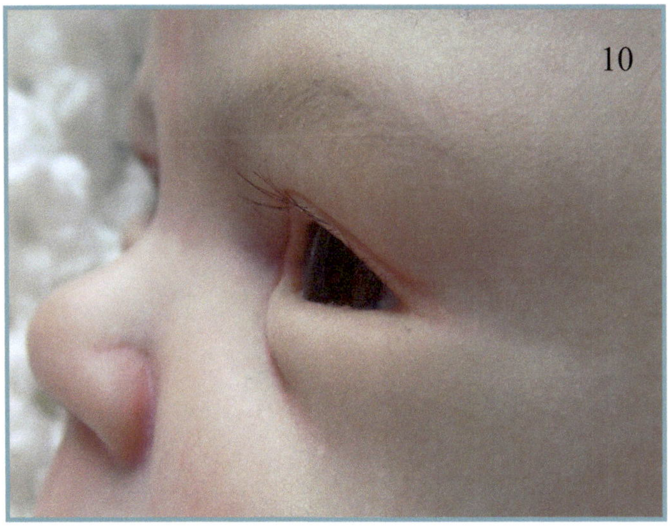

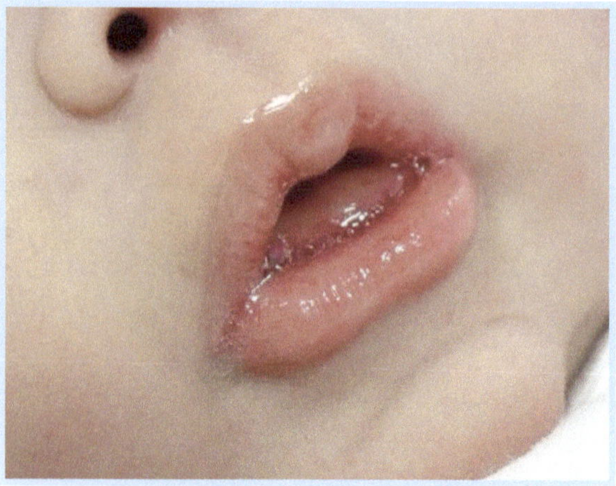

Making Spit Bubbles

by Debbie Henshaw

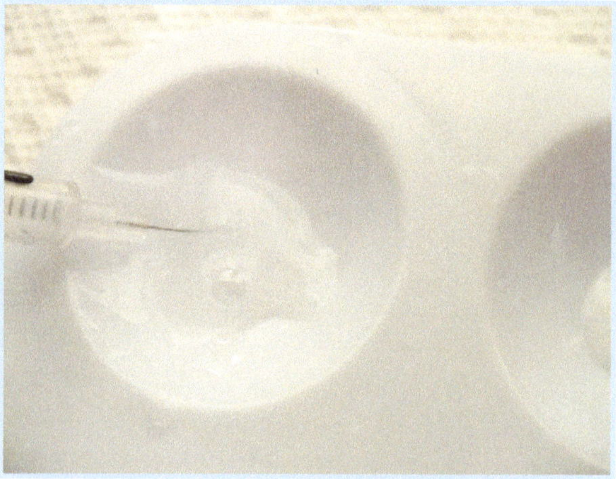

Spit bubbles are the hottest thing on the market right now~giggle giggle~and not quite so easy to make!

My favorite way to make them is to shake up a FRESH bottle of Alene's Paper Glaze (found at Michael's or online), untwist and remove the cap and let it rest elevated. Bubbles will form inside the cap. (for the sake of photography, I shook the bottle, poured some in a dish and used my syringe to create more bubbles).

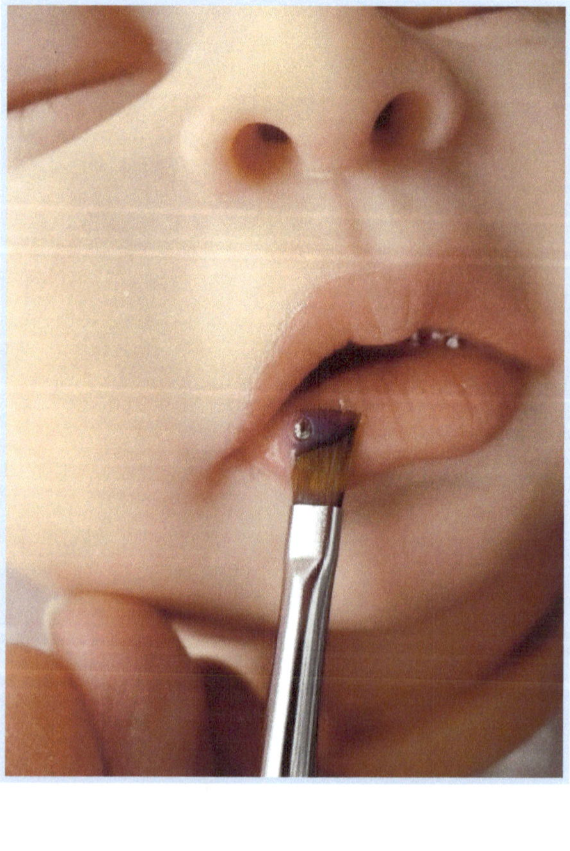

I dampen a small, flat paintbrush and insert it under a bubble that I choose for the specific place in the dolls mouth. I gently scoop up the bubble and gently slide the paint brush to the selected area of placement.

Using a toothpick, I help the bubble off every so gently. The most I put on at a time are two bigger bubbles or a brush full of teeny bubbles.

Rinse the paint brush often in hot water and damp dry on a lint free cloth. Keep applying bubbles until you are happy with the results.

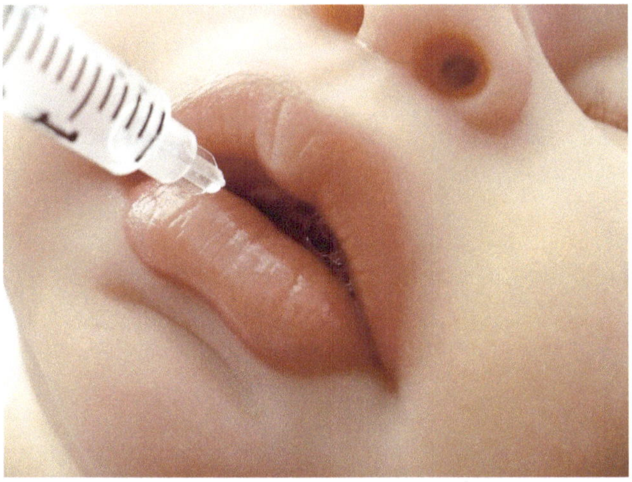

Let the head rest in an undisturbed place free of movement and wind. Make sure the head is angled so that the bubbles won't slide where you don't want them. Let this dry for the remainder of the day or night. Replace any bubbles that popped (does not happen often to me at all) or add more bubbles if needed when drying is complete.

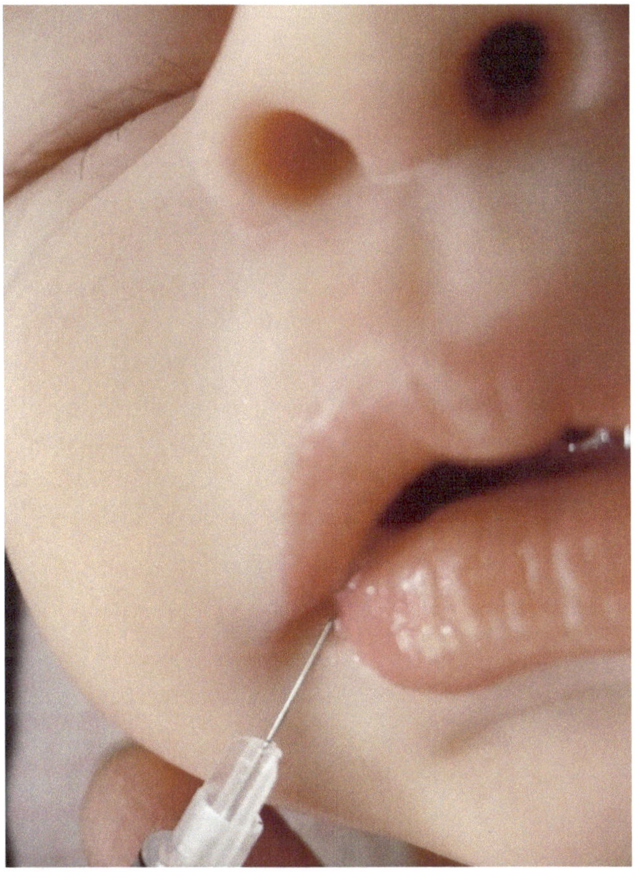

The second way to do bubbles is with an insulin syringe. Using a small, damp brush, apply some Alene's Paper Glaze into the selected area of the mouth of the doll. VERY slowly and gently, inject air into the glaze forming bubbles. When you have achieved the amount of bubbles you desire, allow them to dry as listed above. Keep the syringe cleaned off in hot water and a lint free cloth.

Debbie Henshaw
www.theynevergrowupnursery.com

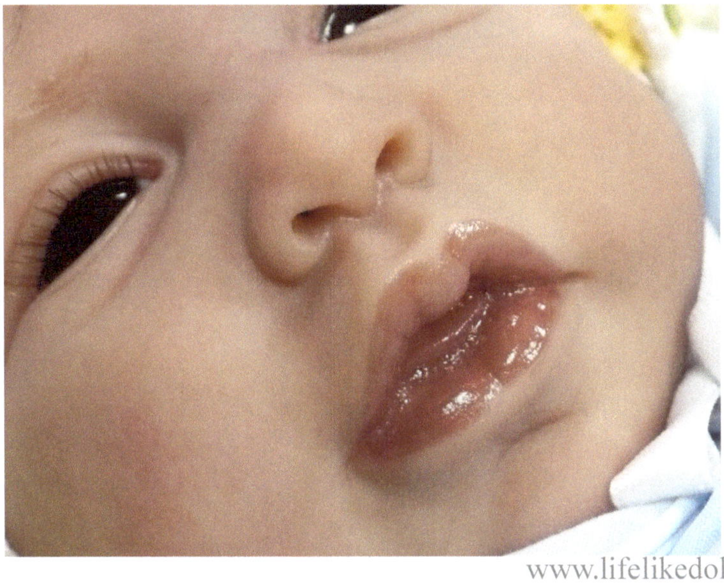

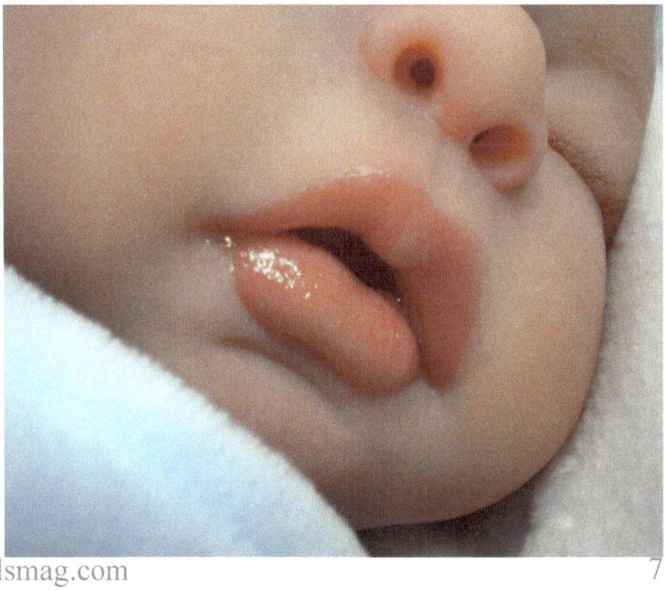

Inserting Eyes in Reborn Dolls

by Rachel Maynard, Precious Little Babies
www.preciouslittlebabies.co.uk

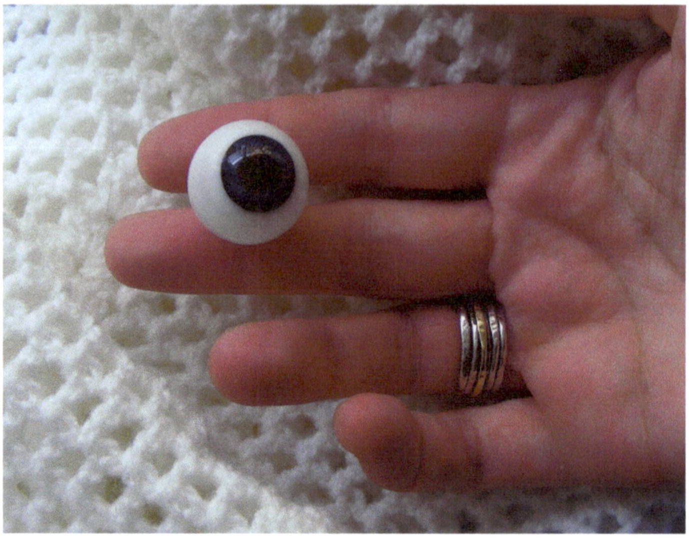

Start by cutting a cross shape in the back of your eye sockets. You have to make sure that this is done before you root your lashes as the easiest way to get to the back of the eye is to push the vinyl in on itself so that you can access the eye from the inside through the neck ring. You can use a craft knife or scissors whichever you find easier. Some eyes are ready cut so you can just pop the back out.

Once you have the sockets cut, take your glass eye and using your fingers, wedge the eyes into the holes. You may find that some of the little flaps get tucked in. I tend to use a broken rooting needle or pair of tweezers to pull them out. This is all done through the inside of the head and can be very fiddly, its best to do this on carpet as glass eyes will smash on hard floors.

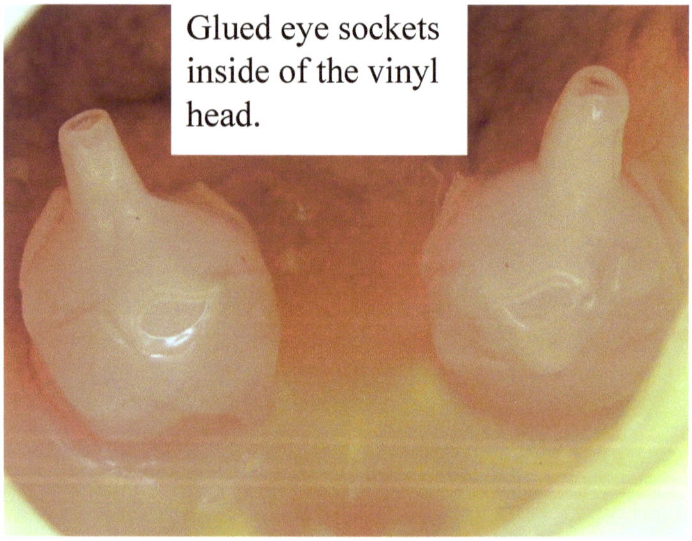

Glued eye sockets inside of the vinyl head.

Once you have your eyes securely in the sockets you need to make sure they're straight before gluing into place. Make sure that your babies eyes are in a nice position by moving the eyes to make it look like the doll is looking at you.

If the eyes are a little too small for the sockets or a little odd shaped, you can pack out the back by using tweezers to wedge some fibrefill behind the vinyl flaps to make sure they're nicely fitted, before gluing.

Once you are happy with the placement of your eyes you can glue them in place. I usually pour E6000 onto the backs of the eyes and use an old paintbrush to make sure they're fully covered and that some of the glue has seeped behind the vinyl to secure it to the eye. (see picture above.

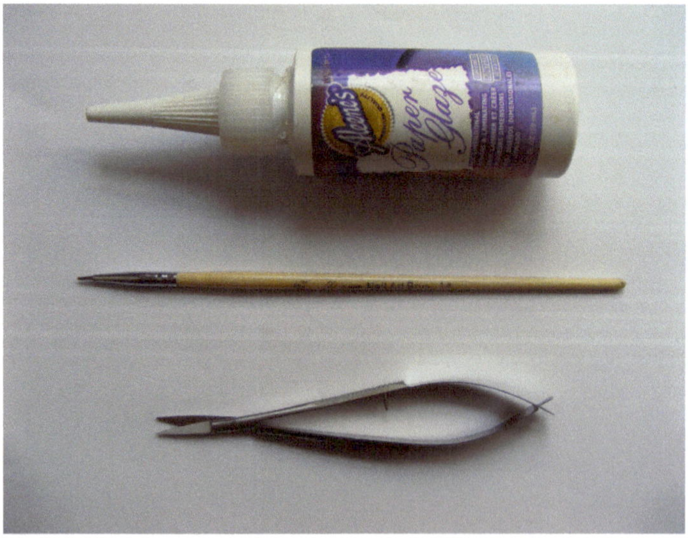

Once your eyes are glued and dry you can decide if you would like to add some paper glaze (baby tears) to your eyes. I don't often use it but it is handy for filling the tiny gaps that can be left either side of the glass eye. Use a paintbrush to drop the paper glaze into position and allow to dry, do not put the paper glaze on too thick or it stays white and is easily peeled off.

Reborning Tutorial
Painting Creases

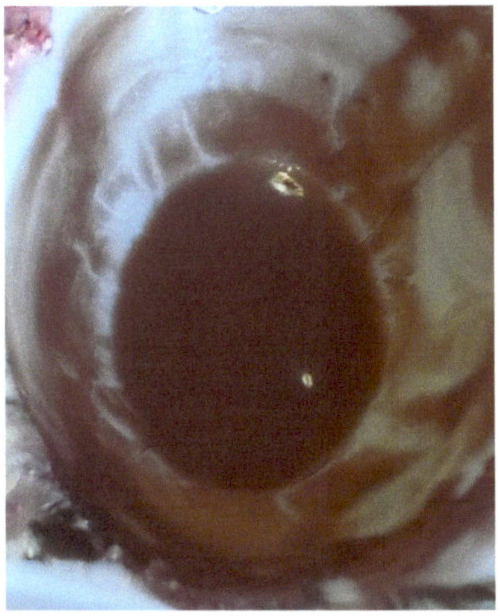

1. This crease colour is one I have had mixed for quite awhile, and I'm not sure what mixture it is. If you are mixing from scratch, try flesh 07 with a touch of burnt umber and red.

2. Paint over all creases and folds, and on the lips.

3. Use a mop brush and/or a sponge to remove the excess paint.

4. Bake at 268 for 8 minutes. Check the paint with a wet q-tip to make sure the paint sealed.

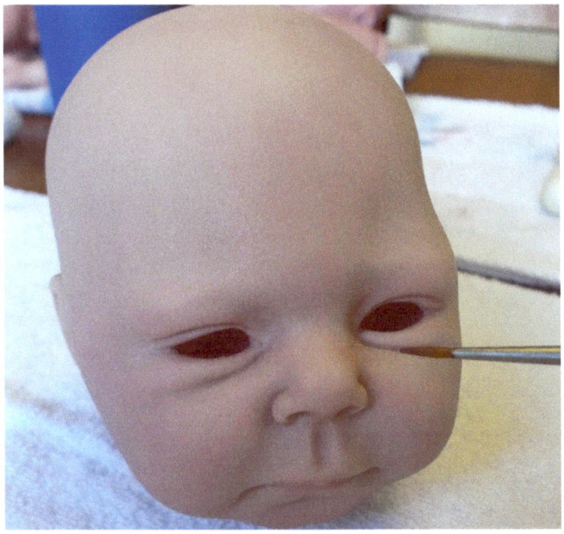

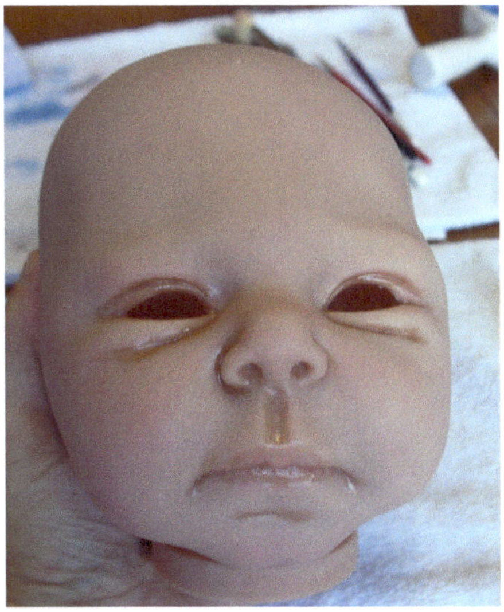

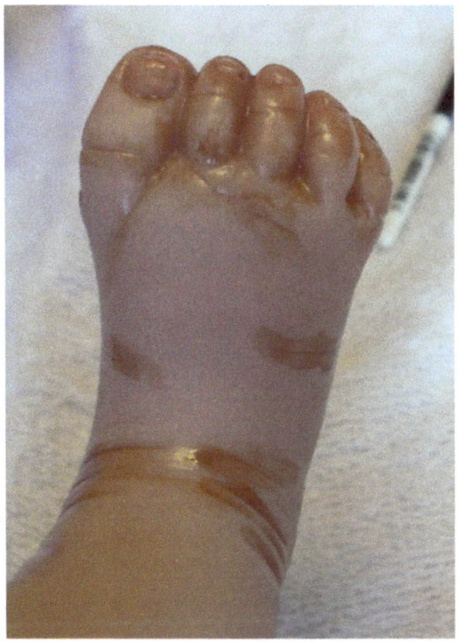

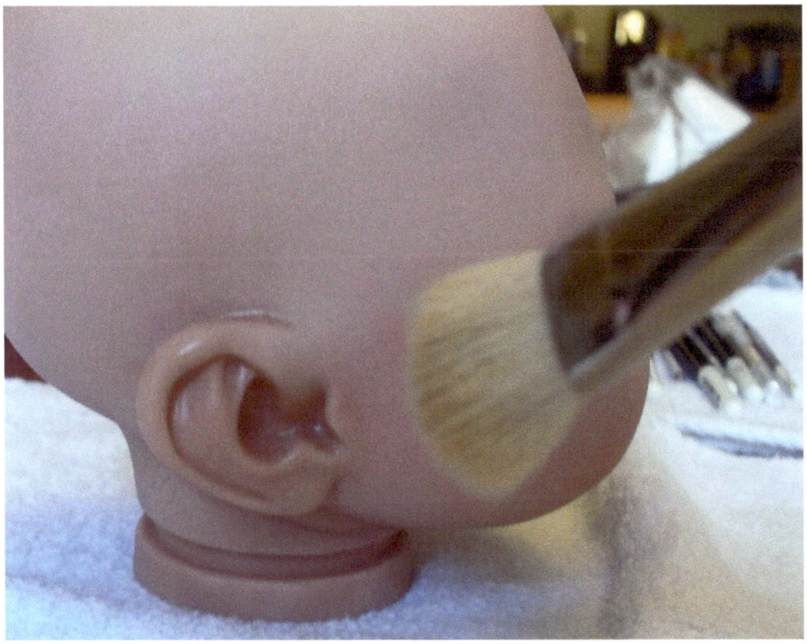

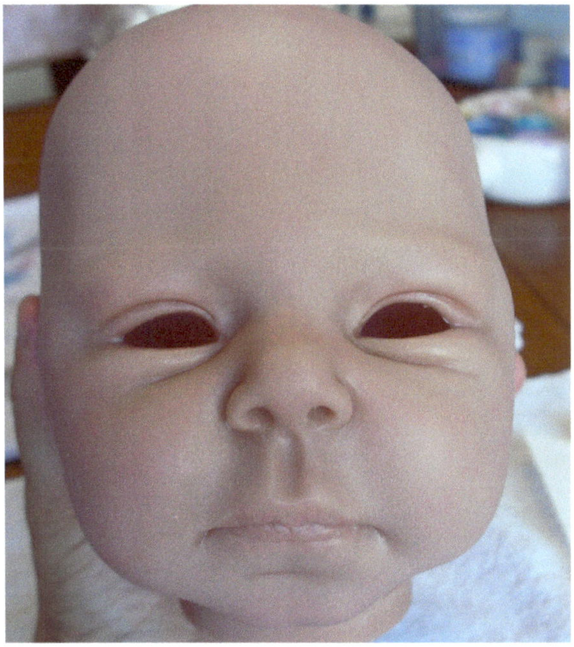

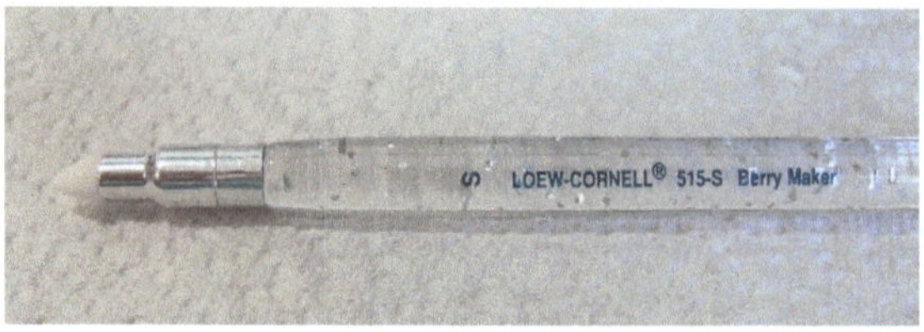

USING THE BERRYMAKERS™

to create newborn skin mottling on your Reborn Baby

by Stephanie Sullivan

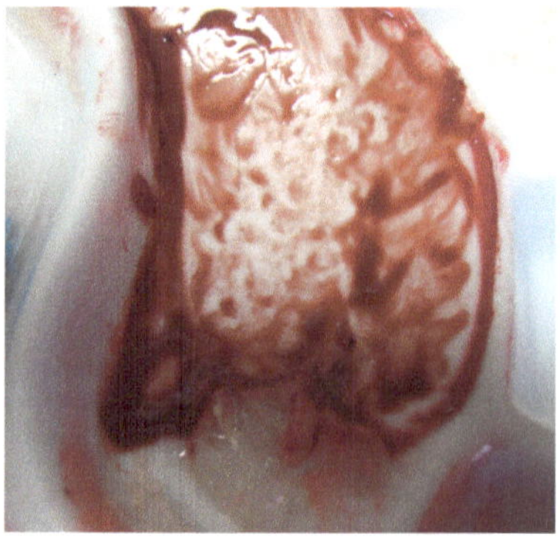

I did this tutorial using Genesis Heatset Paints. There's no reason the technique wouldn't work with other paint mediums, though.

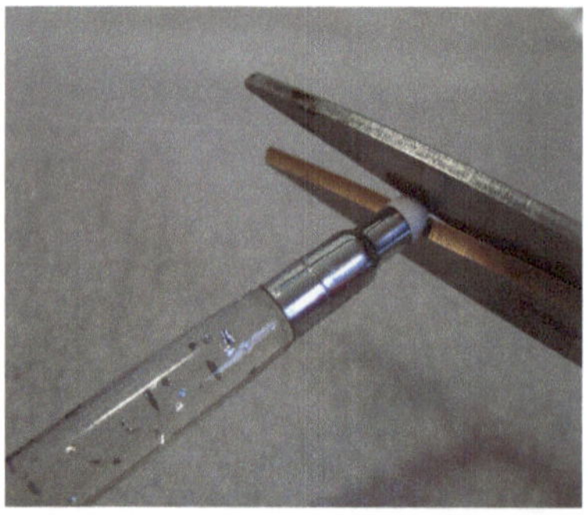

This effect is normally done after you have laid down at least one foundation of flesh coloring. I add it after my second flesh layer and after painting all creases and wrinkles. When I do this effect, it takes the place of a final blushing with brushes or sponges.

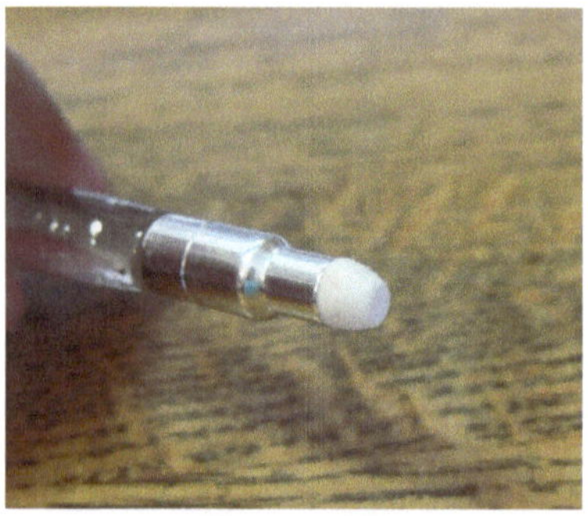

Mix up a glaze with your blushing color and Genesis Thinning Medium. Ratio of paint to thinner should be approximately 60:40. Mix well. You want a transparent effect. (Note: if you are using Air Dry paints, mix up a glaze using similar products and adapt the ratio of paint to glaze according to your paint's instructions).

Through a process of trial and error, I found that using the Berry Makers required a bit of "re-engineering" to achieve a natural mottling effect on vinyl. Because real baby skin has a sort of lacy pattern of white dots surrounded by pinkish-purple circular shapes (a vascular effect usually intensified by the skin chilling) and not actual circles, I think reshaping the Berry Maker tool this way creates a more realistic effect.

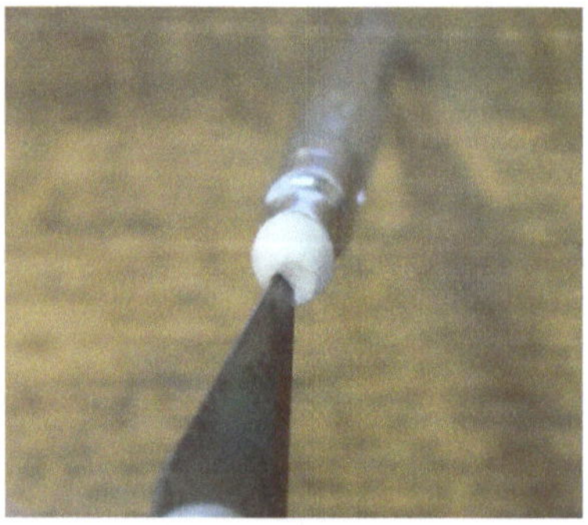

I normally don't apply this effect to older looking dolls. I reserve this effect for doll kits and reborns that appear to be younger than a year old.

I start by cutting the tip off of a small or medium sized Berry Maker with scissors.

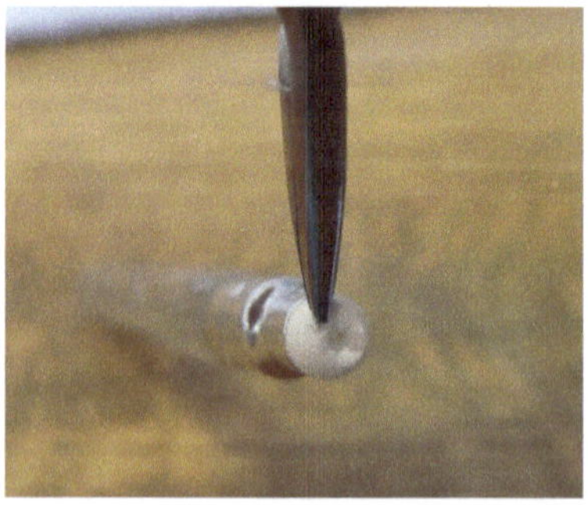

Then I carve a small hole in the center of the foam (using a pointed craft knife) and pop it out with the tip of the knife, or pluck it out with a tweezers.

Finally, I pull off 3-4 tiny sections of the resulting "donut shape" Berry Maker tip with the tweezers to create a slightly irregular roundish stamp.

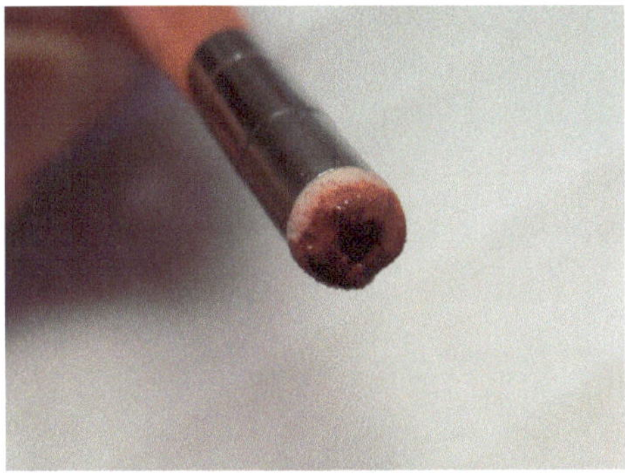

Re-engineered Berry Maker, ready to paint with.

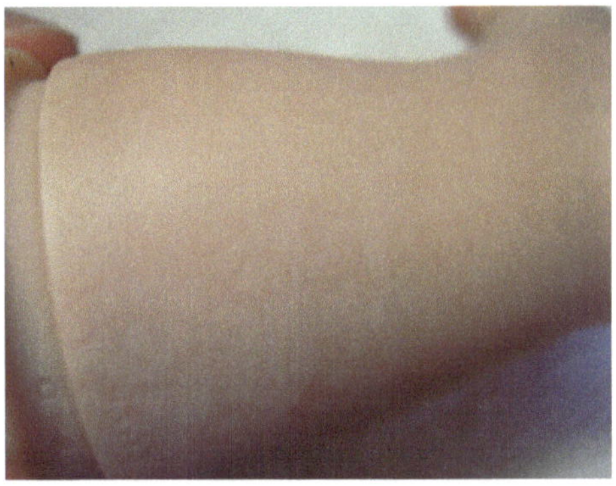

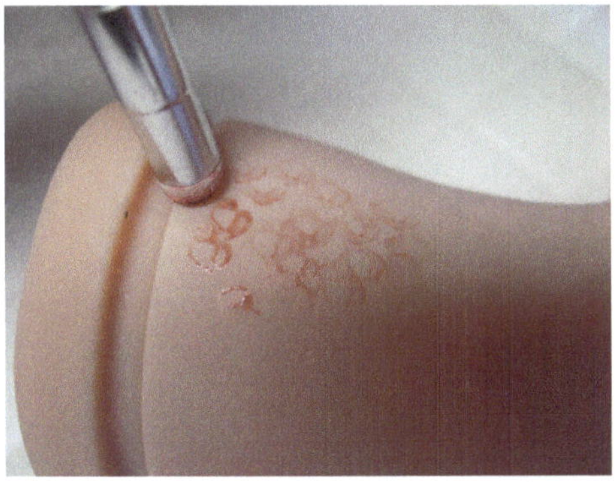

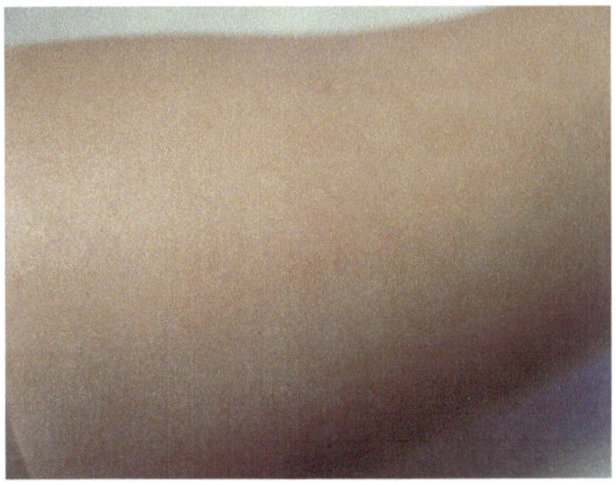

Dip the end of the Berry Maker into the glaze and load it with paint.

Tap small overlapping circles of the glaze on a small area – not much more than a few inches. A straight up-and-down stamping motion is what you want. Stop when you aren't transferring any more paint.

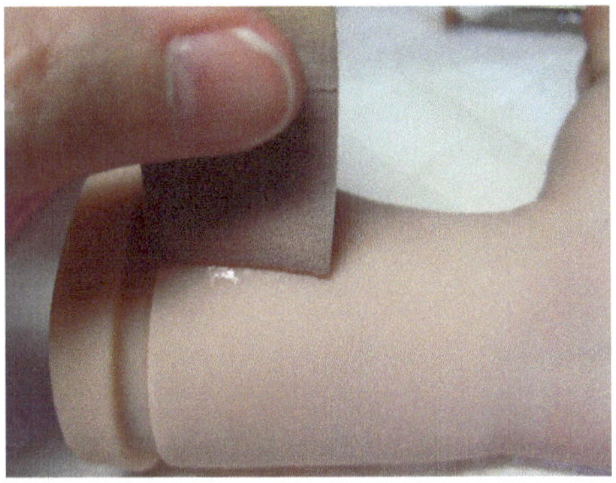

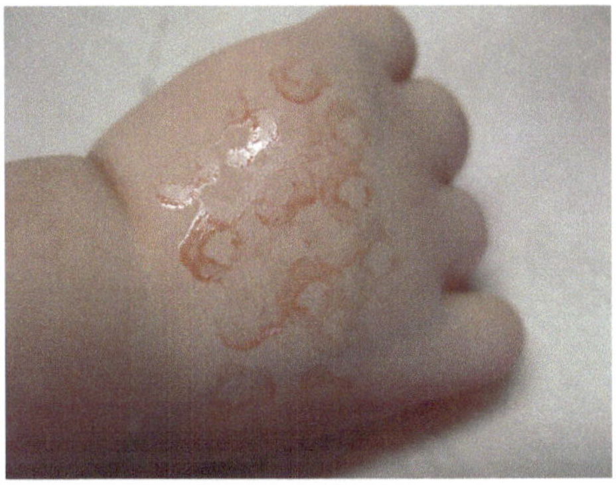

Now, using a cosmetic sponge wedge, just barely blend the dots of color you have made until they start to blend together just a LITTLE. If you over-blend, you will ruin the effect, and have to wipe it all off and start again.

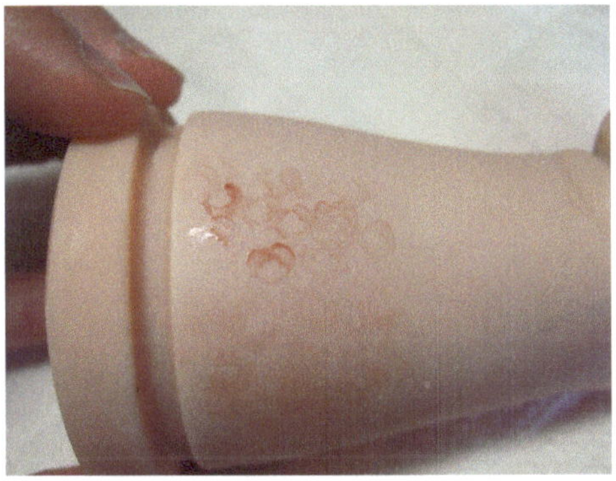

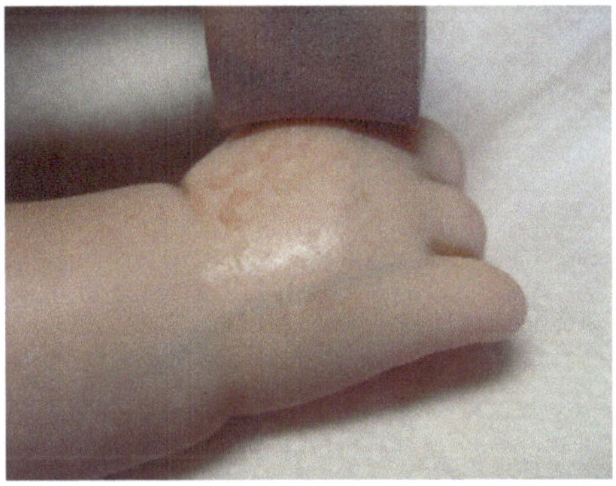

Continue to apply the glaze in small areas, slightly overlapping the previously painted areas. Blend all over the arms and legs, but not on the soles of the feet or the palms of the hands.

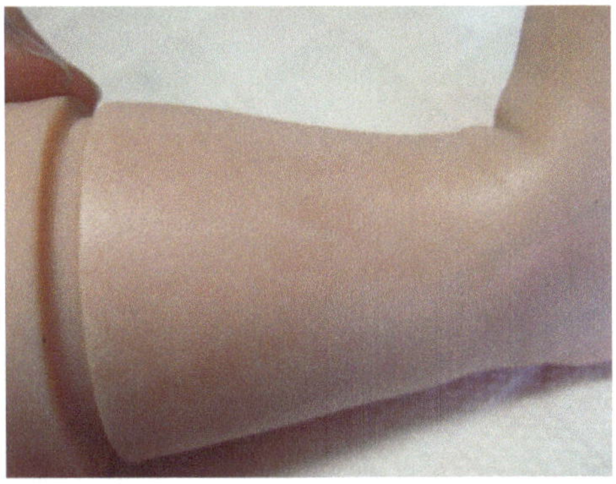

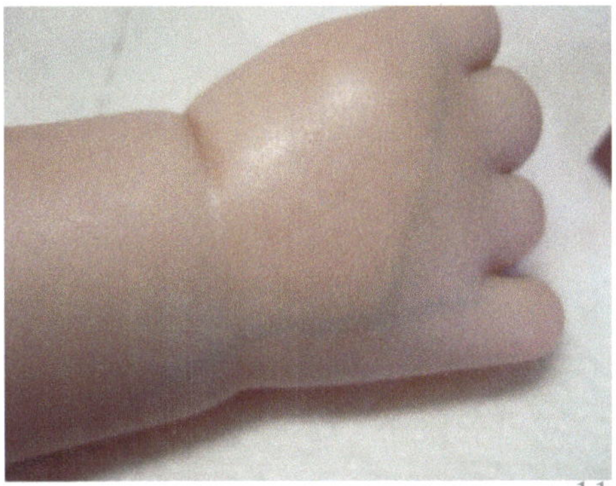

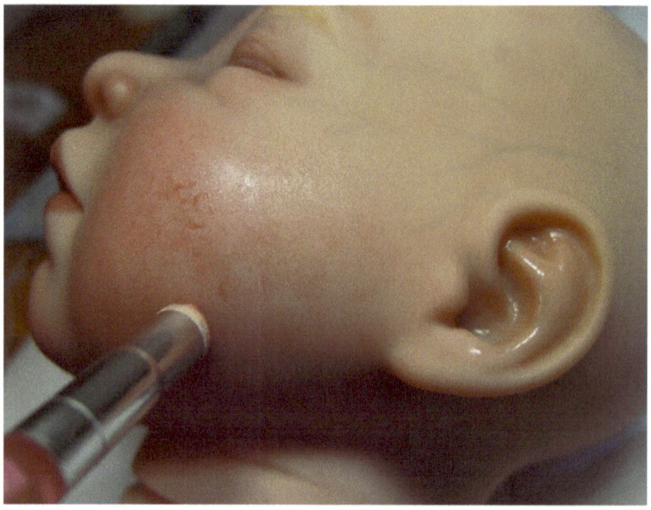

Mostly this effect is observed on a baby's limbs (excluding palms of hands and soles of feet) and to a much lesser extent on the face.

Once you have completed the mottling on the limbs (and face, if you do it there), heatset the parts as you do any Genesis paint, or allow to air-dry if you are using acrylics or Air-Dry paints.

It does take some practice! But when you get it right, it's very satisfying, and will give you the appearance of real newborn baby skin mottling!

Photo Credits:
Fig. 1 Loew Cornell Co. "Berry Maker" ™
Doll used in demonstration: Secrist Doll Co. "Jasmine" doll kit with Infant Limb pack

Nails

by Cheryl Bage

I love doing the nails on my babies! It usually means I am almost finished creating a new little wonder.

Here are some basic steps to creating a realistic nail.
I will demonstrate on the toe nails as they are usually a little larger and easier to see.

I am working on an unpainted limb because I, unfortunately, forgot to take some pictures when I worked on my last baby. You should still be able to get the general idea.

I use Genesis Heat Set Paints. You will need to cure the paint with your heat gun (or preferred method) in between each step.

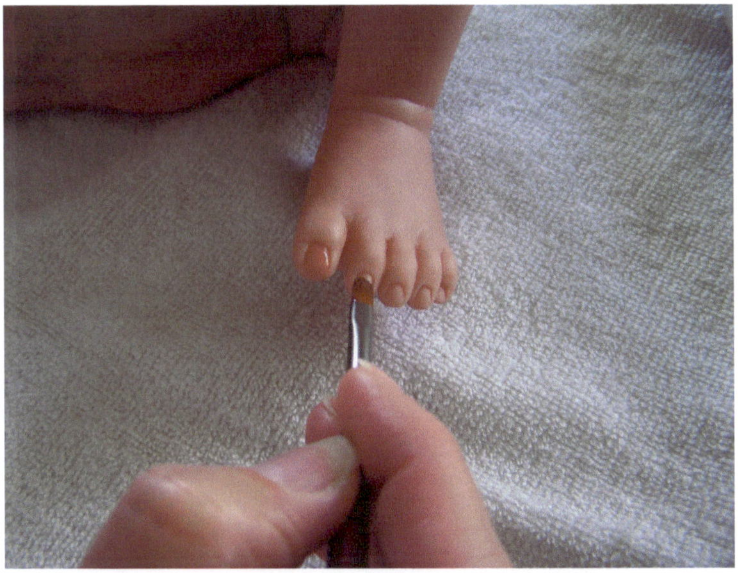

I start by doing a base coat on the nails of a colour I make using a bit of each Pyrrole Red 02, Burnt Umber, Pyrrole Orange Yellow 07, and a touch of Phthalo Blue 03 mixed with the Genesis Thinning Meduim. I use this medium for doing the nails because it gives you more control of the paint and it goes on in a nice even coat.

I use a filbert (or cats tongue) brush for the nails because the rounded end and flat bristles fit the contour of the nail perfectly.

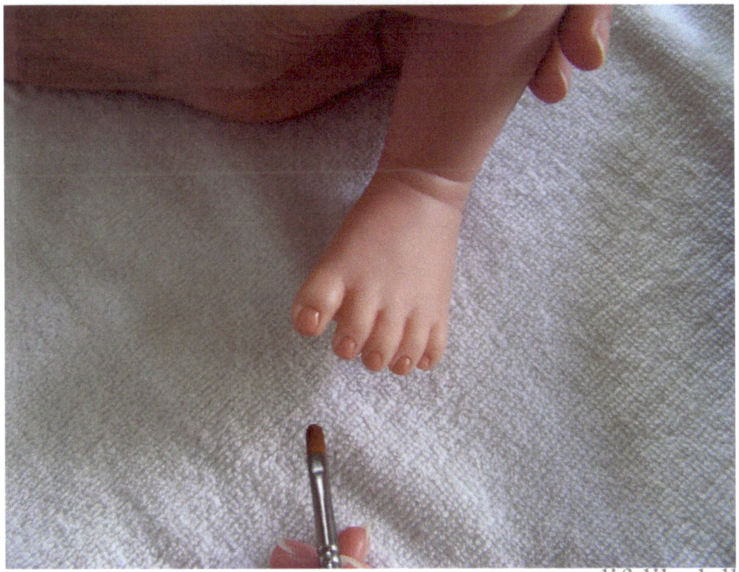

Here you can see all the nails have an even coat of base colour. Now heat-set the paint.

Now I will mix an off white to do the nail tips. We don't want a stark white that looks like a french manicure. To keep it natural, I mix a bit of Flesh 08 into some white. I also mix this with a touch of Genesis Thinning Medium but not too much because you don't want this paint to be very translucent.

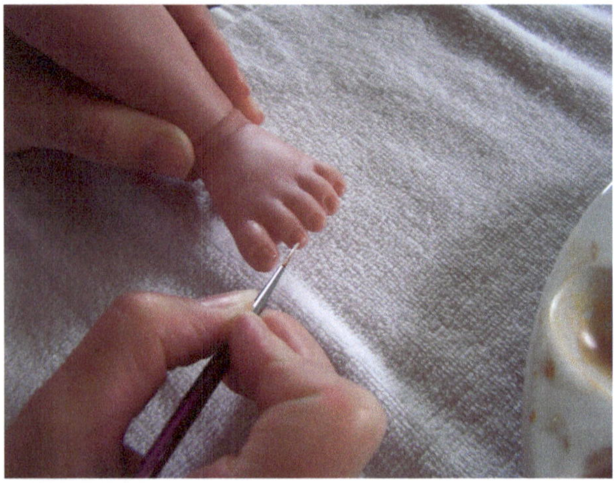

Using a fine liner brushI now do a very narrow line across the bottom tip of the nail. If you get a little over the edge onto the "skin" area you can use a toothpick to take it off.

Do all the tips and then set the paint with the heat gun.

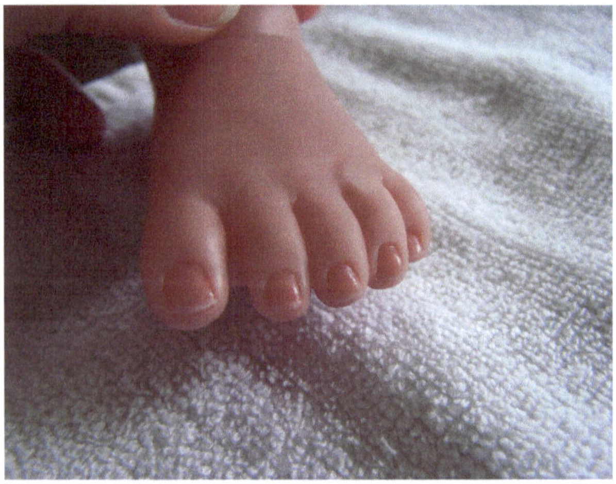

Here you can see all the nails are finished painting.

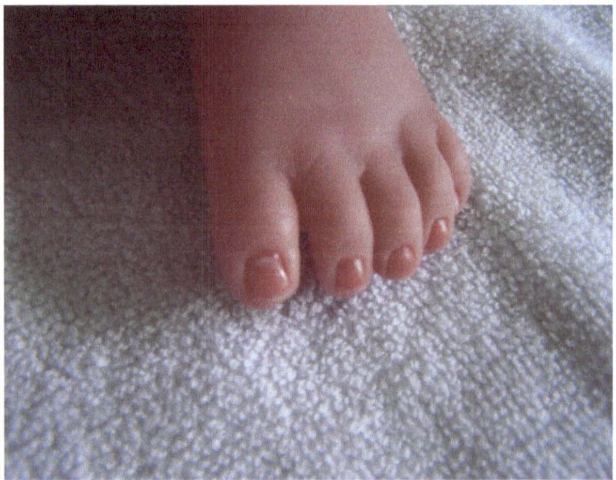

Something I've noticed that is becoming very popular is to paint the little half moon at the cuticle. I do this by putting a little of the tip paint colour across at the cuticle.

I then use a small mop brush and lightly soften it so that it is much lighter and less noticeable.

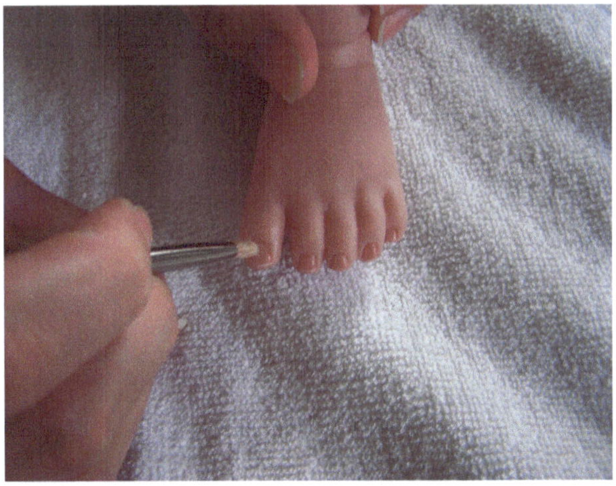

Here is the finished result. Make sure to heat set with the heat gun when finished.

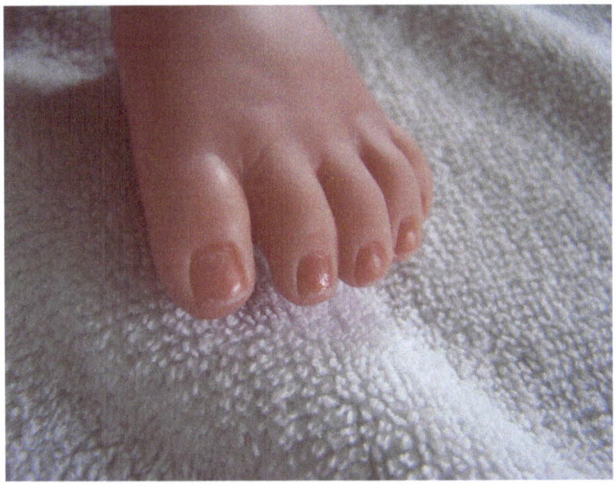

Once you are finished painting you can use an acrylic gloss varnish to finish them off.

This picture shows the finished nails, including the half moons, on a painted baby.
These nails do not have the gloss varnish.

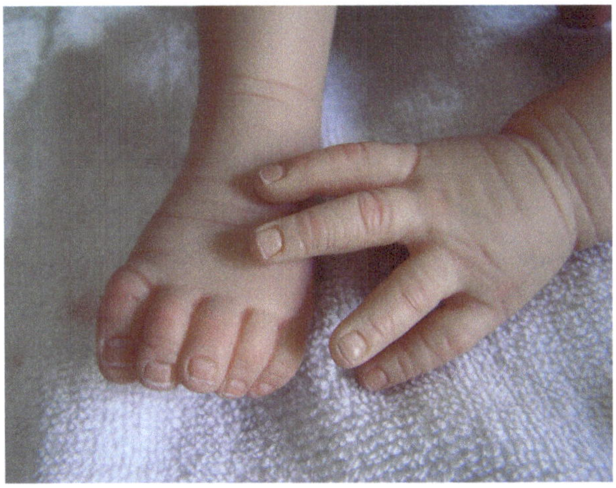

These nails are finished with gloss varnish but do not have the half moons.

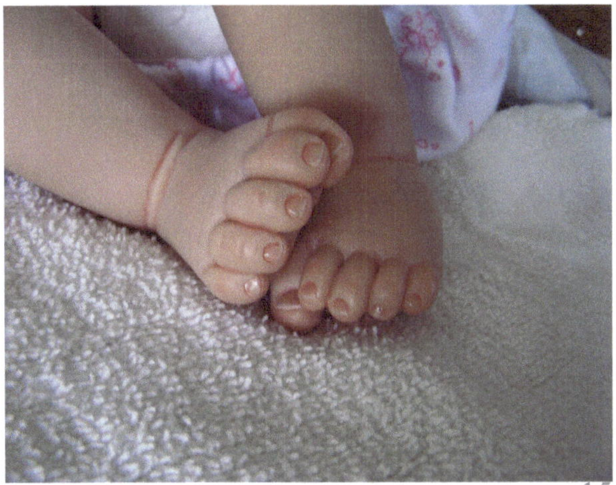

Making an Umbilical Cord

for your reborn doll

by Ruth Seyffert
Blessed Baby Creations

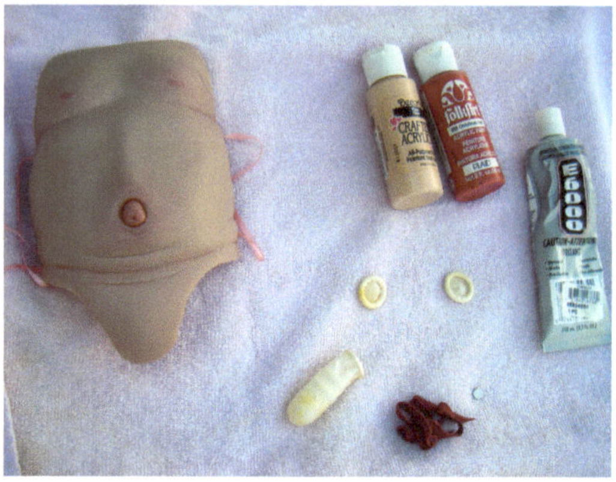

You will need the following:

2-3 fingers cut from latex gloves
A pair of earth magnets
A few thin strips of red material
E-6000 glue
Acrylic paints - red and flesh
An umbilical clamp
A body plate

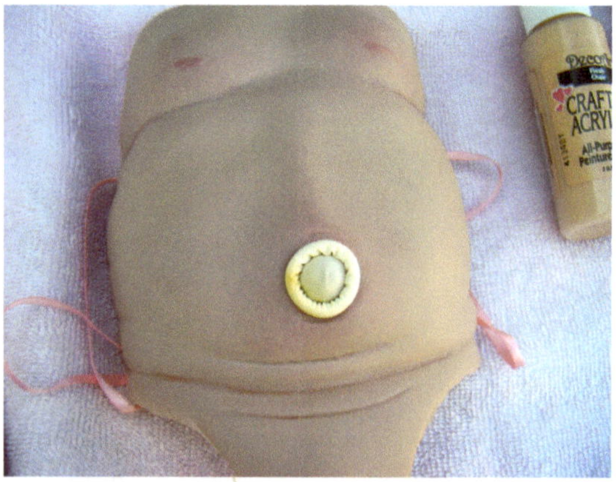

I glued the one magnet to the inside of the body plate first.

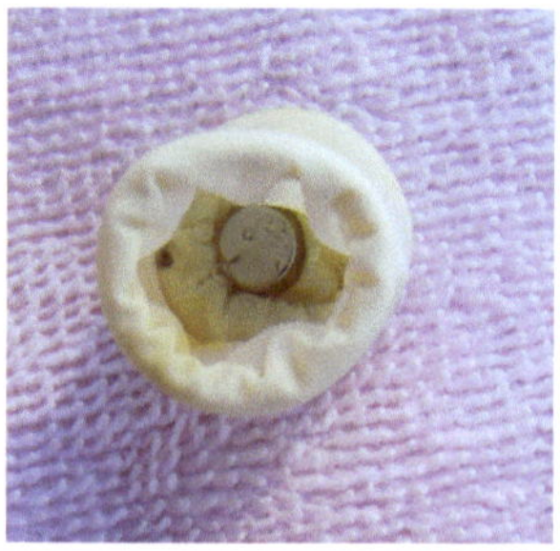

Roll up one finger piece and set it onto the body plate

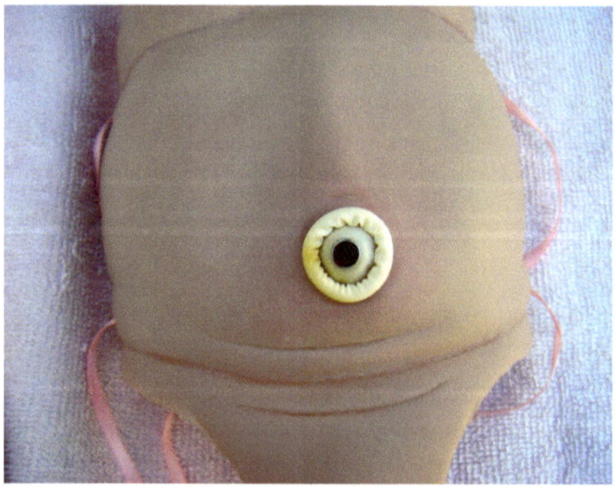

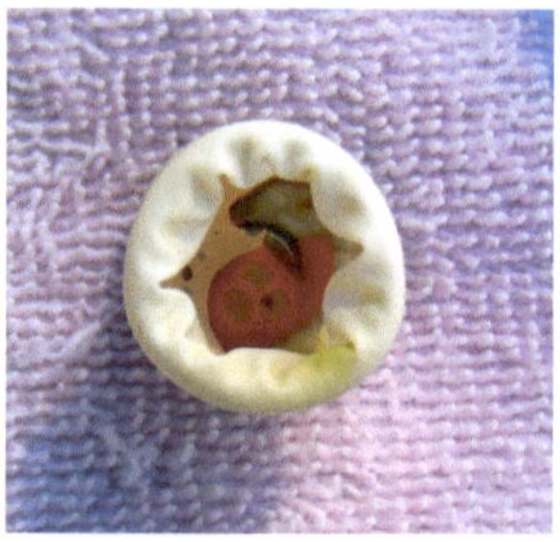

Put some glue onto the rolled up finger piece and set the second magnet into the glue. That will ensure that the magnet is the right way. Let it dry while sitting on the body plate to keep the shape fitting against the body.

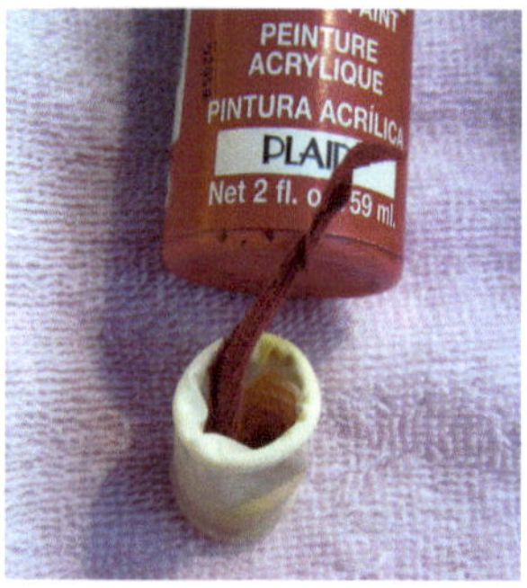

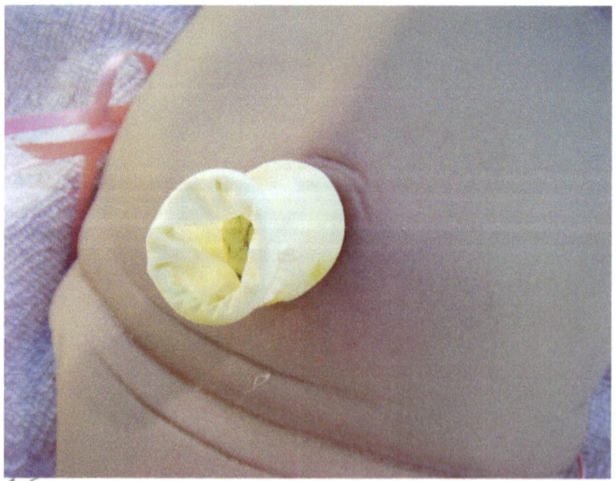

Once it is dry turn it over and put a drop of glue on the other side. Roll up a second finger piece and carefully roll it onto the first piece joining it onto the fresh glue.

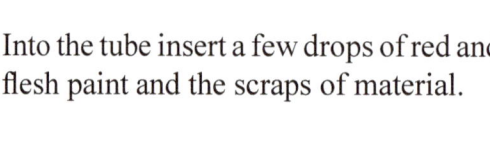

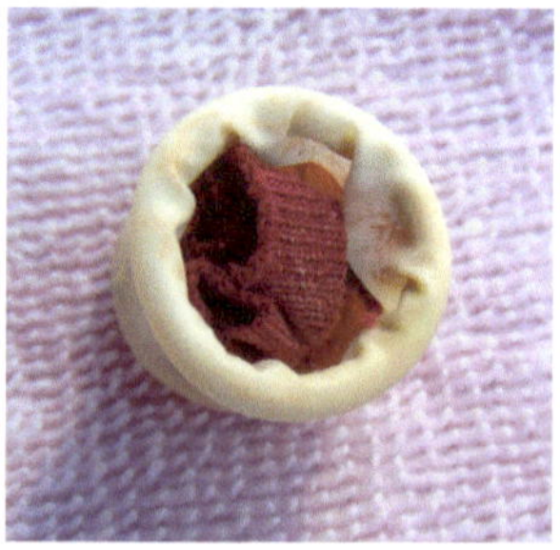

Into the tube insert a few drops of red and flesh paint and the scraps of material.

Squish it around to mix it then squirt some e-6000 glue into the tube and squish it again. Shape it the way you want it to look, try the clamp on but don't close it until you have it the way you want.

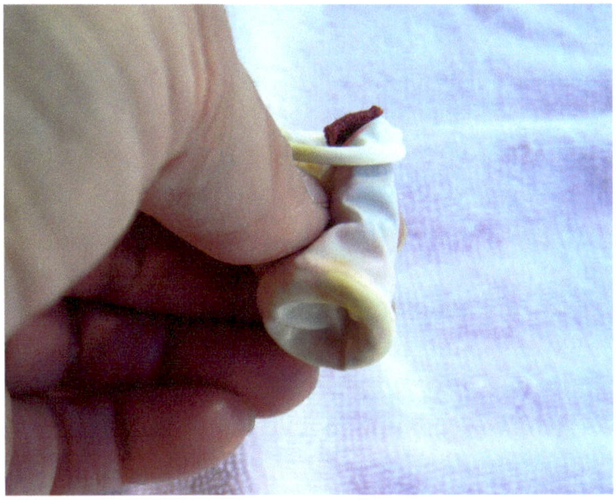

You will need to trim off the excess part of the tube and if needed add a little more glue to the ends to pull it together again.

Once dry you may want to paint a bit on the outside to match your skin color so wait to close the clamp until after you paint.

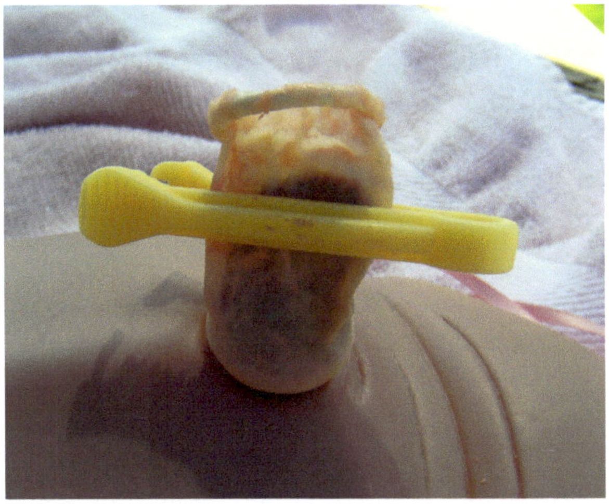

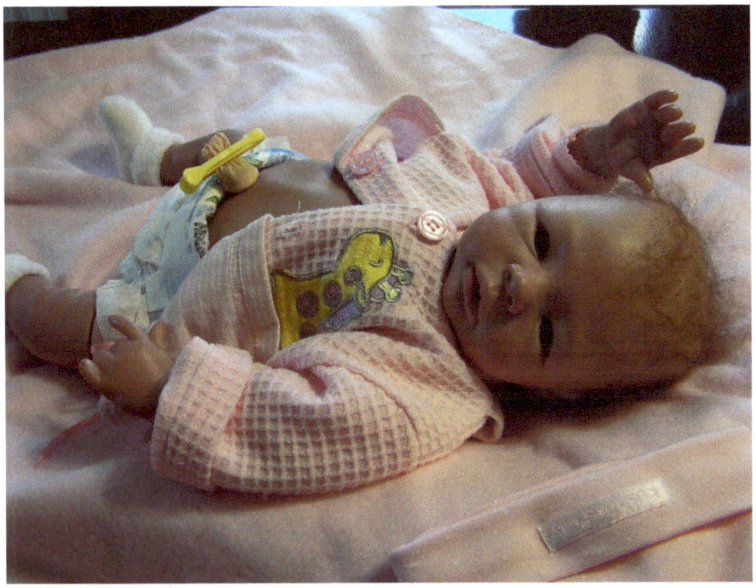

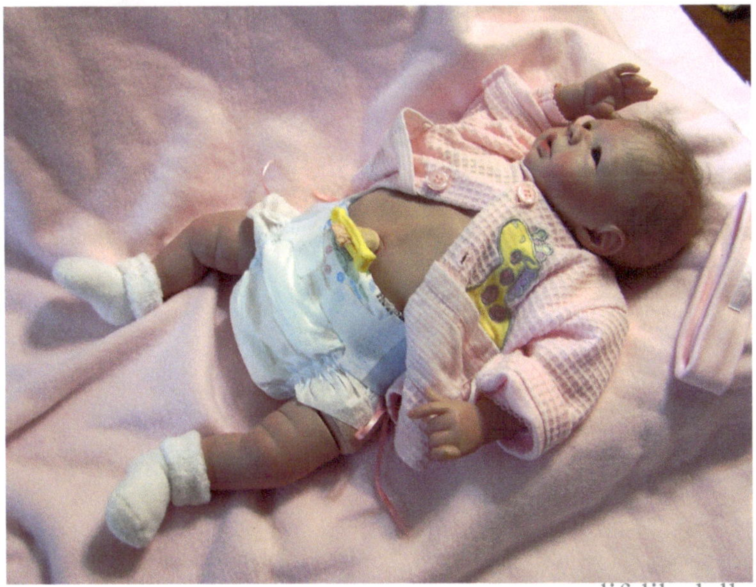

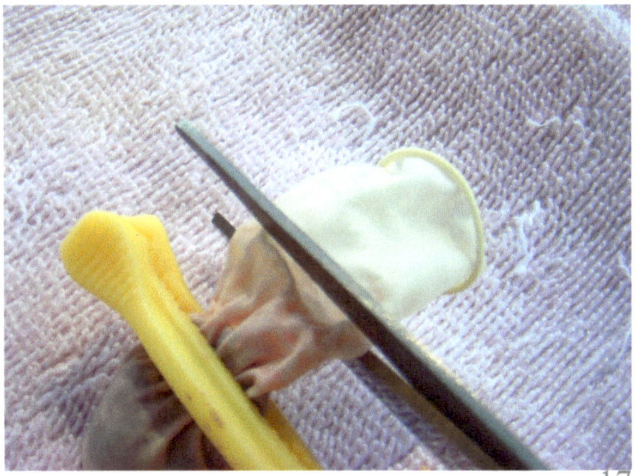

Adding Fairy Ears to Your Reborn

Sometimes a special little baby calls for something a little different. And what could be more enchanting than discovering a tiny newborn fairy sleeping in the garden. So what to do when you hear the whimsical call of the enchanted forest…create a baby fairy of your own naturally! Aside from a lovely gossamer petal dress, and delicate floral crown your reborn baby doll will need some lovely fairy ears.
One of the easiest way to achieve this is to sculpt your own using polymer clay. My person favorite brand for this project is Super Sculpey™. It is soft and easy to sculpt with and has a great base color. It blends in seamlessly and cures in your home oven to a life-like translucent finish which resembles human skin. Please feel free to experiment with various brands of polymer clay to see which type you prefer.

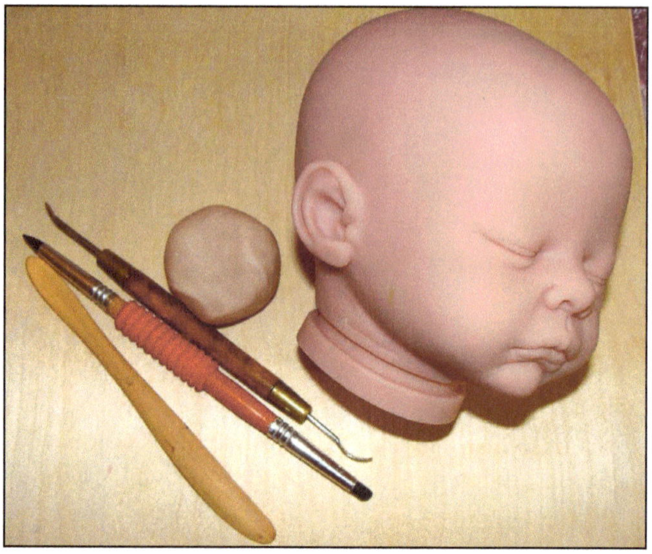

So let's begin:

Here you can see the small ball of clay, a rubber tipped tool, a 3-in-1 tool and a wooden sculpting tool.

Assemble your tools; a vinyl doll head, a small ball of polymer clay a few basic sculpting tools and your usual reborning Genesis paints (or your paint of choice). Nothing special is needed, really anything that will allow you to get into the creases and add detail. If you're working on a life-size doll and you are in a pinch, you could even get away with using your fingers and the end of a knitting needle. Another optional supply is some Orange Hand Cleaner which smoothes and removes fingerprints beautifully, but again this is not a necessity.

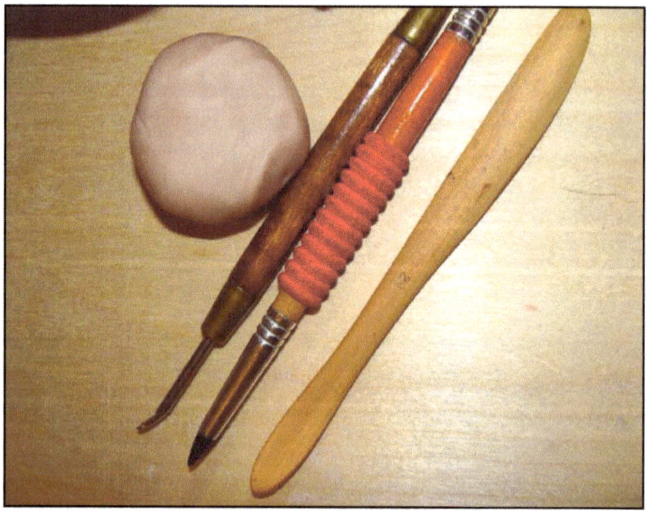

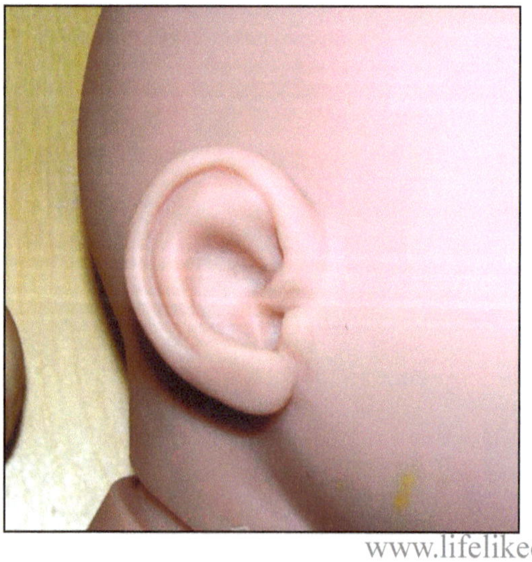

Take a close look at your baby's ears (or anyone's ears for that matter) to get an idea for the detailing and shape. Because we are creating fairy ears, we have a bit of creative license as they are fantasy characters. So just get a basic idea of the landscape of the ear.

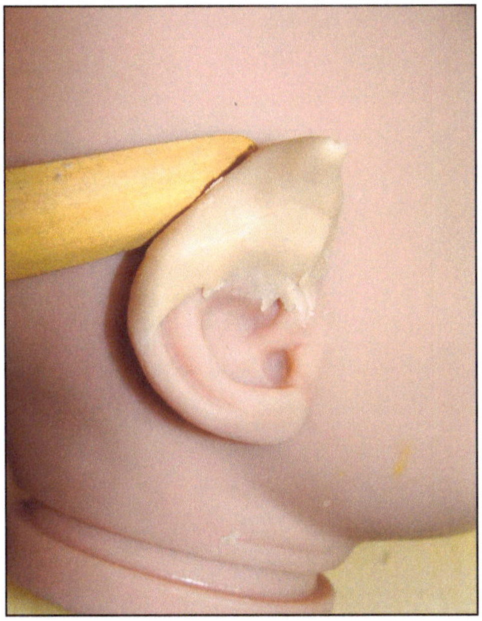

Condition a small piece of clay by kneading it with your hands this will soften the clay, warm it up and make it easier to blend and adhere to the vinyl. Add your clay to the upper ear.

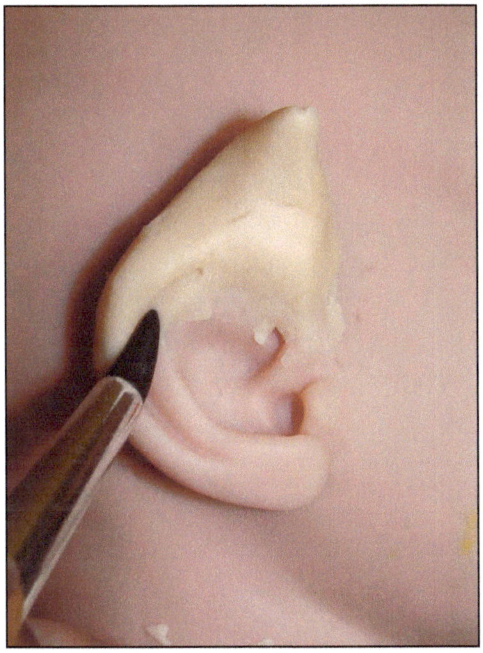

Using your tools or fingers, begin to gently shape the clay to the ear, forming the pointed tips and blend the clay into the inner ear and behind the ear.

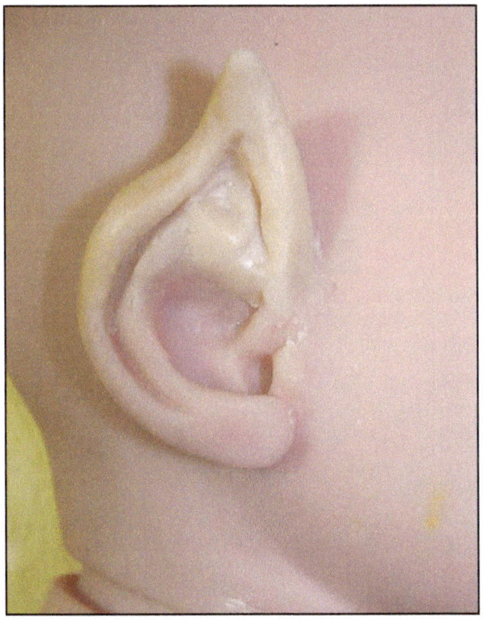

Try working on both ears at the same time, to get the sizing approximately the same. No need to stress about this of course because even humans are not perfectly symmetrical. Continue defining and smoothing and blending the edges into the ear until they are no longer visible.

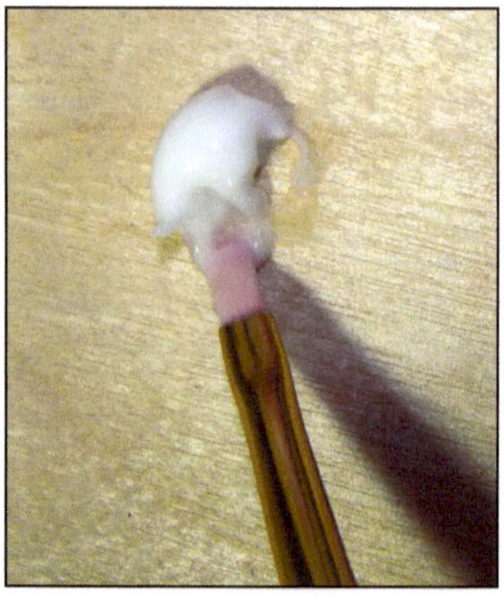

Once you have your fairy ears as you want them, it's time for the smoothing. If you wish, add a tiny amount of the Orange Hand Cleaner to a soft bristle paintbrush. Make sure you only use a small scant amount otherwise you will risk making your clay very sticky. Otherwise use your tools or fingers to smooth and remove any fingerprints.

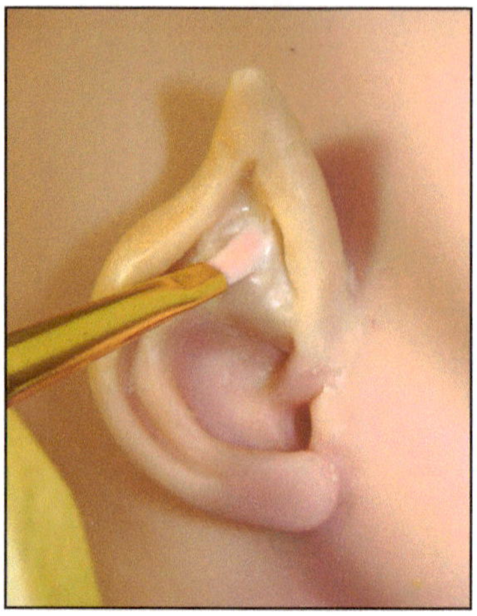

With your seams blended and clay smoothed, it's time to bake your ears. Follow the manufactures recommended baking time and temperature, but always keep a very close watch on things. Your vinyl (and clay) will be safe at the recommended temperature, but could very easily burn if left for too long, releasing toxic fumes. Generally, you will be baking 15 minutes for a ¼ thickness of clay. You could place your head on a towel lined baking sheet.

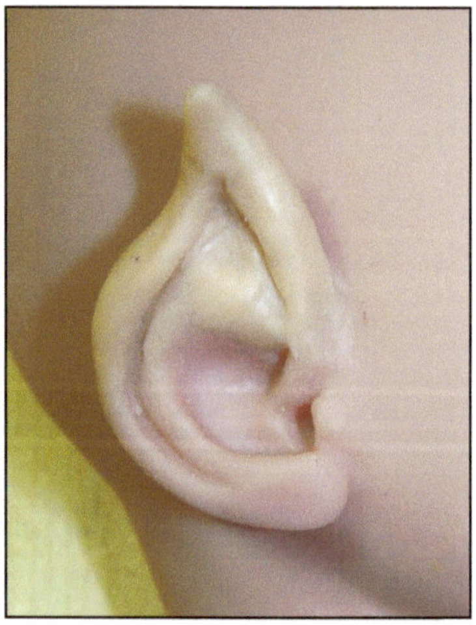

Once your clay has been cured in the oven, allow it to fully cool. Then you are ready to paint. If you apply your ears before painting your doll's head, you will have much better success with blending the colors of your ears to the rest of your doll's skin color. Here I have quickly demonstrated how easy it can be to make your clay almost disappear using paints. The shine is because the Genesis paints used haven't been cured, and my lighting is a bit off, but I'm sure you get the general idea.

Lifelike Dolls Magazine published a previous article on coloring correction and matching which you may wish to revisit. By the time you are finished your baby fairy will look as though her fairy ears were a part of the original vinyl mold.

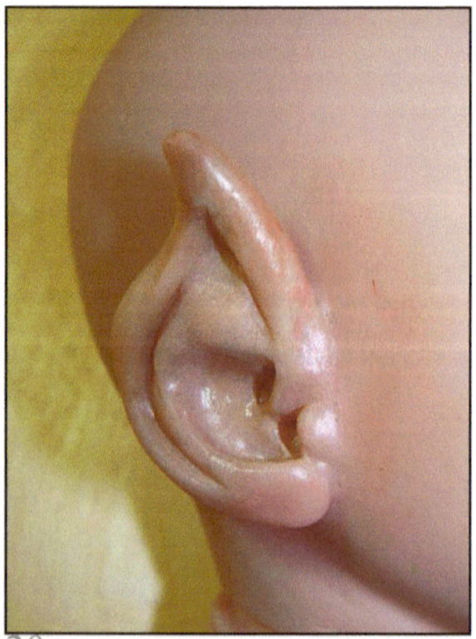

Have fun with this project and I wish you magical fairy creating!

Michele Barrow-Belisle

Masquerade Doll Studio
www.MasqueradeStudio.com
info@masqueradestudio.com

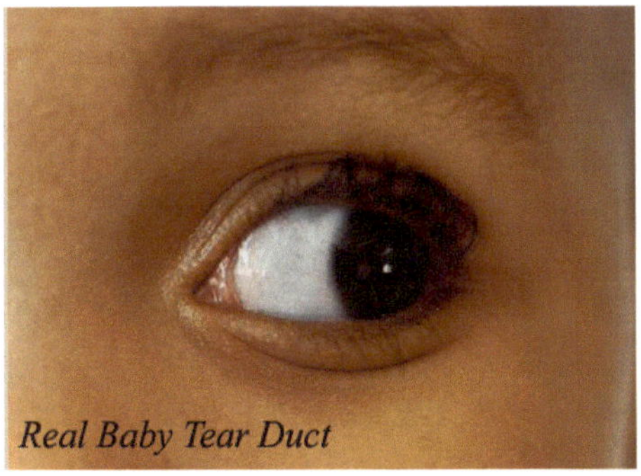
Real Baby Tear Duct

Creating Tear Ducts

by Daria Makarenkova

SUPPLIES

- Open eyed Vinyl doll kit
- Eyes that fit the kit (any kind)
- Flesh colored sculpey
- Tooth Pick
- Liquid Sculpey
- Wipeout tool

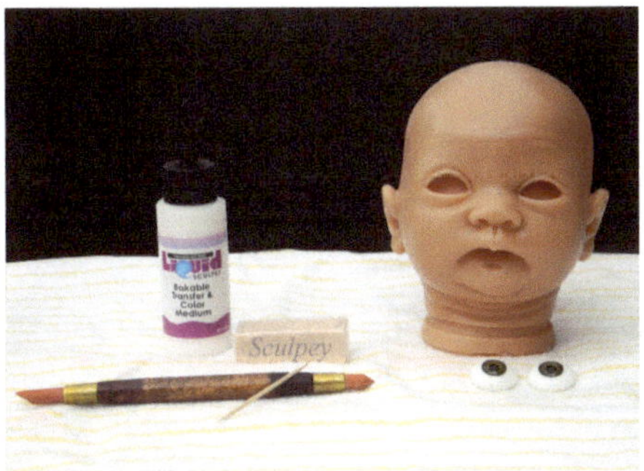

In this Tutorial I will be using a Martha Viola doll By Linda Webb. She requires 22mm oval flat back glass eyes.

The first thing to do is to insert the eyes in the sockets. Once they are inserted, align them and glue them in. Make sure you are happy with the placement because it will be permanent! Also make sure there are no gaps between the eyes and the sockets--the eyes have to be flush with the socket. I used E6000 glue to secure the eyes on the inside of the head. Then I baked the head for 10 minutes at 265°F to set the glue.*

The best way to paint or sculpt realistic babies is to find a real baby to use as a model--or at least a good picture. At top left, there is an image I found on Google of a real baby. The tear duct is somewhat exaggerated because the baby is looking of to the side and this stretches the tear duct and makes it look larger. However, this is a good clear image. There are many more like this online, or another good source is baby magazines.

Liquid Sculpey is what holds the clay in place. Put a drop in the corner of the eye you are working on. Then take a tiny bit of Sculpey, roll it in to a ball and apply to the corner of the eye.

Using a toothpick press the clay in to the corner of the eye. You can use the toothpick and/or any other tool you are comfortable with to shape the tear-duct. First sculpt the general curved shape. Looking at your image of a real tear-duct start adding detail. There is a little raised knob toward the corner of the eye and a lower "ribbon" wrapping around it. Look at your own tear-duct for added visuals.

After you have finished sculpting the tear-duct seal it with liquid Sculpey using a small brush. If you got any Liquid Scuplpey on the eye just dip a brush or a cotton swab in some alcohol and wipe the eye (be careful not to damage the tear-duct!). Bake.

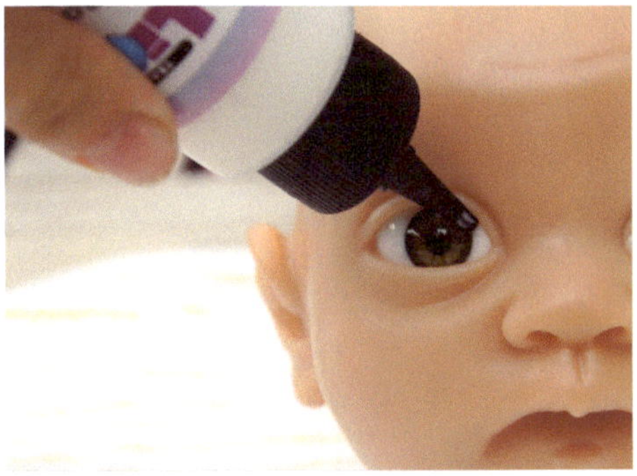

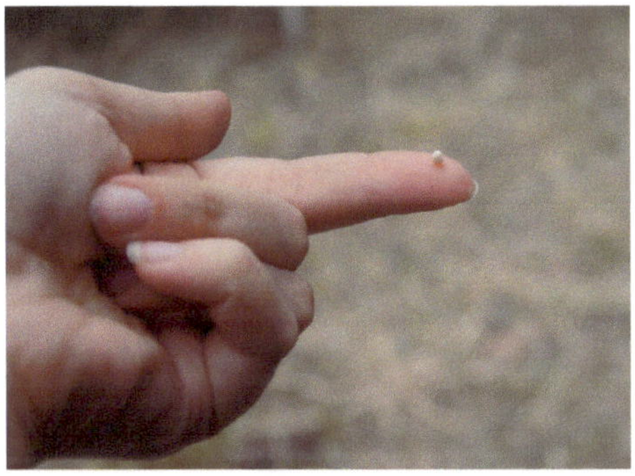

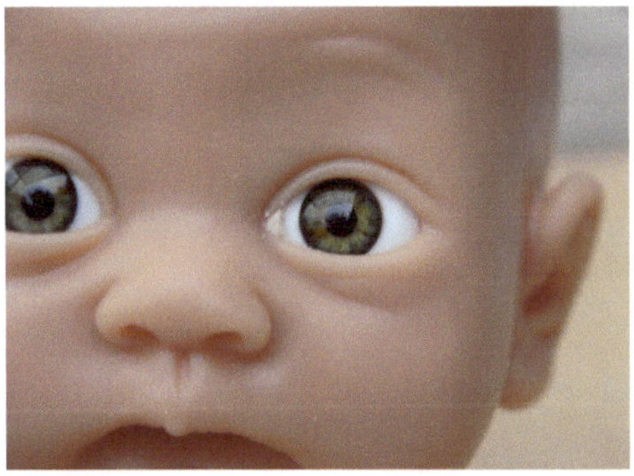

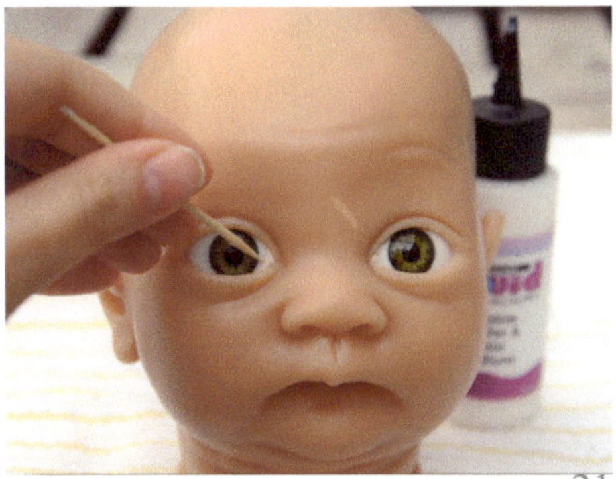

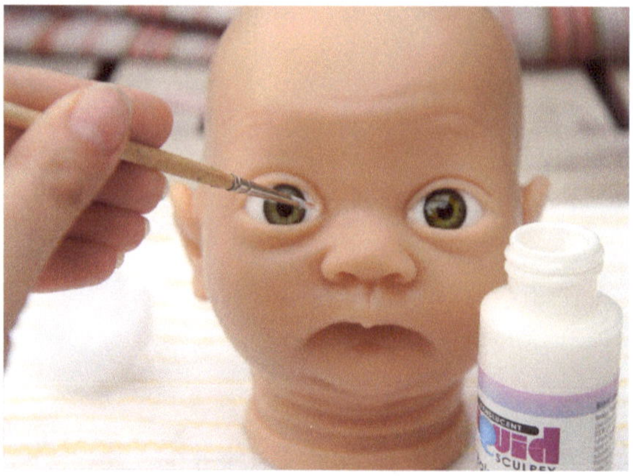

Once you have baked the tear-ducts, which were sealed with Liquid Sculpey, start applying your skin layers as normal. You do not need to apply flesh tones to the tear-ducts. Be careful of the tear ducts as you paint. They will NOT be dry even after a number of bakings. The curing temperature of the Geneses Heat Set paints is different from that of Sculpey!

As you progress in your reborning, start (very carefully) applying reds to your tear-ducts. Do not use very bright reds or your baby will look like he has an eye infection. Use many thin coats of paint. For matching colors refer to your pictures of real babies.

When you are happy with your reborn and you are done baking, the next step is to glaze the eyes and the ducts. If you are planing to root your eyelashes or to use strip lashes attach them prior to this next step.

Once the lashes are on you are ready for the final step! You will need Aleen's Paper Glaze, Genesis Vein Blue and black.

Now if you look at your eyes, or the eyes of any baby, you will notice that the whites are not really white, they are grey-bluish. The glass eyes do not reflect this fact. The whites are much to white. To fix this I like to tint my Glaze. I mix a small amount of vein blue and black with some thinner in my pallet. I take the head and lay it down in my lap face up. Then I pour the glaze directly in to the eye. This helps prevent streaking. I dip the brush in to my tinted thinner and use this brush to very quickly spread the glaze around the eye. The glaze will look whitish while drying--it will dry clear.

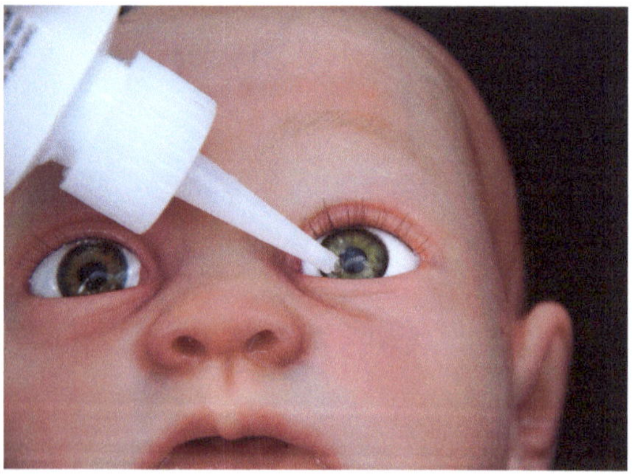

Daria Makarenkova
Daria's Boutique
ebay ID emwohl

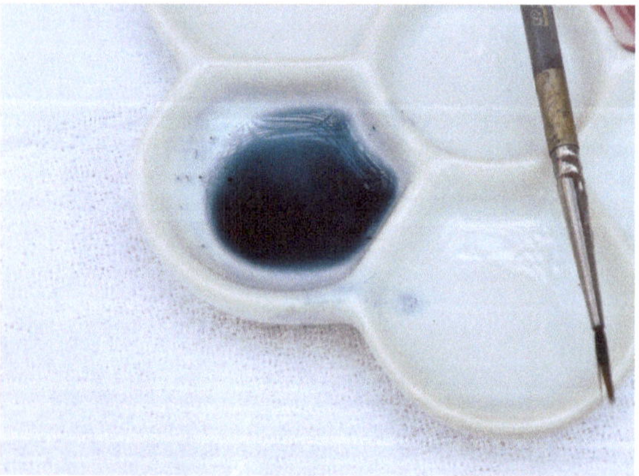

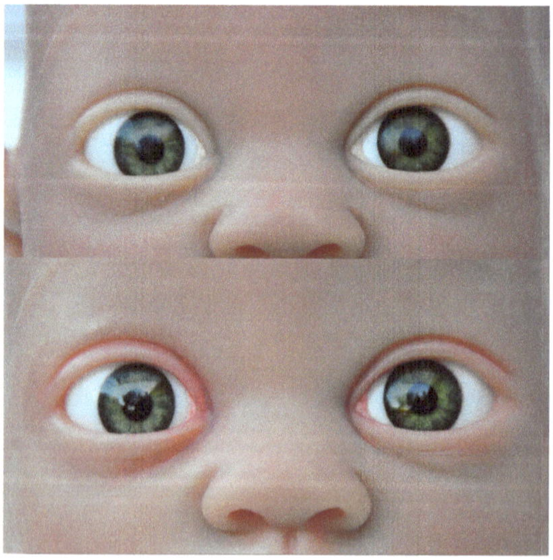

Read manufacturers instructions before heating any adhesives in the oven.

TREASURE-HOUSE
Dukker & bamser

We invite you inside our Danish doll and teddy universe.

Here you will find a rich selection of materials for manufacture of Reborn - newborn dolls and teddies.

Use our Google translation ..... and do not hesitate to contact us if you have any questions. We ship worldwide.

miaculti©

Christel and Dorthe
www.treasure-house.dk
info@treasure-house.dk

SCULPTING TINY EARS

by Dorothy Steven
DOT'S TINY TOTS

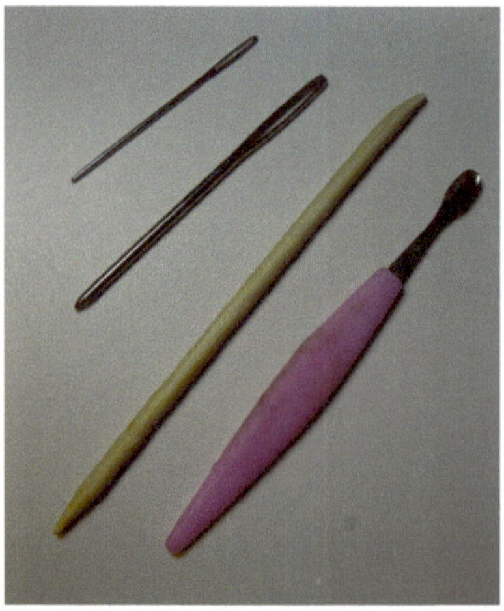

Here are my tools, I love these plus I use a a eye shadow brush and a rubber tipped paint smoother. For these ears I used the wooden cuticle pusher which I sanded real smooth and shaped with the sand paper and the smaller darning needle.

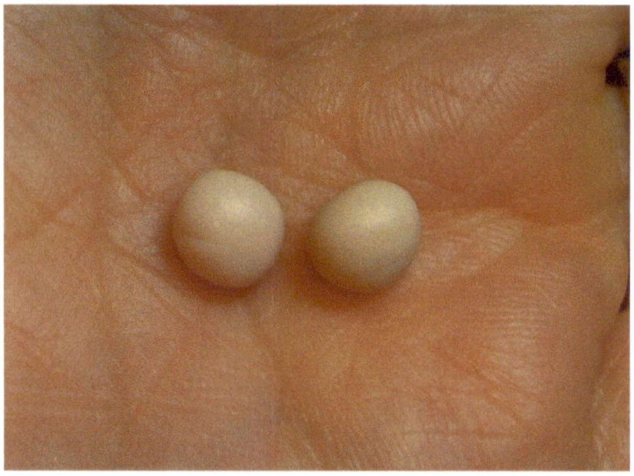

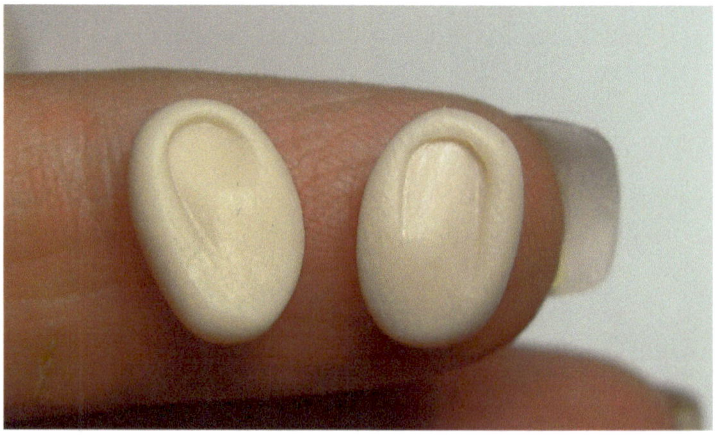

Step 1: Roll out two small balls of clay, keeping them the same size.

Step 2: Flatten them some what and elongate them. I used a wood cuticle pusher to make this indent in upper part of the ear and along the outside edge.

Step 3: Attach them to the head at the point halfway back from the front of the face on the side of the head. The top of the ear should be level with the eye.

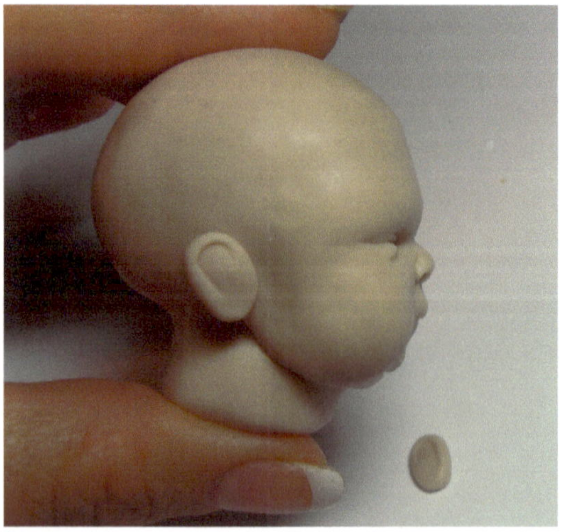

Step 4: You can see here that the eye is level with the eye, and I also smoothed the front of the ear into the side of the head.

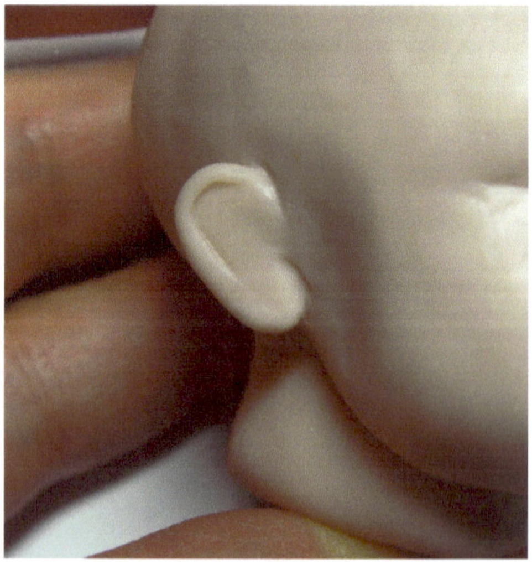

Step 5: Add detail with the cuticle pusher or even a sewing needle. I like the cuticle pusher because it is rounded at the end and it can do all the detail needed for the ear I also use a rubber tipped smoother to smooth out the edges.

Step 6: Add more detail. I like to keep it simple.

I used to make this ear with a wood cuticle pusher. If the shape is off sand paper works great to make the end rounded and smooth. The last thing I sculpt on my baby is the ears, those seem to be the easiest to smushed by accident, so I leave them for last.

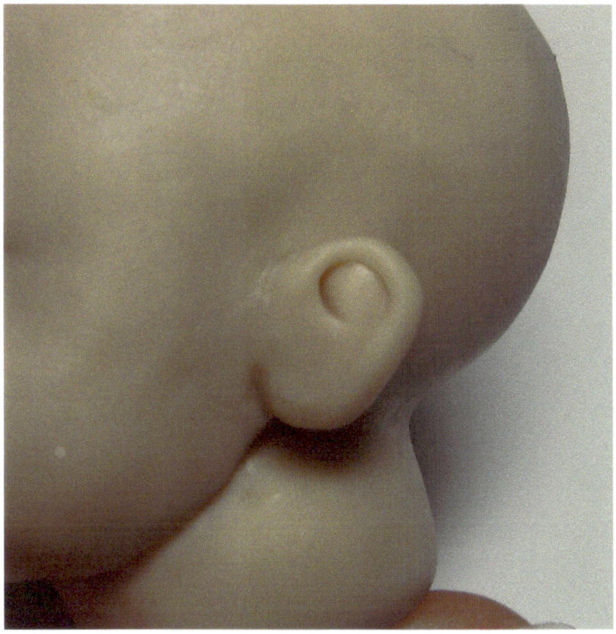

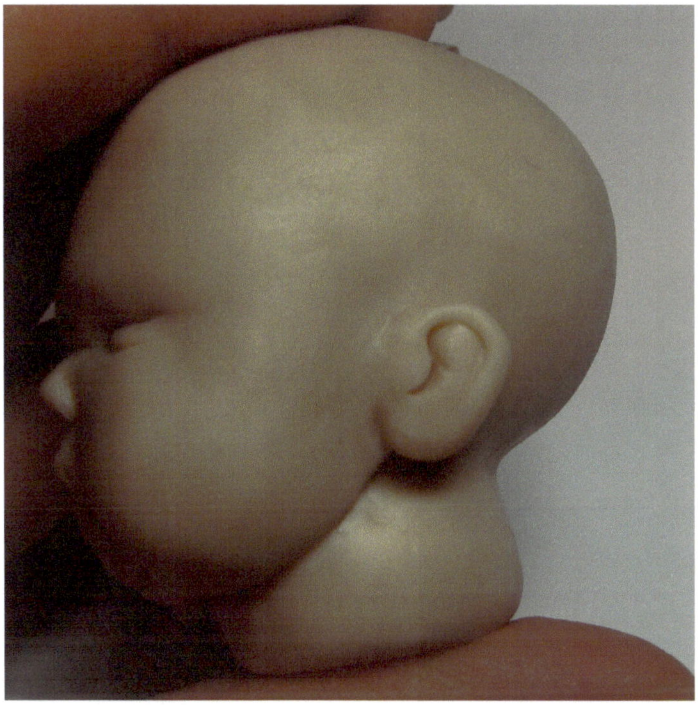

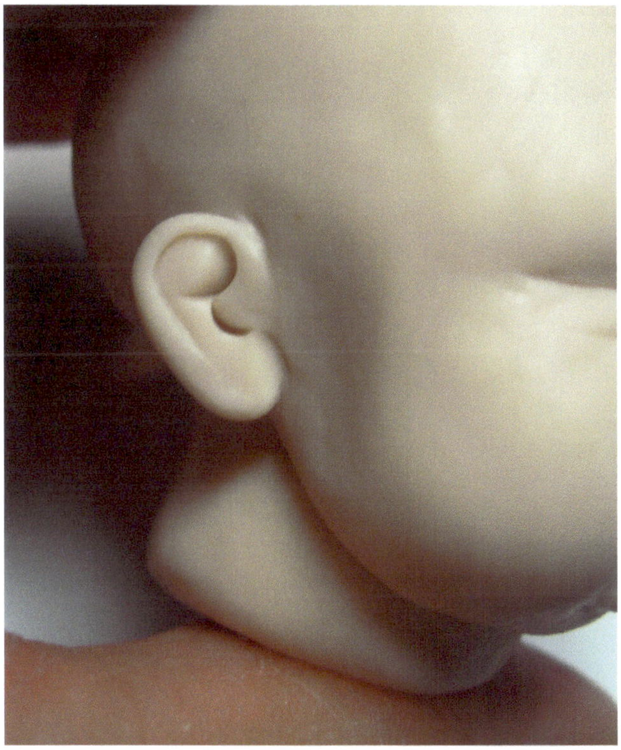

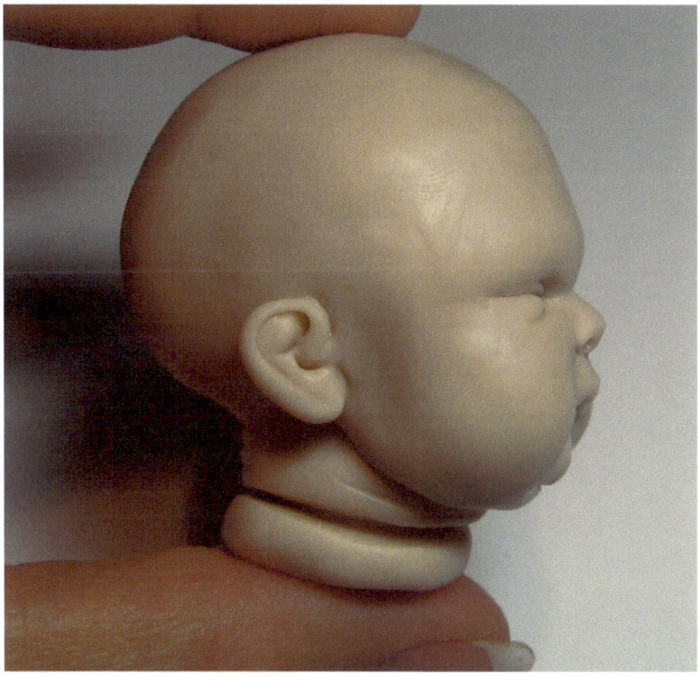

Making a Tiny Wig for a Mini OOAK

with Dorothy Steven

Here are the supplies I use. Make sure to use a thread that matches your mohair.
I also use an iron and a nice flat surface.

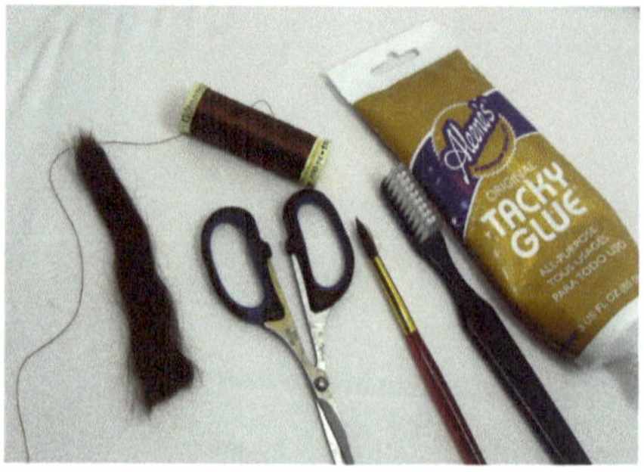

I take a small bundle of mohair and lay it flat. I then use the thread and tie it in the middle of the bundle.

Next fan out both ends like in photo.

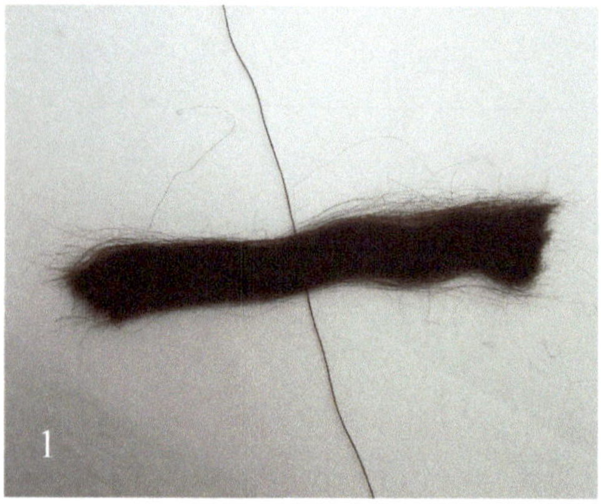

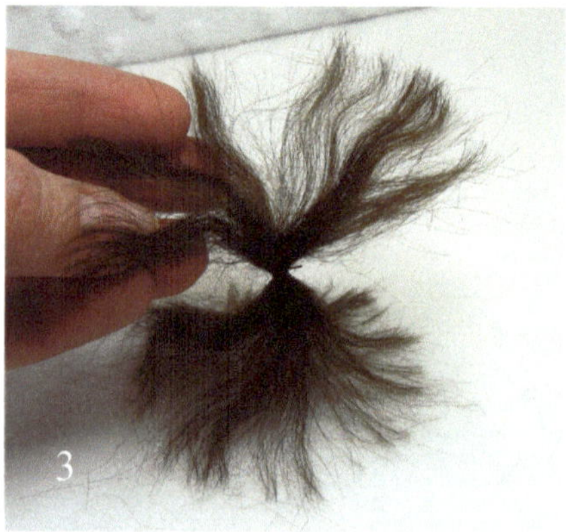

I then flatten the fanned ends like thi., Next, lay the hair on a flat hard surface and set an iron on top to help flatten. I have the iron set to the wool setting.

Here is the flattened hair ready to apply to the doll head. There will be a real tiny circle in the center and that will be the baby's crown.

Using a small brush I then apply the tacky glue. I brush it all over the head where I want the hair to stick.

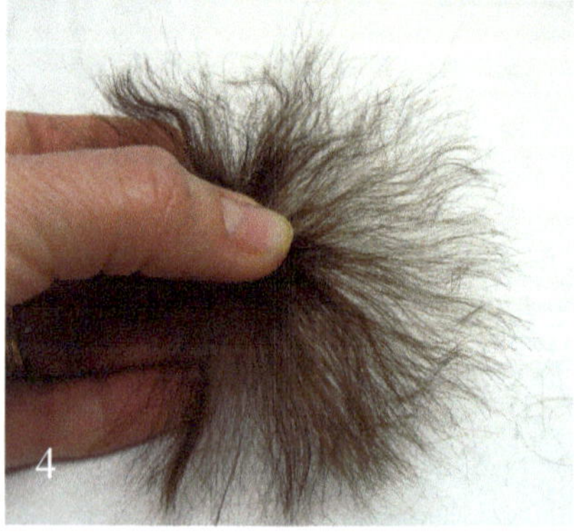

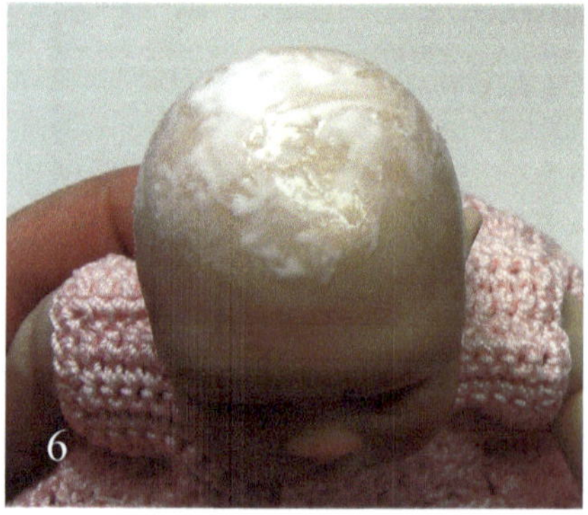

I then apply the hair placing that circle I called the crown at the back upper part of the head. I start there and smooth on the hair using my soft toothbrush. You want it to stick to the tacky glue.

I then start to trim. I use a tiny pair of sharp scissors. I first trim all the length off and then I thin the wig. I cut starting at the bottom on an angle ending towards the crown. I thin out at the temples and at the back of the neck and I trim around the ears. I am aiming for a wispy baby look.

Here is the head after a bit of trimming, you want to cut a wee bit at a time.

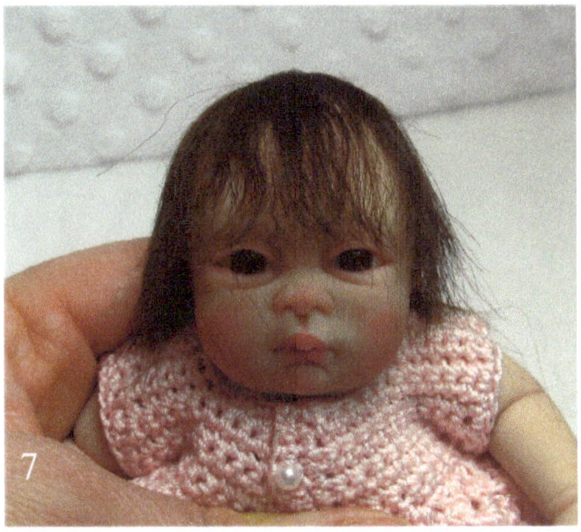

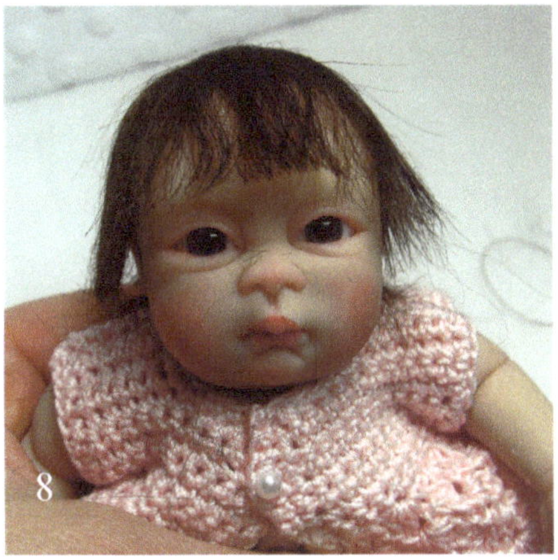

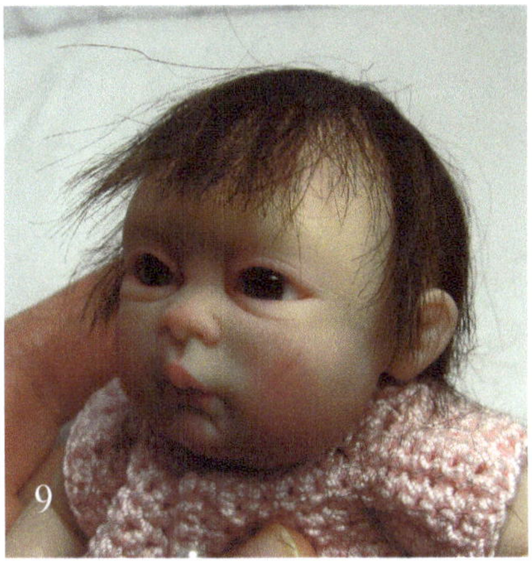

More thinning and trimming on the angle as I described.

More trimming and thinning, side view.

Another view of the little hair cut.

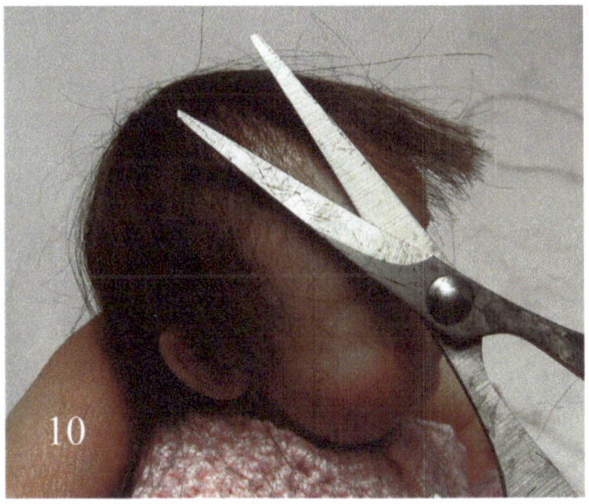

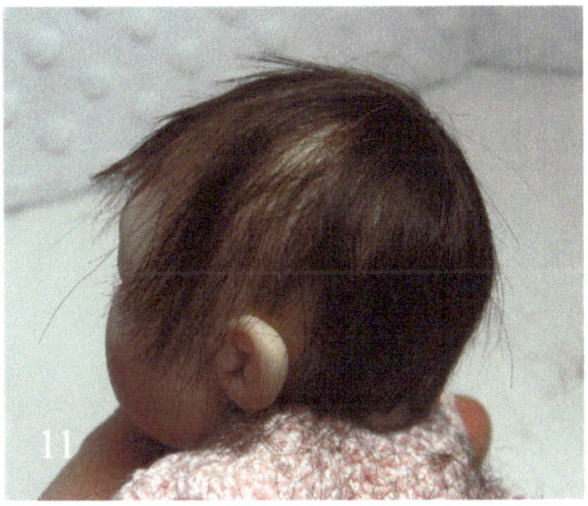

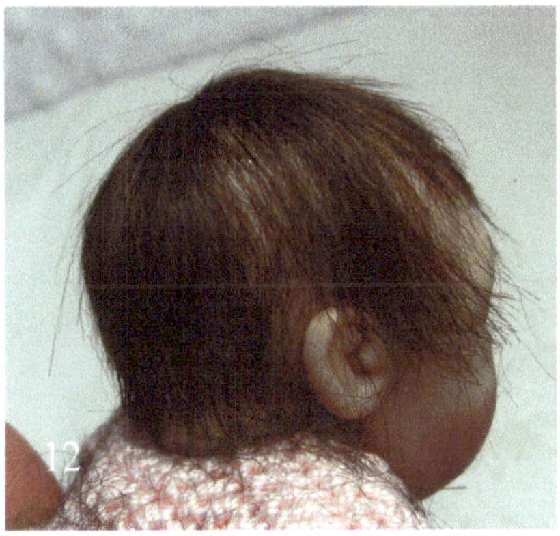

I then wet the hair slightly with a watered down glue mixture. You need more water then glue. I use a paint brush to wet down the hair in the front and at the sides so the baby gets a little style. You can just wet down and style and let air dry but I like to have the hair stay in place so that is why I use the glue.

I use my tooth brush to style her hair some before I let it dry. I use my heat gun but I would let it air dry if you are not familiar with the gun.

Here she is the front view. She has a nice wee baby look to her hair.

Here is a back view of baby's hair.

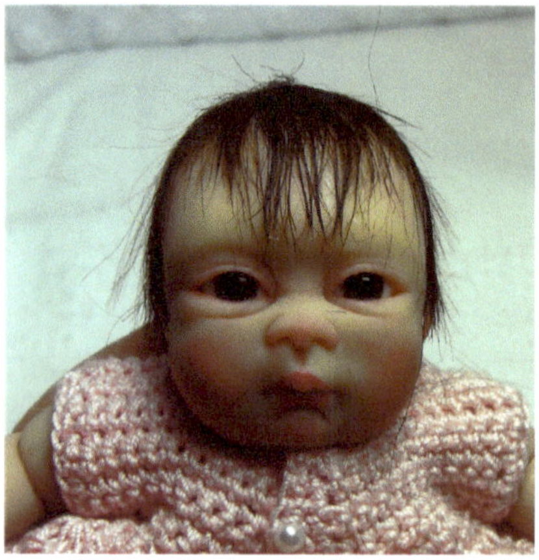

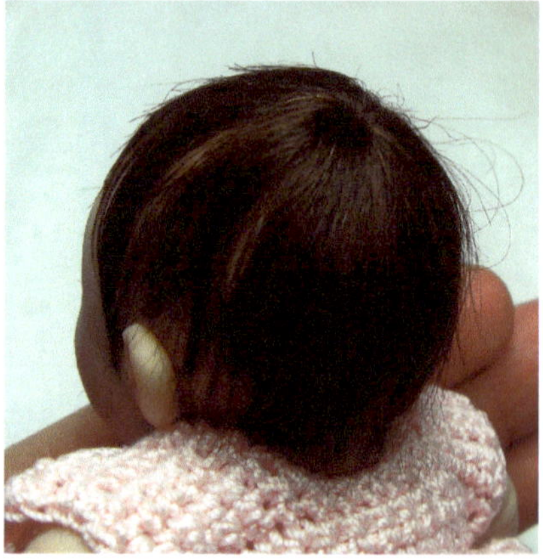

Here she is all finished!

Dorothy Steven
Dot's Tiny Tots

http://dotstinytots.blogspot.com

Creating a Wire Armature

by Michele Barrow-Bélisle

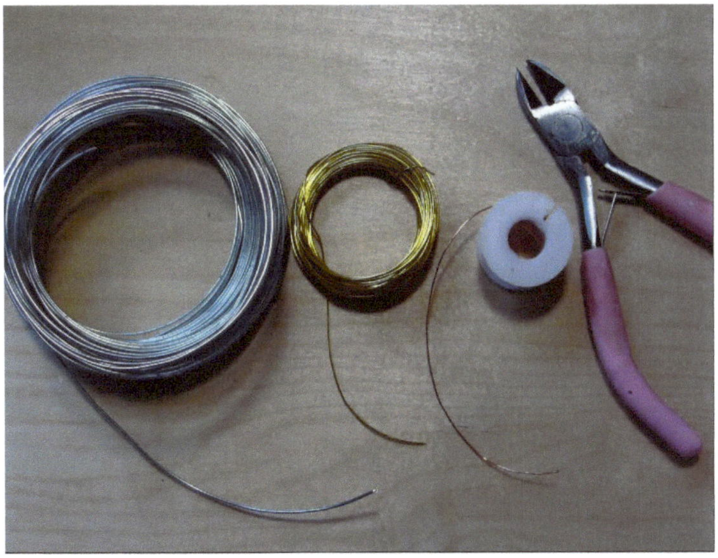

Keeping your dolls and figure sculptures upright can be challenging. Wire armatures are one solution to this problem. They provide a stable inner foundation upon which to build your polymer clay sculpture. I like to think of them as providing the same function as our skeletal system….strong bones offer strong support.

Generally speaking the larger the sculpture, the more critical it becomes to have a solid armature. Clay, being fragile by nature needs the extra support provided by an armature. Tiny polymer sculptures may work out fine without any inner support. Larger scale sculptures require armatures to reduce the amount of clay mass, allowing the piece to fully cure and maintain integrity.

There are a wide variety of materials which can be used for creating an armature; wire, coated wire, tinfoil, vinyl forms, Styrofoam forms (*specifically created for oven use), copper or metal rods, electrical grade rope wire or even PVC or metal pipes.

In this article we will focus on creating a wire armature suitable for smaller scale figures, under 12 inches in size. With a heavier gauge wire you may even be able to use a similar armature for a larger sculpture. Of course there are many other factors which come into play, including the overall design and the intended pose of your sculpture.

Select a firm wire which will easily be concealed by your sculpture, but with enough strength to hold your desired pose. As a general rule of thumb, the higher the number, the finer the wire.

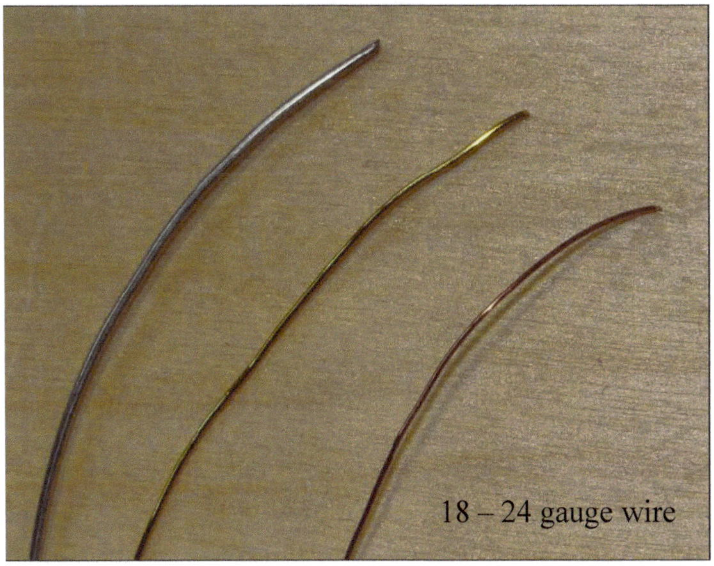

18 – 24 gauge wire

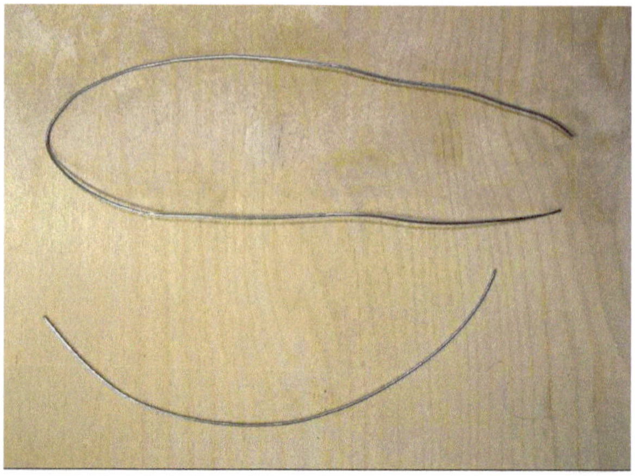

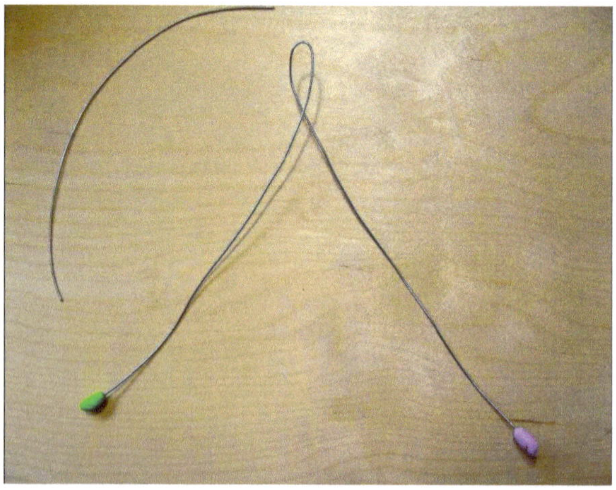

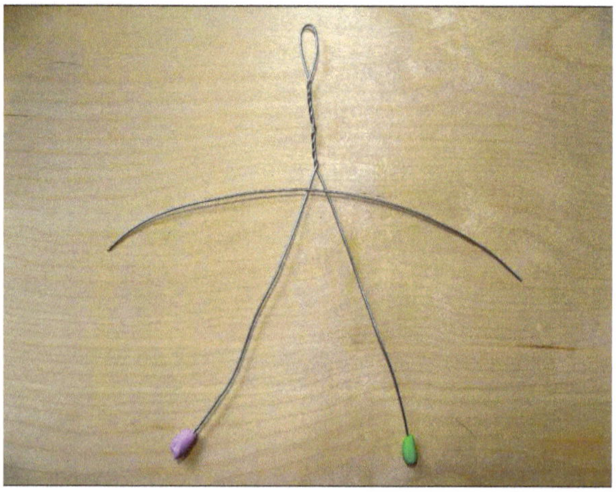

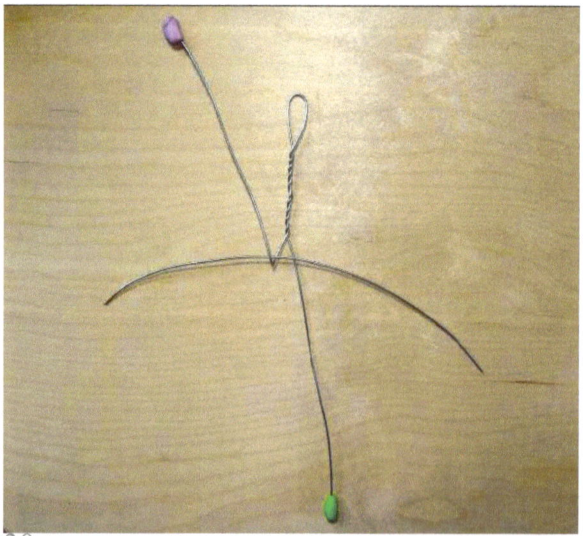

Begin with a length of wire which will run up one leg to the head and down through to the other leg, leaving ample excess for creating a loop. A loop is useful during sculpting, giving you a hands-free way to work on your piece. It can also be handy for hanging your piece in the oven during curing.

Cut another length of wire for the arms.

It may be helpful to have a scale drawing or sketch of your figure to use as a guide. Beginning at the top of the bend, twist the wires to form a small loop at the top. (I've added colored bits of clay to the ends of the wire in order to make it easier to follow the movement.)

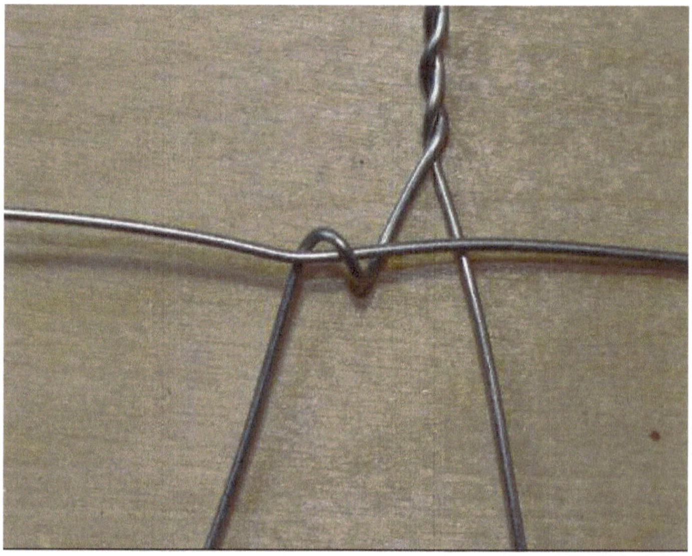

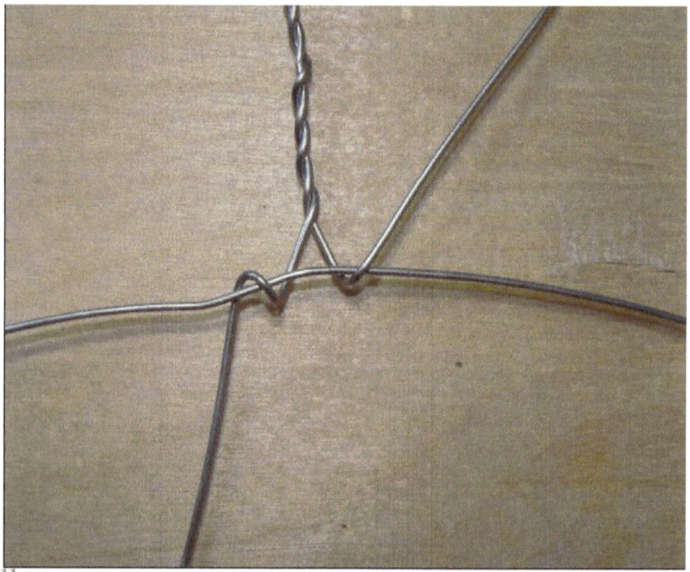

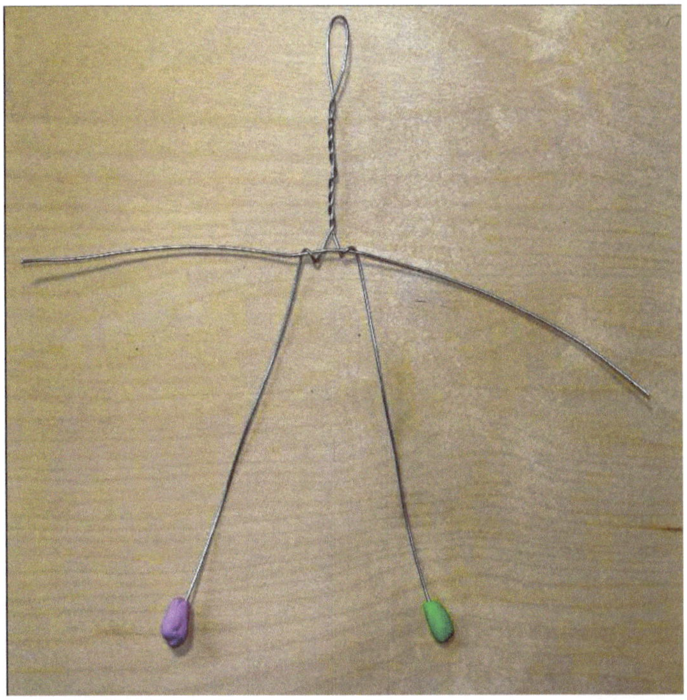

Continue to twist the top loop until you reach the neck/shoulder area of your figure.

Continue turning the top loop, twisting the legs to form the torso.

Place the arm wire across the body, forming a small triangle in the centre. Bend one leg up over the arm wire, wrapping around it and then back to it's place.

Repeat the same with the other leg, wrapping it around the other arm wire. Wrap each arm twice with each leg.

Shape the wires to form the hip joints, elbows and knees.

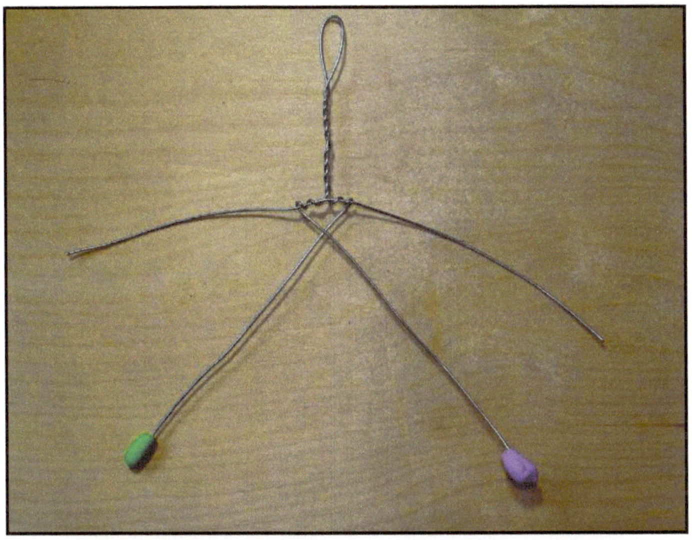

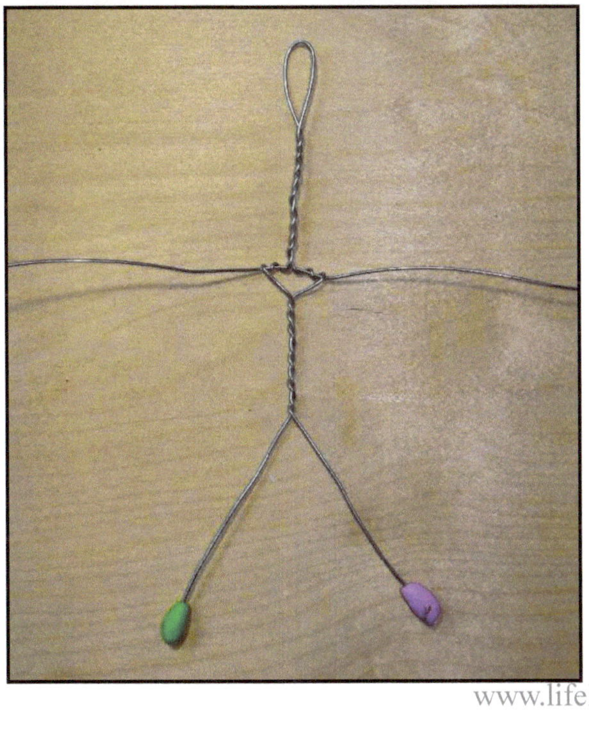

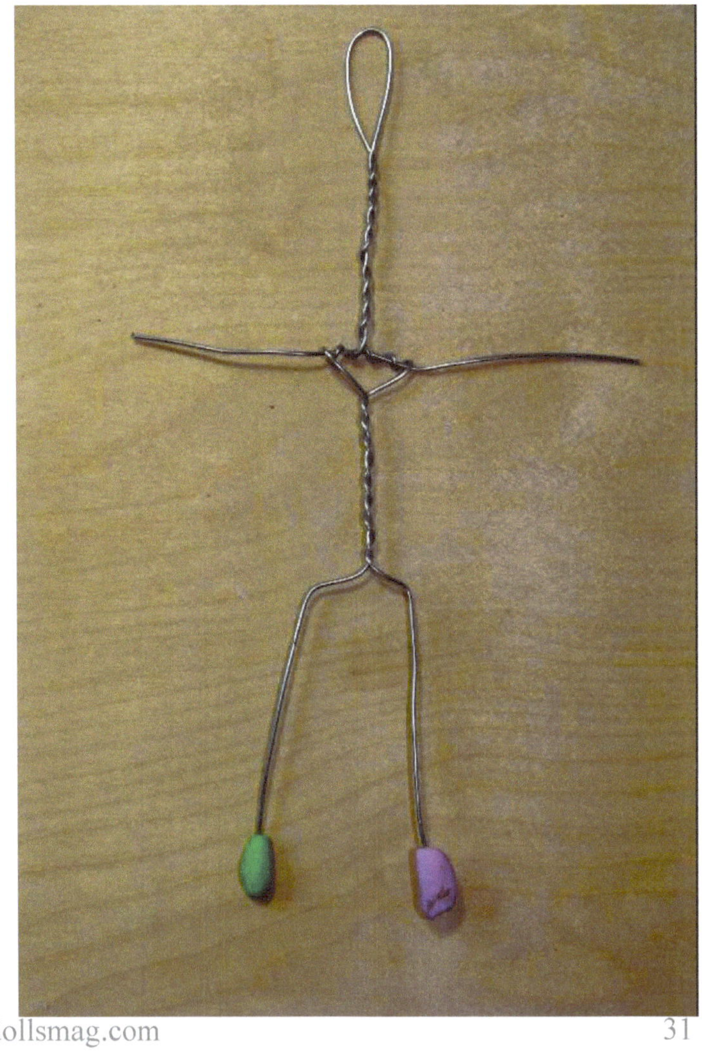

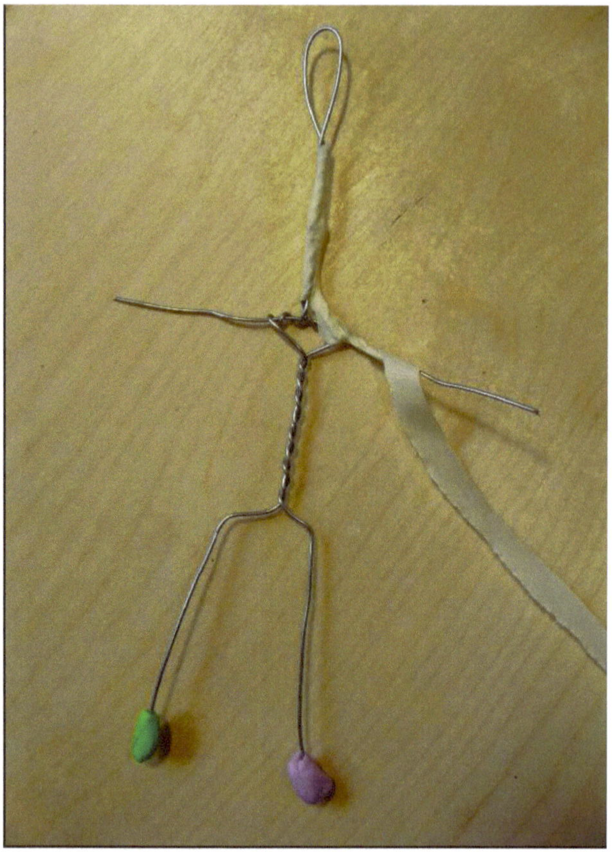

From this point you could cover the armature with floral tape or masking tape to give the clay something to grab onto.

Alternatively, you could create a solid clay under armature, leaving a space at the shoulder, elbow, hip and knee joints to position your armature later. Fire this at a high temperature and cool before beginning your sculpture.

Wire armatures for a sculpture to be assembled on a cloth body can be created for smaller scale sculpts. Find a suitable gauge wire and cut to double the length of the limb. Twist in the same manner and bend into the desired shape. Once again this top loop comes in handy.

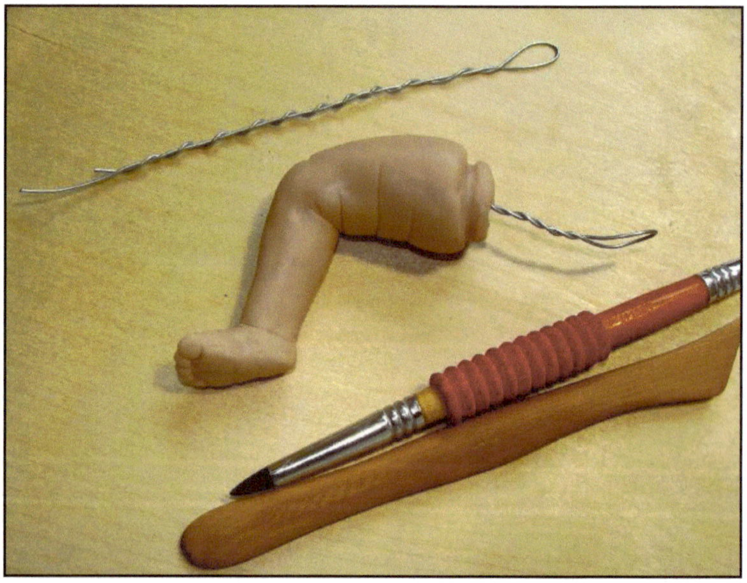

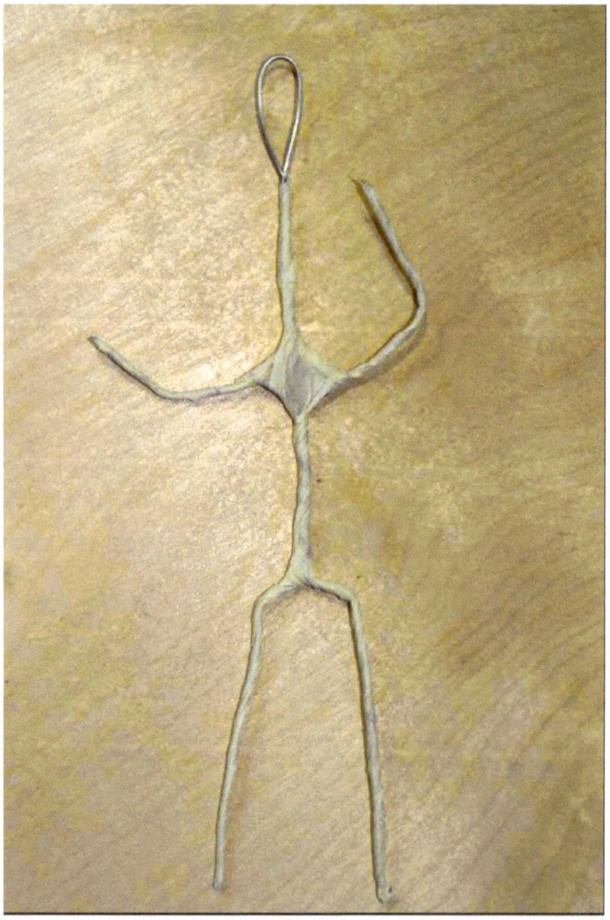

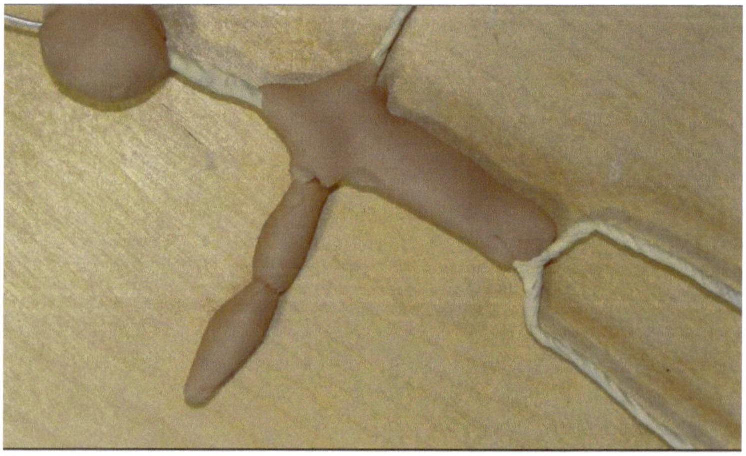

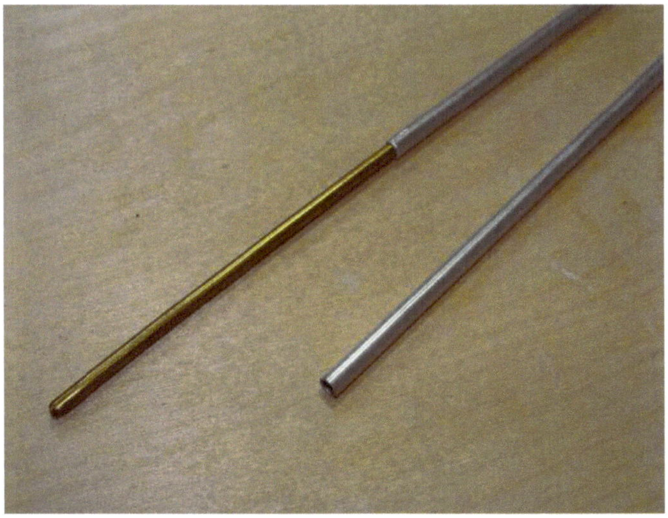

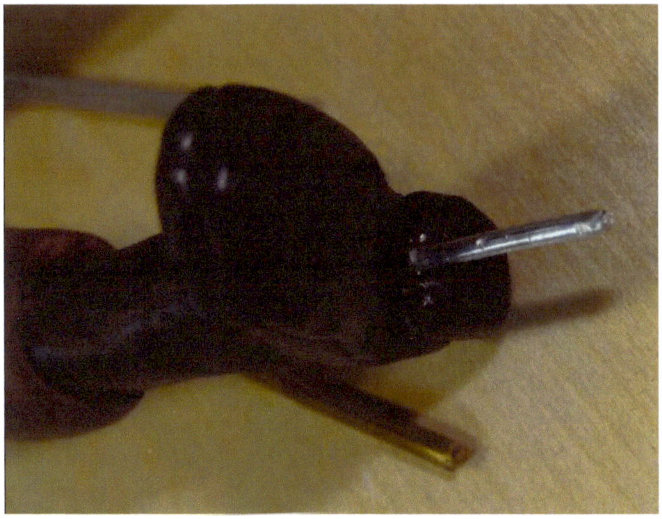

A larger full body sculpt may require metal rods to give greater support. The tube and rod can be used for the dual purpose of creating an armature and providing a support for a free-standing piece.

Once you've created an armature for your piece, you are ready to bring your figure to life, confident that it has the support of a solid foundation. And a solid foundation is pretty much what all good things are built on!

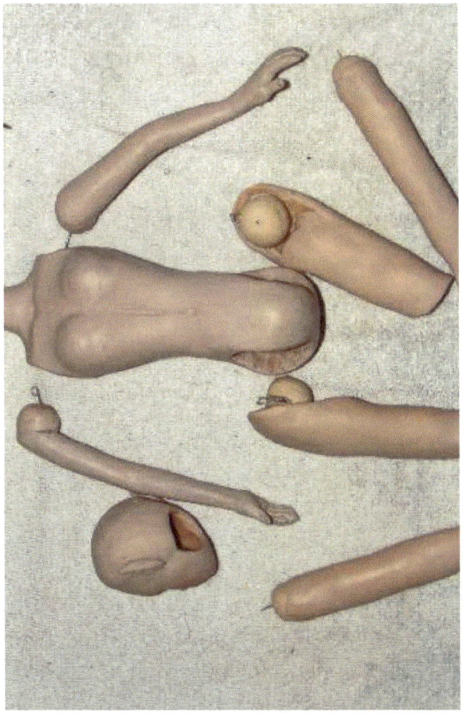

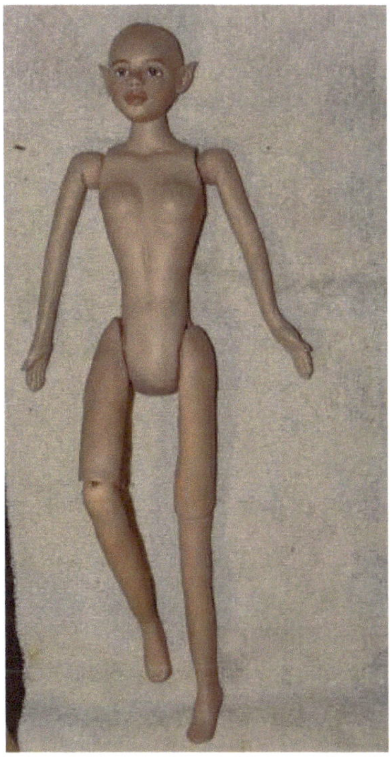

Michele Barrow-Bélisle

MBB Doll Design Inc.
www.mbbdolldesign.com

Sculpting A Ball Jointed Doll
A Five Part Series by Michele Barrow-Belisle

Introduction:

Welcome to the amazing adventure of sculpting a ball jointed doll in polymer clay. My first attempt left me wanting to pull my hair out and run screaming from the room. But after a few deep breaths, and a glass of red wine, I persevered and managed to accomplish what I had set out to do. I invite you to join me in this journey that will offer as much frustration as rewards. In the end you too will have created your own ball-jointed doll in polymer clay.

Traditionally, ball jointed dolls are sculpted from a wet clay. Given the fact that each body part must be hollow, it is easy to see why this would be an ideal medium. But my love of polymer clay set me on a mission to figure out a way to work with it. I am by no means an expert. And this tutorial journey we are on is by no means the only way to produce polymer clay BJD. I really wouldn't necessarily claim it's the best or the easiest way. It's just one way, a method to spark ideas. Explore and experiment and find the method that works the best for you. Some steps can be completed in a different sequence.

A little about these dolls before we begin: Ball Jointed Dolls are high end collector dolls, most often produced in resin, and originating from Japan. Created as one of a kind and limited edition pieces, they began with a company called Volks. The figures were created to resemble popular anime characters; featuring stylized and cartoon-like face sculpts. The popularity of these dolls has grown substantially. They are now produced in a variety of countries and with a diversity of looks, no longer limited to the original Japanese anime styled features. Sizes range from 4 inches to 27 inches and everything in between. Ready to wear fashions and accessories are easy to find for the more popular bjd sizes. It's fun to create your own doll within these specifications, to take advantage of using trendy manufactured outfits expanding your dolls wardrobe easily. It also makes eye and wig selection easier too as the popular sizes offer the most options, variety and styles.

BJDs as so named because of the ball joints, or circular pieces located at each joint, most often the knees, elbows, shoulders and occasionally at the ankles, wrists and hips and chest. This jointing allows the doll's body to move. The dolls can hold a multitude of poses due to the elastic stringing that runs through each limb, into the neck and anchored in the head of the doll. The tension on these strings combined with the slotted round ball joints allow the doll to stand, sit and hold a variety of other positions. This results in a doll that is extremely versatile, allowing you to place it in a wide variety of settings or scenes to convey a desired emotion, message or mood. More recently bjd's can be found in a wide variety of face sculpts and styles from traditional anime to ultra realistic to fantasy to mythological creatures. While these dolls are typically very expressive and dramatic, the overall look is really up to you and your own personal preference.

Before these dolls are cast in resin, an original doll must be sculpted. And this is where we begin. While I do not plan on covering resin casting in this article, you certainly could take your original sculpt and have it cast in resin either professionally or using a do-it-yourself method. This results in a finer, smoother more professional finish to the doll, as well as allowing the possibility of creating multiple casts for a limited edition production or artist edition collection.

Michele Barrow-Belisle
Masquerade Studio
www.masqueradestudio.com
info@masqueradestudio.com

Sculpting a BJD: Part One

Supplies:

- Super Sculpey Polymer Clay
- Template (ideally front view and profile drawn to scale)
- Assorted sculpting tools
- 2 bags of mixed wooden beads, one small size, one large size (not needed if you sculpt your ball joints from clay)
- Tin foil
- Heavy gauge wire (gauge will vary depending upon the size of your doll)
- Glass or high quality acrylic doll eyes (size depends upon your doll's eye size)
- Eyelashes
- Sand paper med, fine & extra fine
- Scalpel or Exacto knife
- Talcum Powder
- Optional: Dremel tool
- Small drill & drill bit mini mite, and collection of sanding and grinding head
- Genesis, or acrylic paints
- Assorted brushes
- Drill bits
- Acetone
- 2 yards of 3mm round elastic
- Tweezers
- Wire
- Needle nose pliers

Preparing your template:

Decide on the look you want to have for your doll. Choose the body type, figure and style. Sketch or trace a front view and profile, giving yourself a rough guideline to follow. It helps if your drawing is to the scale of your doll. That way you can use it as a template while sculpting.

Create a story around your doll. Let images and ideas float in your mind as you plan. Your doll will likely want to tell you her story, so listen carefully to her (or him) and take notes!

Once you have a template drawn or copied to scale, we are ready to begin.

Sculpting

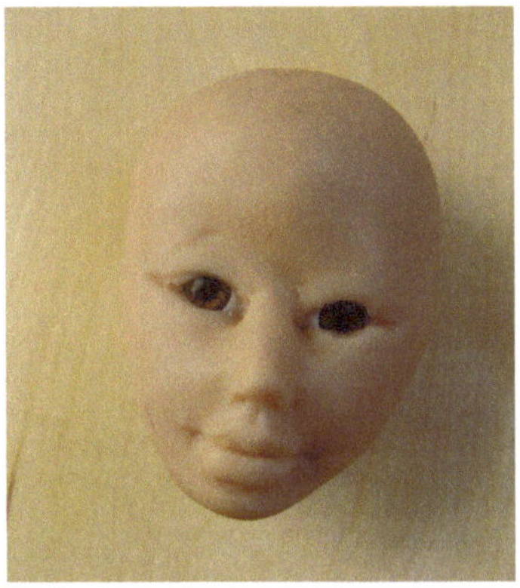

Create a foil armature for the head and the torso. The rest of the body parts can be created with solid clay and then drilled through or a hole made using a knitting needle or similar tool.

Cover the front of a foil ball with clay and create your dolls face…but only the front of the face. The rest of the head will be completed in a second stage. You can sculpt the face and ears. Refer to photos as reference to get the look you are after.

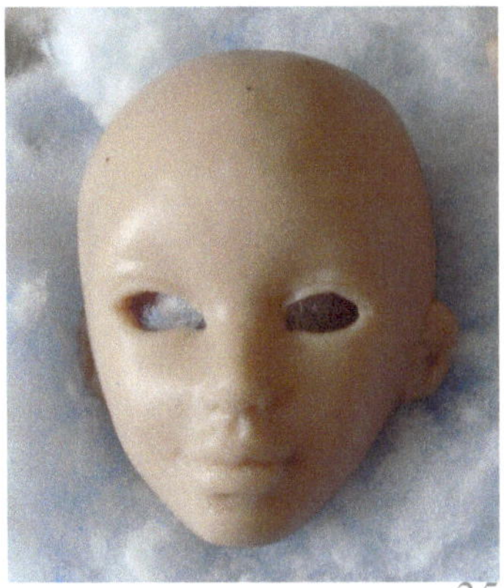

Inset the eyes now, or wait until later. If you want to be able to change the eyes, make sure not to bake them into your clay head (remove them before baking). Once you are satisfied with your doll's face you can bake following the manufacturer's directions.This might be a good time to mention a word about the clay. I have used Super Sculpey for this project, but due to some uneven discoloration during baking, I will have to paint the entire doll before assembling. This may not be an issue with even baking or when using another clay brand. Just something to consider.

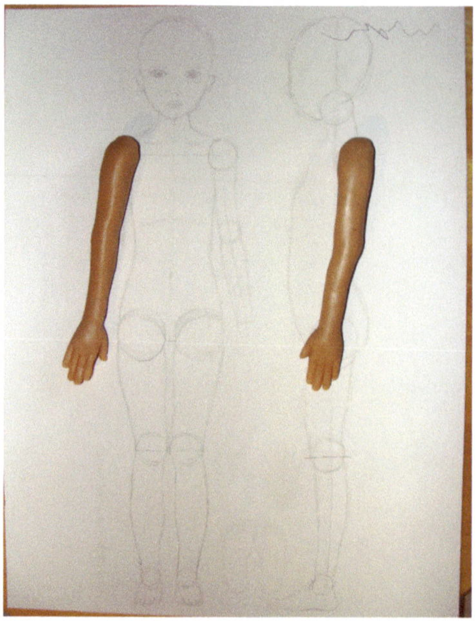

Use your template as a reference to sculpt arms for your doll. As I mentioned, you have the option of using wooden beads as your ball joints or sculpting your own from clay. You could purchase a special device for making perfectly round clay beads; however I just created my own for the purpose of demonstrating.

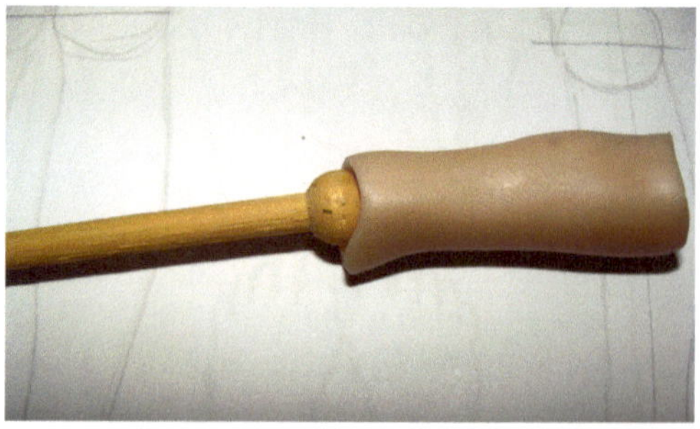

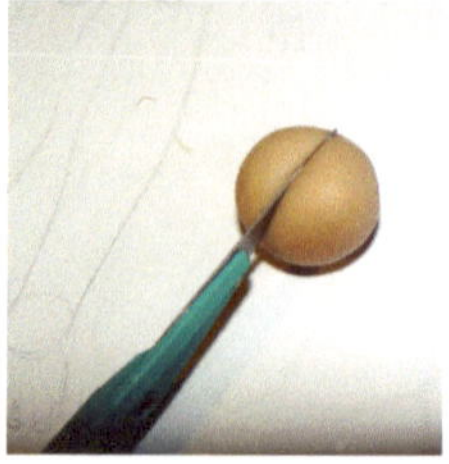

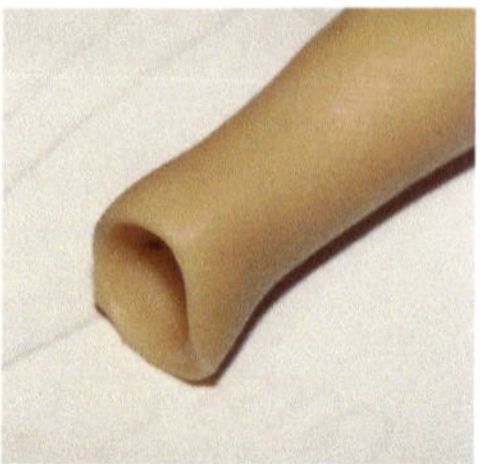

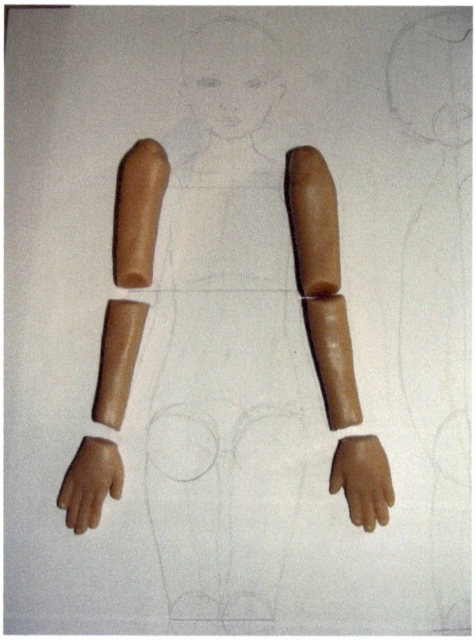

Divide the arm into sections where the joints are going to be placed by slicing with an exacto knife or scalpel.

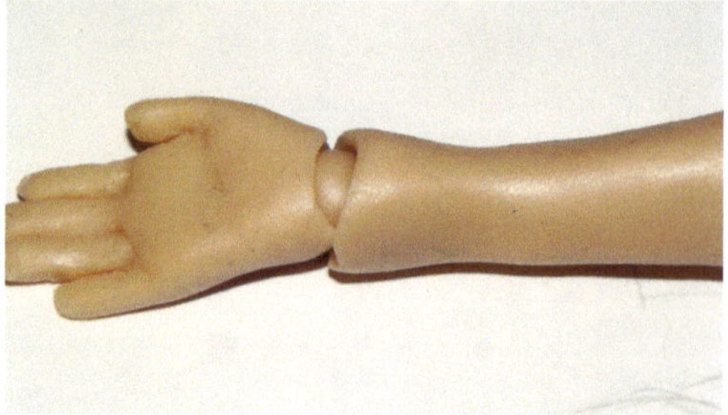

Use a tool to bore a hole through the centre of each arm section with the exception of the hand.Use a ball tool to create a round socket at each end of each joint. Pay close attention to the ball joint sizes in your template.

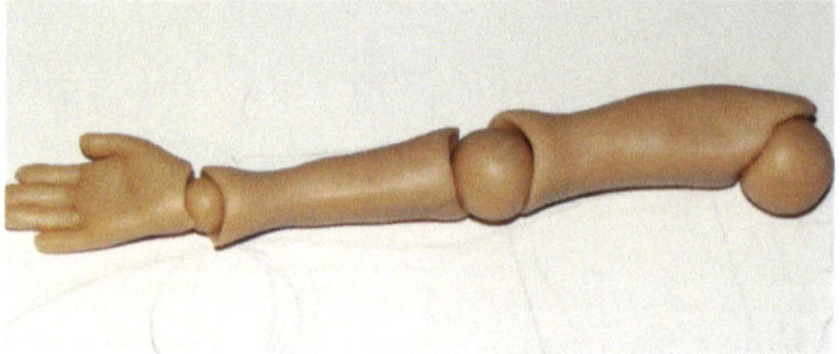

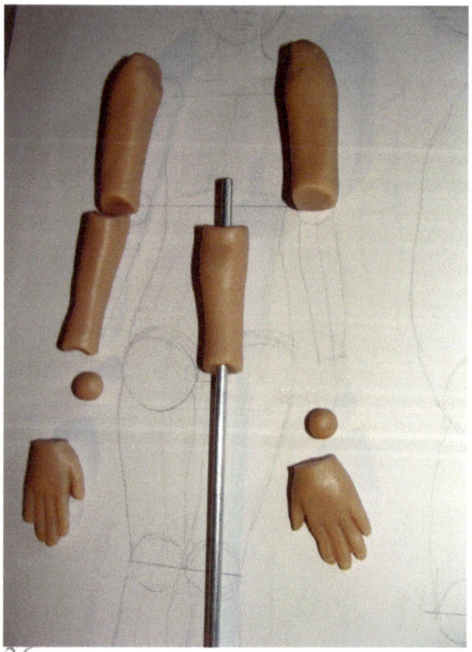

Create (or select) the appropriate sized balls to use for your joints. Dust each ball socket with talcum powder to prevent the uncured clay from sticking to itself. We are not ready to bake yet, so we want to be able to remove our ball joints so that we can add holes for stringing.

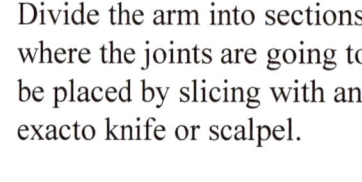

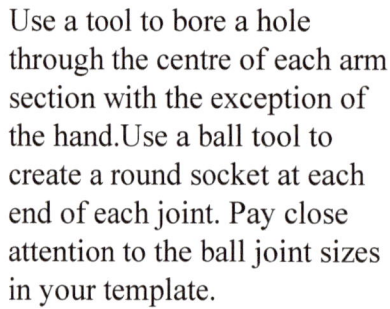

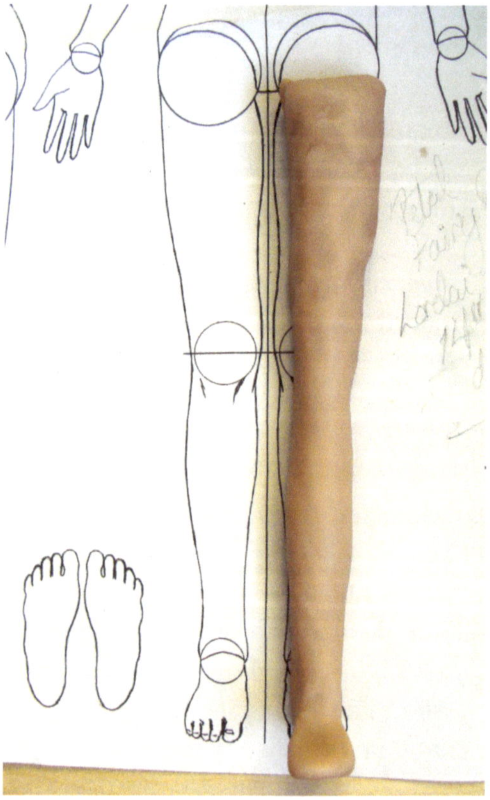

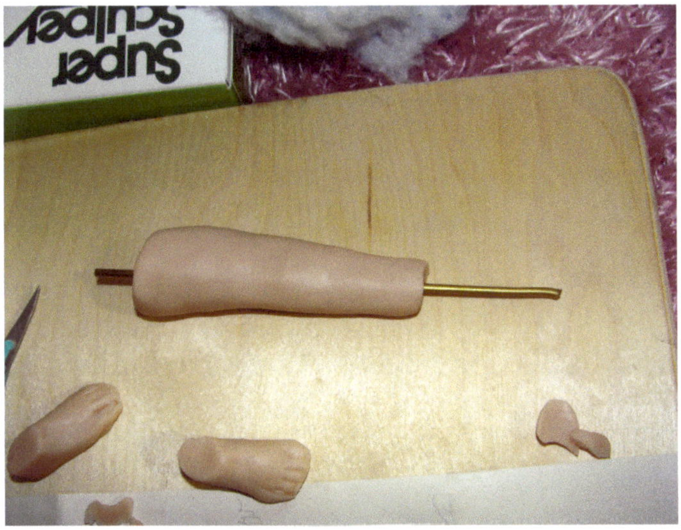

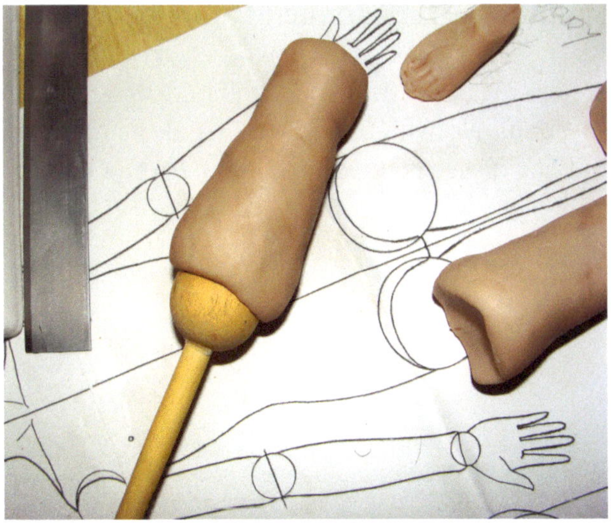

Use the same method for creating the legs. Begin by sculpting the legs to fit your template.

Divide the leg as we did with the arms, at the joints. Create a "V" shaped cut at the back of the knee for ease in bending. Using a ball tool, create the sockets in each end of the leg sections and the corresponding ball joints to fit.

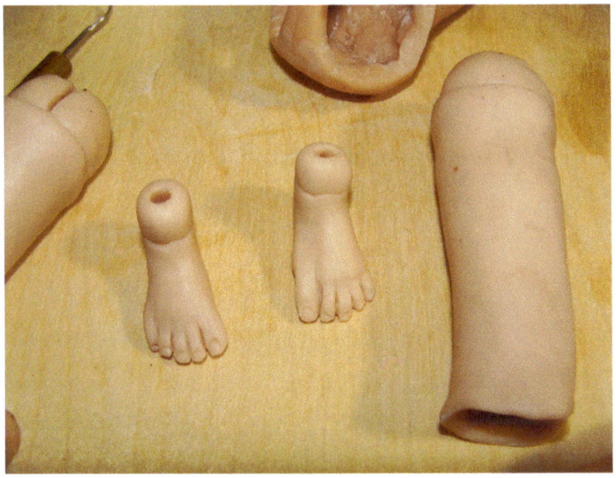

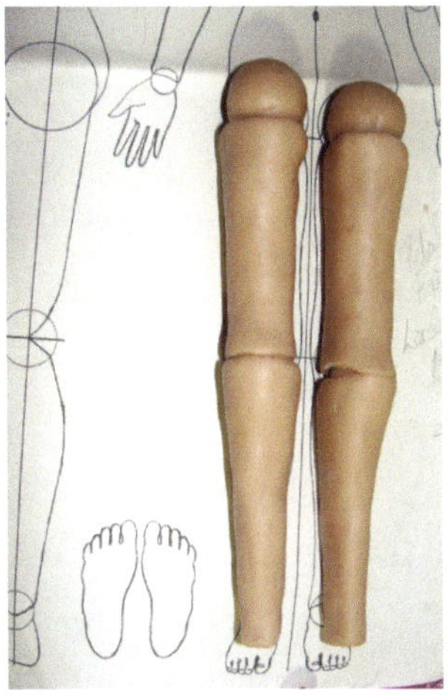

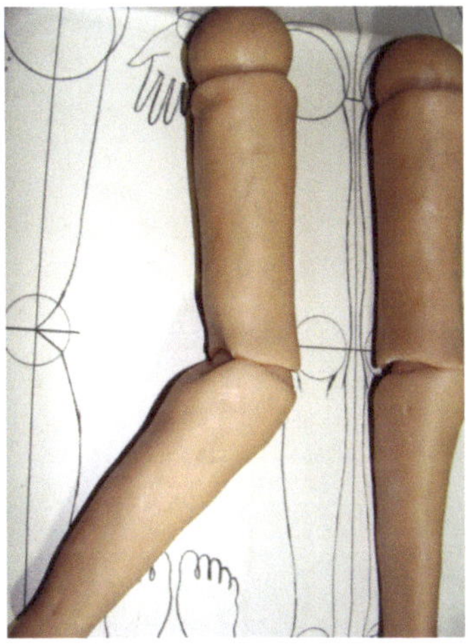

Sculpting a Ball Jointed Doll Part 2

Welcome back! Grab your sculpting supplies and a cup of coffee, tea or my personal favourite, red wine and let's continue with our ball jointed doll project. When we last left off, we had completed the face, arms and legs and had dissected the limbs into pieces in order to add our ball joints. Next we will sculpt the torso.

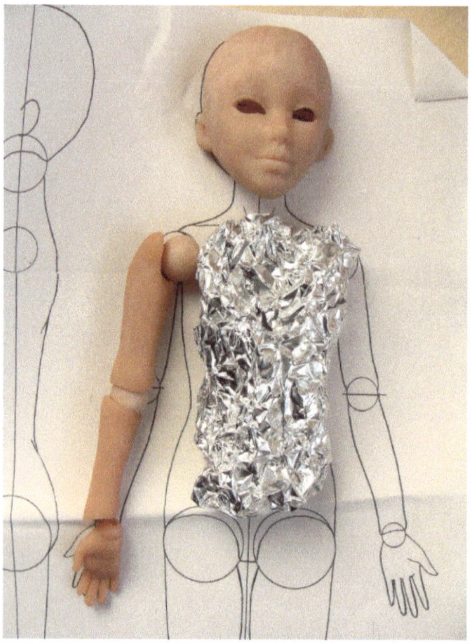

Refer to your sketch or model in order to follow the correct proportion for your doll. This part of the body will need to be hollow, so one method for accomplishing this is to create a foil armature to sculpt our torso over. Once the torso had been baked, we can remove the foil.

This works well for larger scale dolls, If you were creating an 8 or 10 inch doll, you could sculpt a solid torso, fire lightly and then use carving tools to carefully hollow out the torso if you would like a ball joint at the chest or just use tubing to create hollow channels for inserting the strings through the center up through the neck and through each limb. An example of this will follow in a later lesson just for interests sake.

Here we have the torso armature created, with our baked arm and hand sections and face. Cover the foil with a thin layer of clay and sculpt in the details of your doll"s torso. The proportions, body type/size and physique are all up to you. There are several wonderful anatomy books that reference the human body at various ages and from differing angles. Those used in addition to images and photos will become some of your most treasured sculpting resources.

One thing to keep in mind is where the ball joints will be located, and to make sure the arm and leg openings can accommodate them. You could use premade clay balls or glass marbles as a template to simulate the position of the ball joint are the shoulder and hip sockets. Use a needle tool to create a hole from the foil center up through the neck.

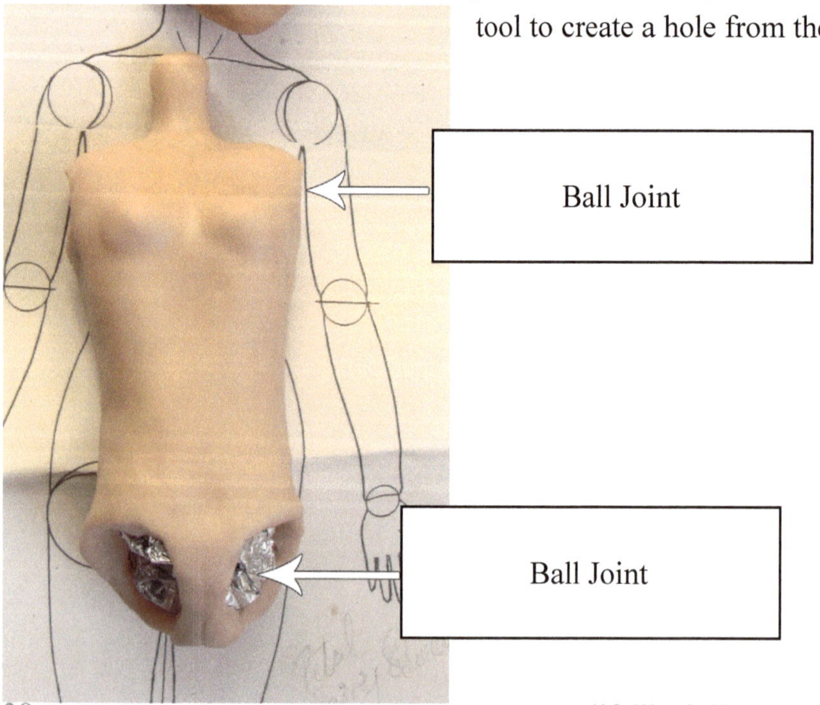

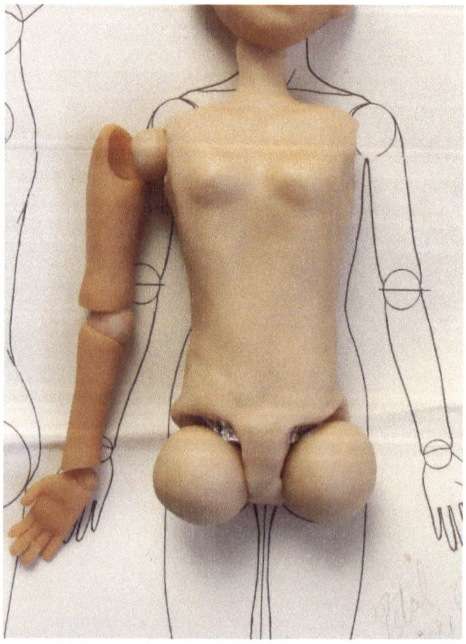

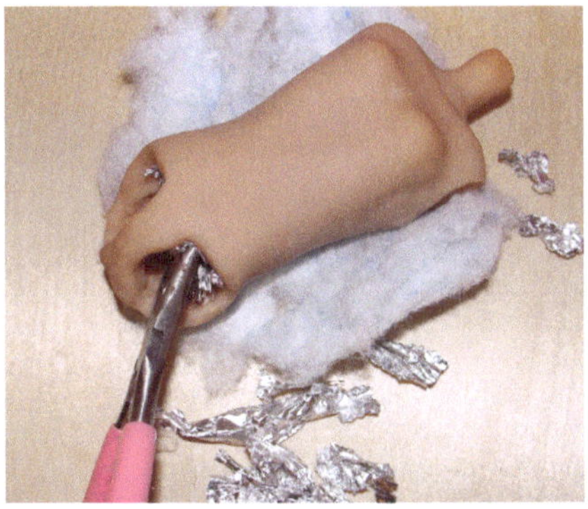
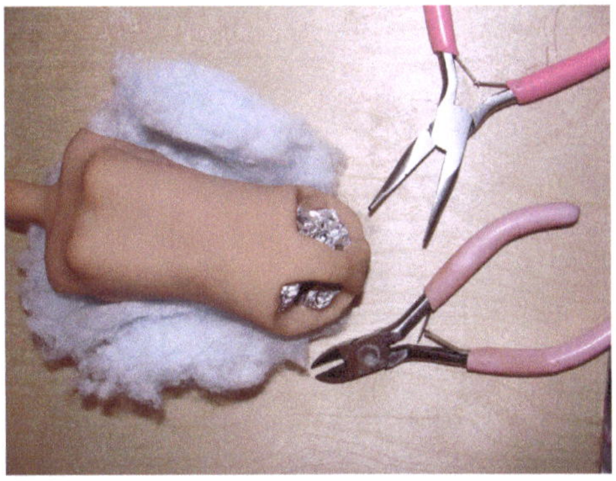
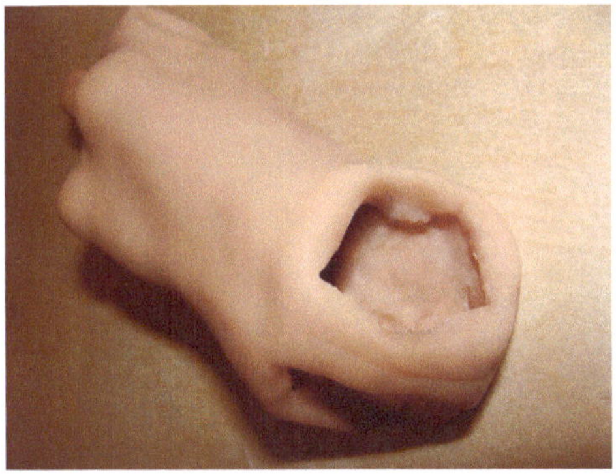
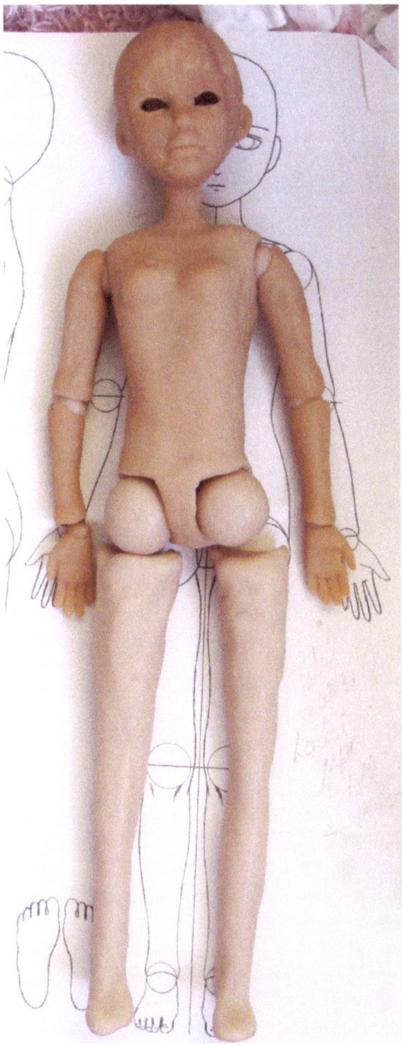

Once you have sculpted your torso, smooth and refine and then bake according to directions provided by the clay manufacturer. Allow the torso to cool and lightly wet sand any uneven areas as needed.

Carefully begin to remove the foil. Using a small pair of needle nose pliers, pull pieces of the foil away from inside the torso, until it is completely hollow. You should be able to see through the hole through the neck, but if not, gently drill an opening. This is necessary for stringing the body together later in a later stage.

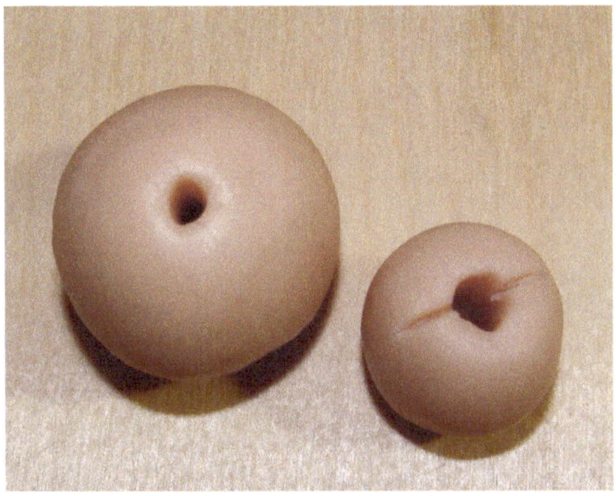

This is a good point to do a first round of baking. This way we can create and fit the ball joints (especially useful if you are creating them from clay). Each ball joint has a hole through it, the knee and elbow joints have slits to allow for bending, and the ankle and wrist ball joints have a pin inserted with s-hook connectors.

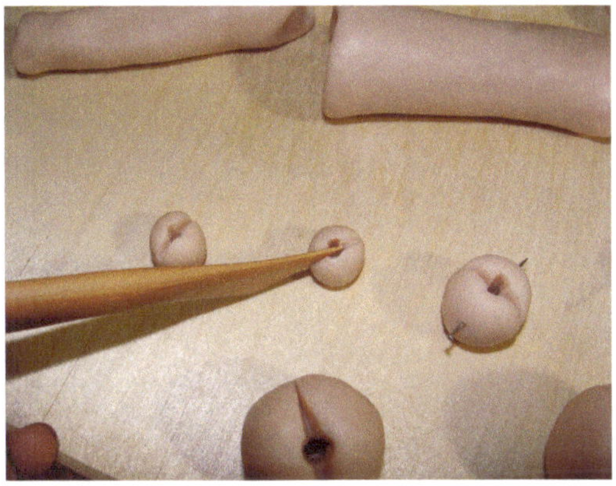
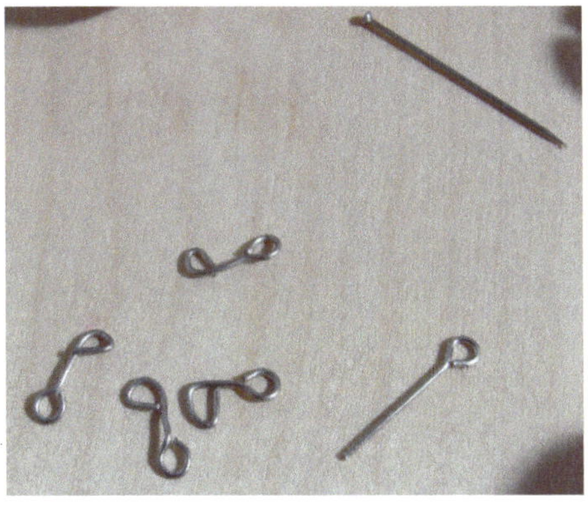
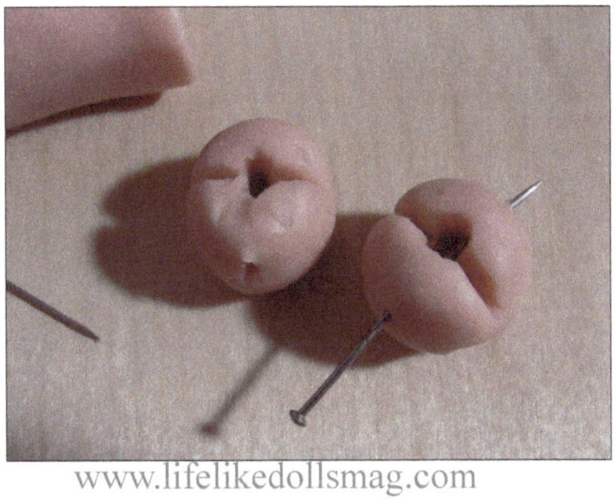
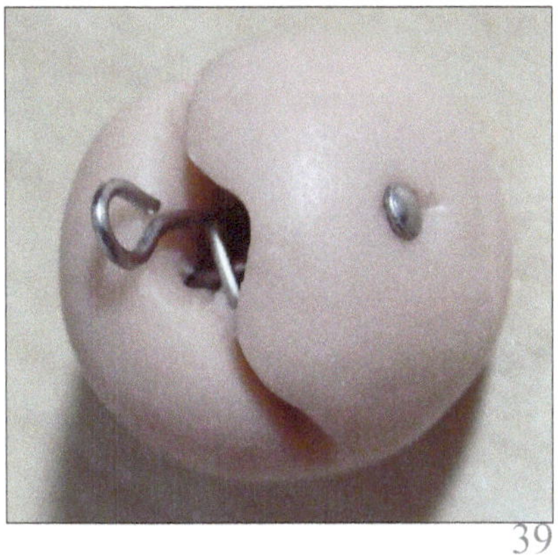

Add a round ball of foil as an armature and add clay to create the back of the head. Leave an opening at the bottom of the head to attach the head to the neck. Cut a circular opening at the top of the head slightly towards the back. This allows access for inserting eyes as well as connecting the elastic strings when assembling the doll. I like to cut out the pieces, dust it with cornstarch or baby power and then put it back in place, baking the whole head. This will allow the piece we cut to easily separate from the rest of the head.

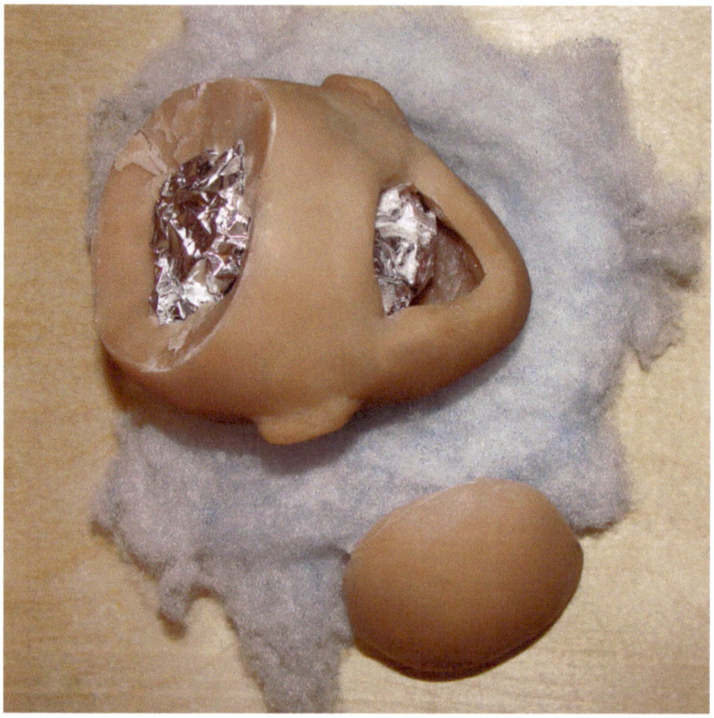

Bake the head. Allow cooling and removing the cap we cut, exposing the foil. Remove the foil using needle nose pliers the same way we did with the torso. Create a ball joint on the neck to attach the head, adding a hole through the center. Cure the ball in order to create a fitting socket in the head.

Fit the ball joint to the head by creating a claysocket for it to sit in. Decide on the eyes you would like to use, and insert them using clay to secure them in place. Fully cure the head. Take your time with this, and make sure to either wrap pieces in batting or insert into an over roasting bag for baking to avoid burning your work. If it does happen (it even happened to me) just breath, have a sip of that coffee, tea or wine and re-sculpt the piece. Or you can do what I did and paint all of the pieces in a matte neutral doll flesh using Genesis paints once you've finished sculpting.

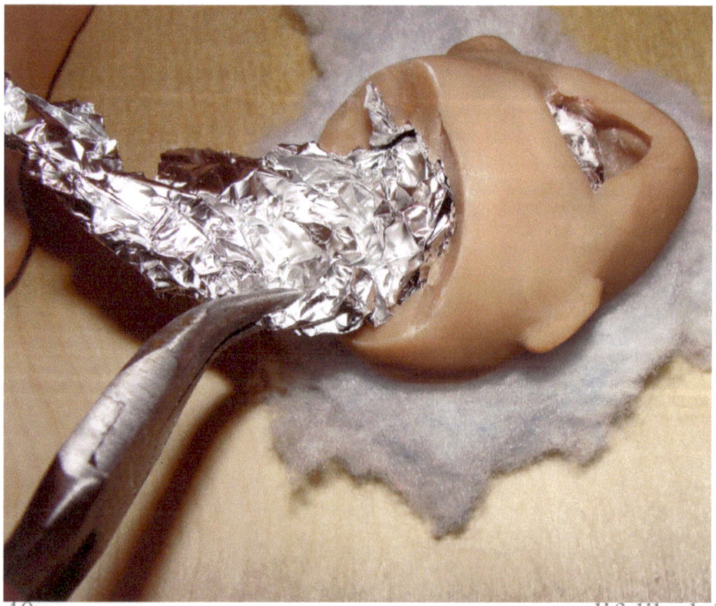

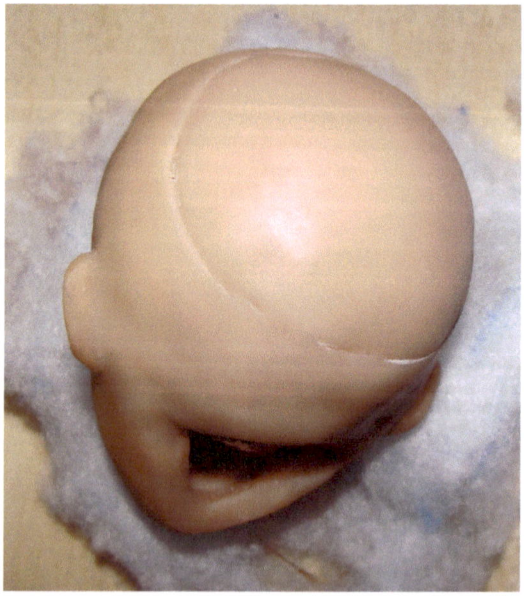

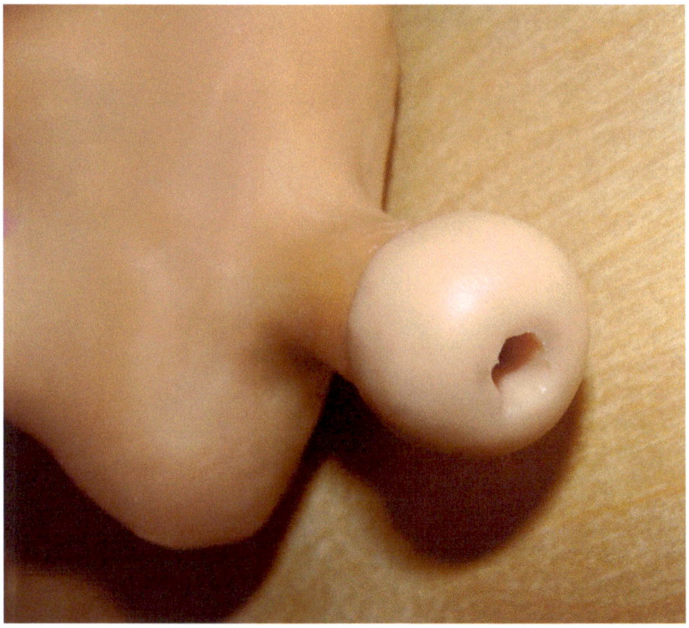

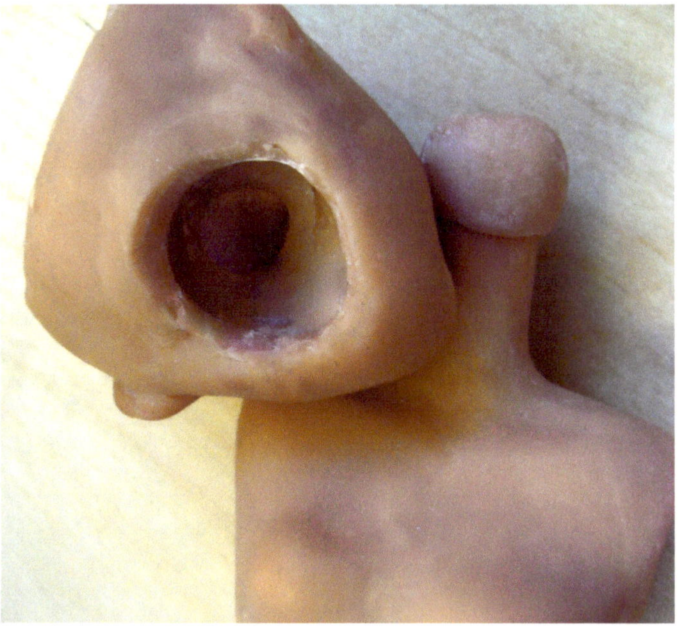

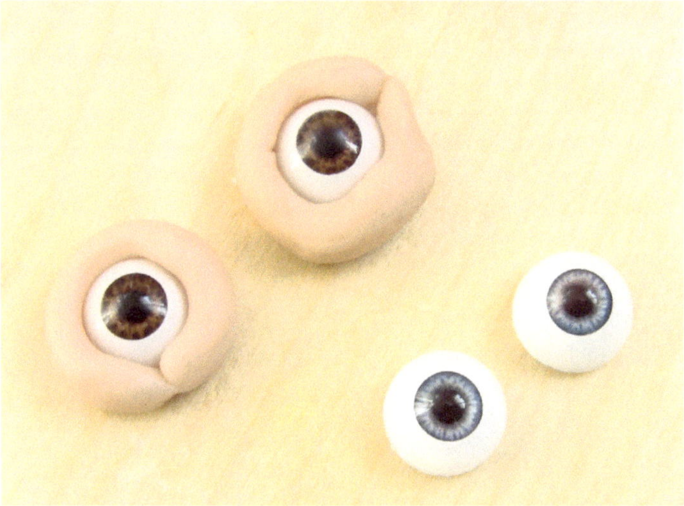

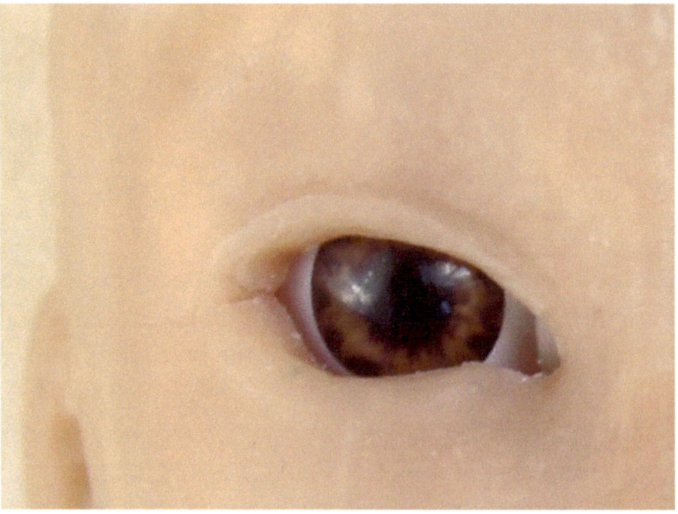

This gives everything an even uniform base color before we move onto painting features and details in our next tutorial.

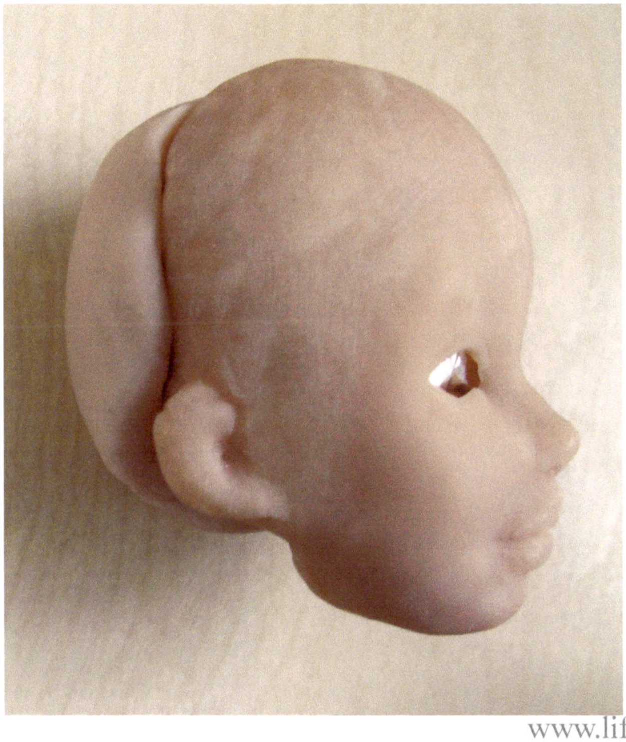

Sculpting a Ball Jointed Doll Part 3

Welcome back! By now you've got all of the essentials at hand…. your sculpting materials and a nerve-soothing beverage, whatever that may be. Today, I've felt the need to add some chocolate to the mix! Ready? Let's dive in.

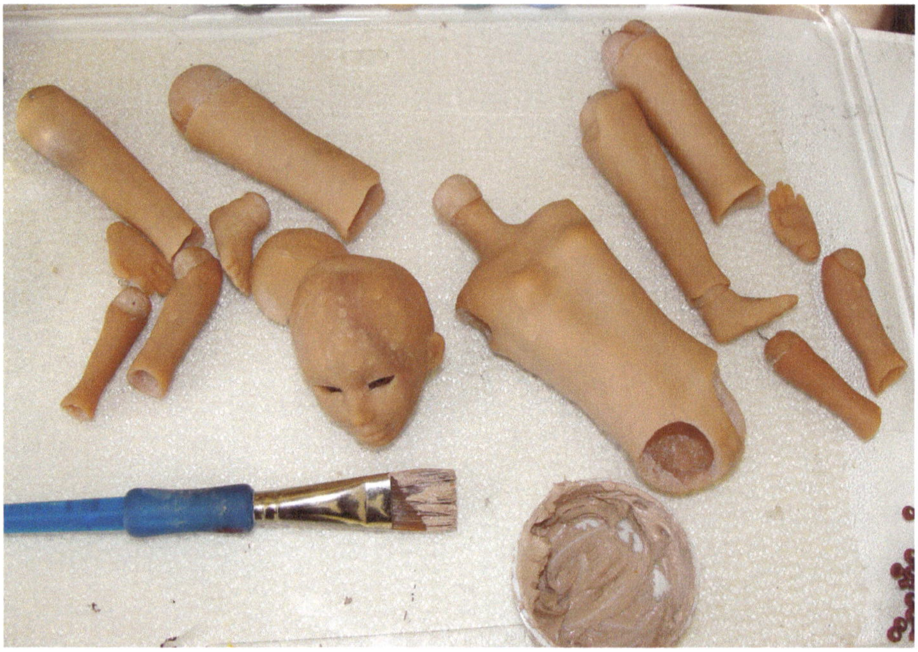

We have completed the sculpting process of our doll; all of her body parts, and ball joints and we have added the pins and s-hooks to the ball joints. I like to attach the ball joints to the limb section, although you could in theory leave them free floating. If the ball joints or limb are wet (as in the clay hasn't been cured) then they will adhere to one another without any problems. I like to add some adhesive just to make sure there is n extra strong bond. I've used both regular Crazy Glue (The gel works best, because it's easier to control and Lisa Pavelka Poly Bonder (hi temp brush on adhesive) made specifically for polymer clay with great success. It's available from their online store at www.lisapavelka.com, and can be used on wet or cured clay. Once this step had been completed you are ready to cure the pieces fully.

This poor girl's head suffered from an exceptionally large number of "moonies", the term used to describe the small crescent shaped discolorations left in the clay after baking, and discoloration. It is something most noticeable with using translucent clays such as Super Sculpey. Sometimes they are tiny and located in places that are fairly inconspicuous. But on other occasions (usually when you least have time for it) they are plentiful and unsightly. Fortunately, I have discovered two tricks to prevent and almost eliminate the dreaded moonies when using Super Sculpey polymer clay. First, prior to baking the clay, brush each piece entirely with the Natural Citrus Hand cleaner. It is available in the hardware stores, and is frequently used for removing paint and grease from hands. There are various brands available, I use MotoMaster Natural Citrus Lotion Hand Cleaner; just be sure not to get the one with pumice (ground apricot seed) added to it. It should be milky white in color. As an added bonus you can use it to clean the clay residue from your hands after sculpting and it smells wonderful! Use a soft bristled brush, and apply a thin layer over each piece. It is important not to over do this step, or your clay will become overly sticky. Let this dry before baking. This step on its own generally prevents any of the moonies from forming, for whatever reason. Secondly, you can use an over roasting bag to cure your clay in. Simply rest your pieces on a bed of polyfil stuffing or batting, and place inside a large oven roasting bag. (These are available in the grocery store usually close to aluminum foil and such.)

I have to tell you, my cooking friends laugh at me when they see the number of kitchen supplies in my sculpting studio. But I mean seriously, where else would you keep your toaster oven, pasta machine, food processor and aluminum foil? <Sigh>

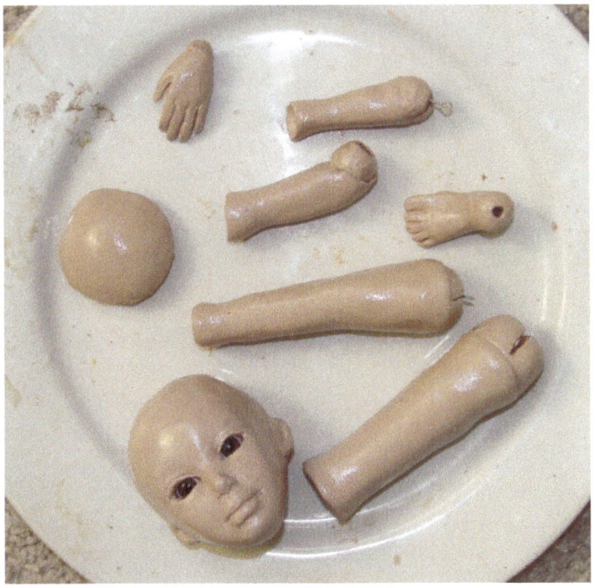

Anyway, the oven bag keeps a constant temperature inside, curing the clay evenly. This also helps to reduce any scorching. Needless to say, in my haste, I failed to take either of these precautions when curing my doll's head. So instead of re-sculpting the piece, which is one choice, I opted to paint the entire doll. You could also do this if you wanted to change the colour of your doll's skin tone, creating a lighter or darker complexion.

Wet sand each piece using wet-dry sandpaper; first with a rough grade paper and then finishing with very fine. Wipe down each piece using a cosmetic sponge dipped in acetone to remove any scratches. If you have sensitive skin, I suggest wearing gloves for this and work in a well ventilated area.

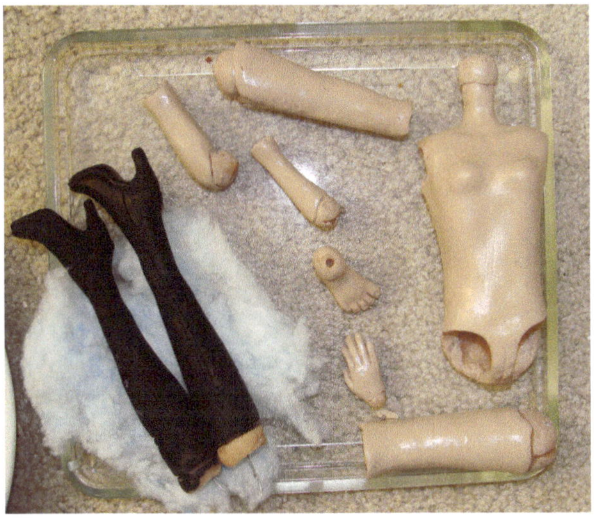

Once smooth and dry, we are ready to paint. The colors you use are up to you, but I'll give you an example of my color selections.

I blended Genesis Paint colors Flesh 08 and Flesh 07 plus a touch of Pyrrole Red 05, with thinning gel and a small amount of odorless thinner and painted each piece with a thin layer. Then I cured the parts in the over at the recommended temperature and time which in my home oven was approximately 10 minutes. I sanded lightly and painted a second coat.

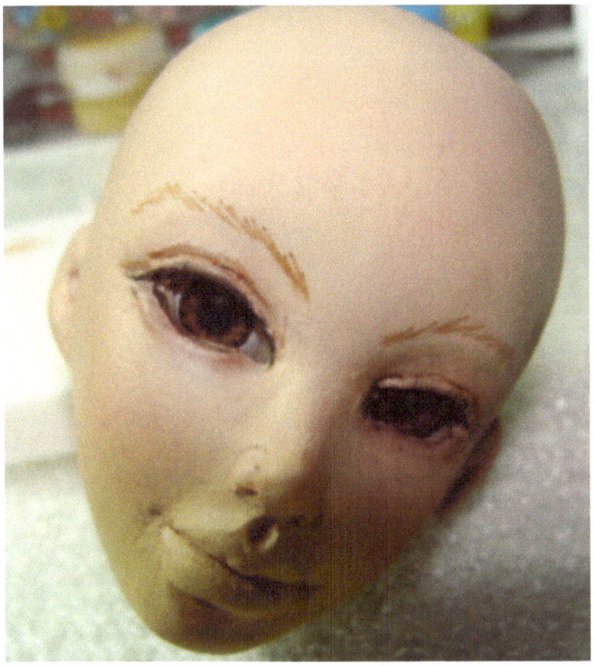

Once this base color has dried, you can add blushing and shading as desired. Depending upon the look you are trying to achieve. For a traditional face up-look on your doll, do a wash of reds/ pinks (such as Pyrrole Red 05 to which I add a touch of Flesh 07 which helps to neutralize the color a little) to blush the doll entirely. There was a wonderful article on Face Ups in a previous issue of Lifelike Dolls Magazine that you can refer back to for ideas. Applying a thin translucent layer of color and wiping are the excess with a clean dry cosmetic sponge. This will leave color in the recessed and creased areas, like around the eyes and in the hollow of the collar bone.

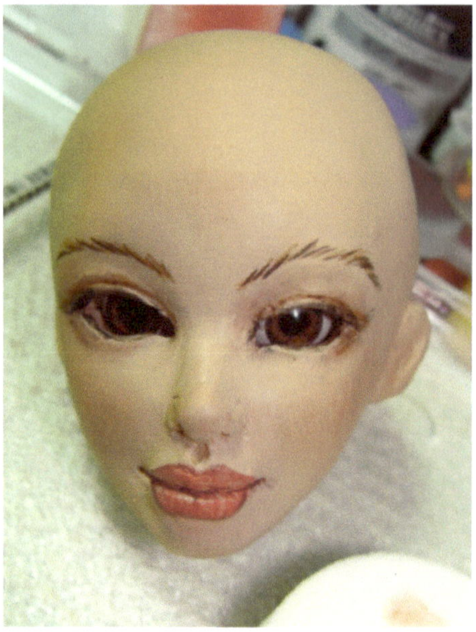

Using the sponge or a small mop brush, apply some of the same blush color to the cheeks and forehead and perhaps the tip of her nose, breasts, stomach, derrière, shoulders, knees, elbows, and the tops and bottoms of her hands and feet (and anywhere else that strikes your fancy).

Returning to the face, you can add additional detailing and lining to the eyes and paint in the eyebrows using an ultra fine brush and tiny strokes, which I did using Burnt Umber. Paint her lips as desired (I blended Flesh 07 with Pyrrrole Red 02 and a touch of Phthalo Green with Glazing Medium for my lip colour). Heat set the paint if using Genesis paints, or allow time to dry if using acrylics. You may want to avoid traditional oil paints, which can react with the polymer clay over time, and cause problems down the road with your piece.

Once the paint has dried you can apply eyelashes to your doll, using a toothpick to apply a thin line of tacky white glue to hold them in place. I went with long diva lashes. You can select whatever style you prefer, or you can paint them on if you choose. To secure the lashes in place you could apply a coat of clear gloss varnish to or Aileen's Paper Glaze to the eyes and lash line which would also add an extra glossy look to the eyes.

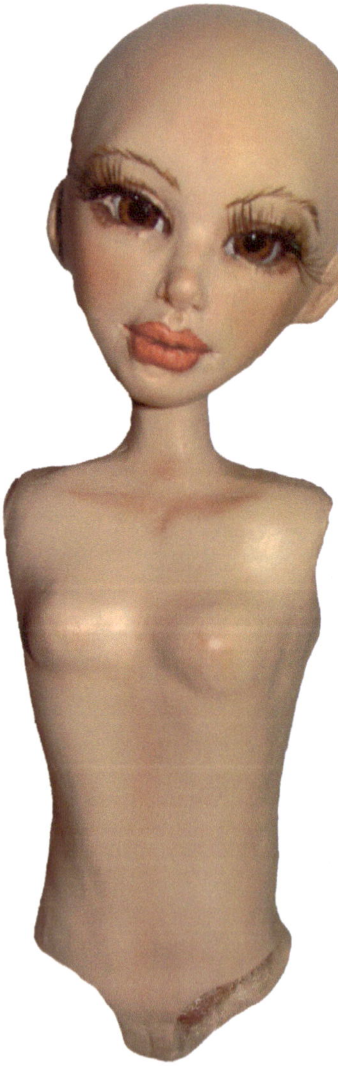

Just for fun, I had to take peek to see how she will look with hair. A definite improvement!

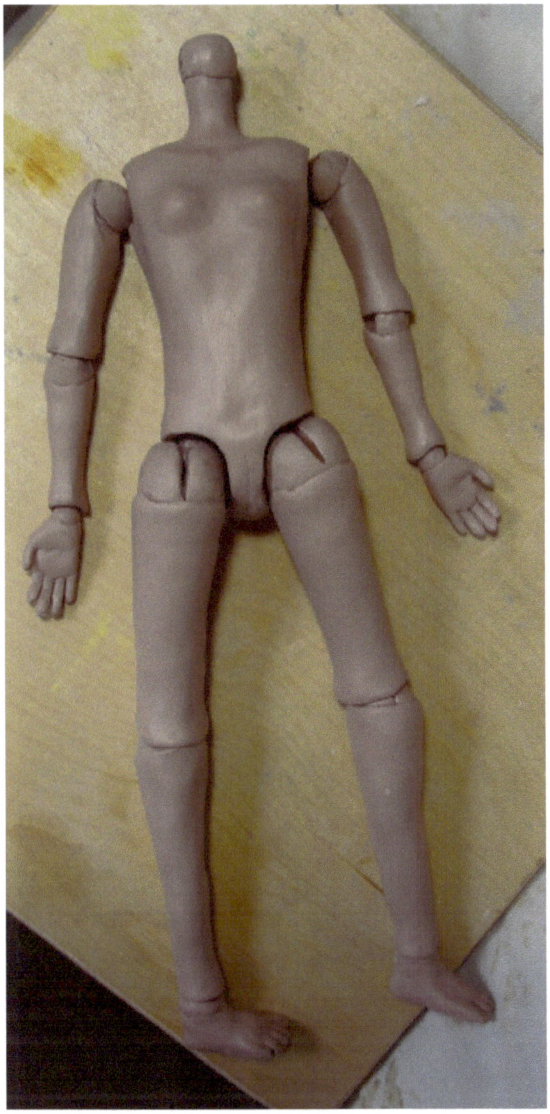

Finally, we're in the home stretch! If you've made it this far you should give yourself a big pat on the back.... *seriously*! And then take a deep breath, because now it's time to assemble everything and bring all of our hard work to life.

Let take a look at how we will be stringing out doll together. You will need thick, round elastic, preferably with out too much give/elasticity. We will be working with the elastic doubled, so check the make sure all of your hollow channels are large enough to accommodate the doubled elastic. If not, then use an appropriate sized drill bit and carefully enlarge each hold, gradually increasing the size of your drill bit as needed. Line up all of your doll parts.

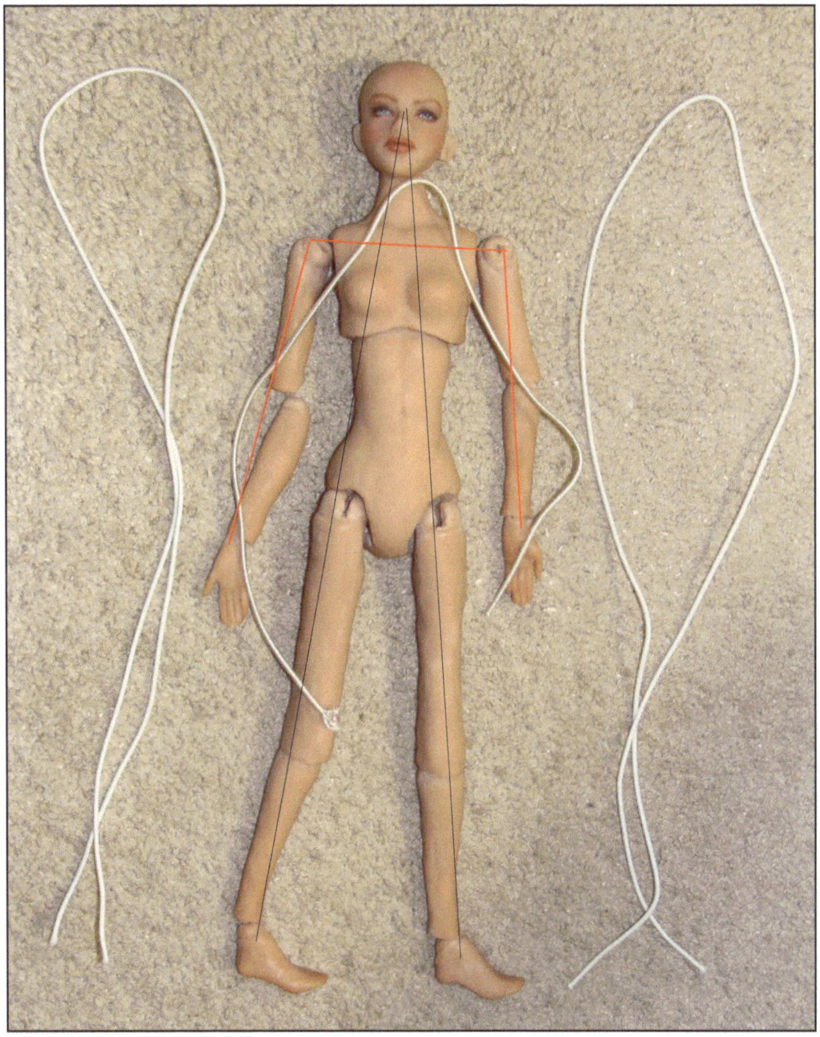

Loosely measure the length of the ankle to the top of the head and double it, cutting a piece of elastic to that length. Repeat for the second leg. Then measure the length up one arm across the chest and down the other arm, double and cut another piece of elastic, for the arms.

There are several ways you can attaché your elastic. You can thread it through the wire loop at the hand and ankles or you can stitch it in place or if you are working with a smaller scale doll you can even use quick setting resin to secure it in place.

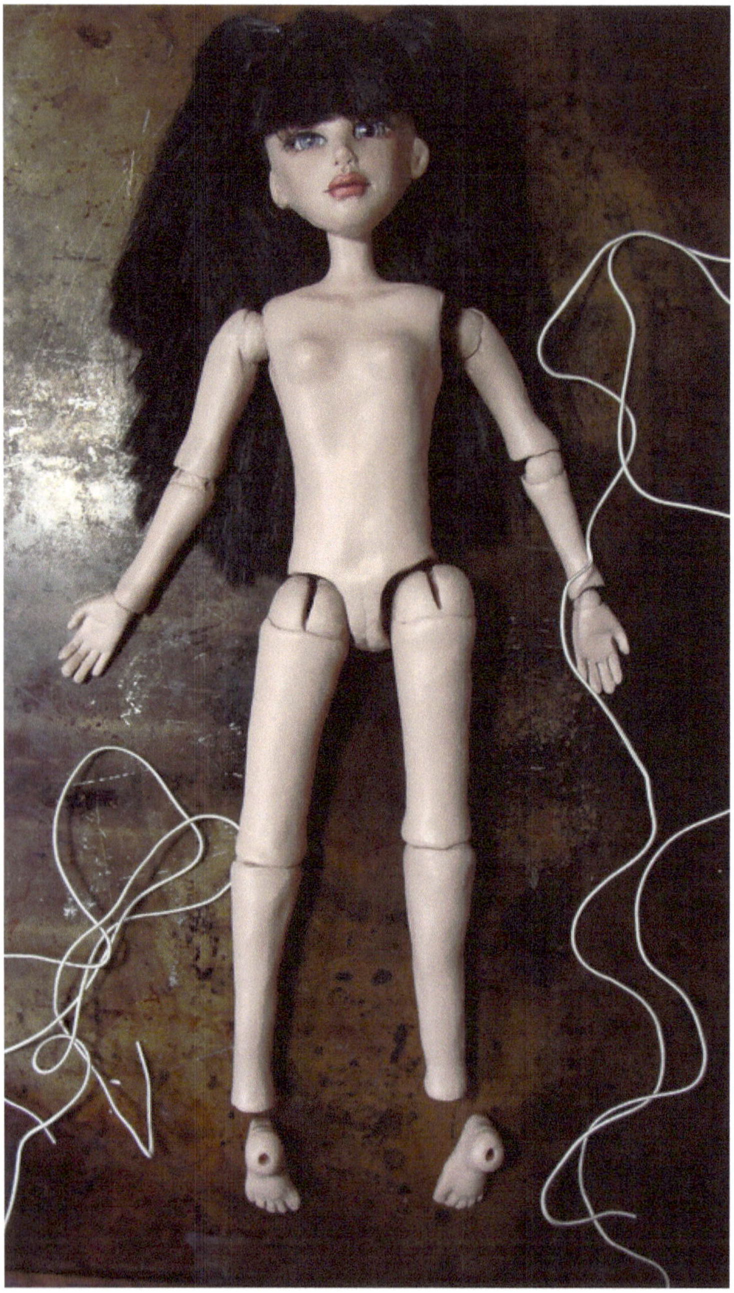

Attach the elastic to each ankle and to one wrist. Line up all of your pieces, making sure you have left and right limbs and parts in the proper place. Using a piece of wire, bent around the loop of the elastic to form a long needle-like extension. This will make it easier to thread the elastic through each piece.

Now begin stringing your doll together as if you were threading beads on a necklace.

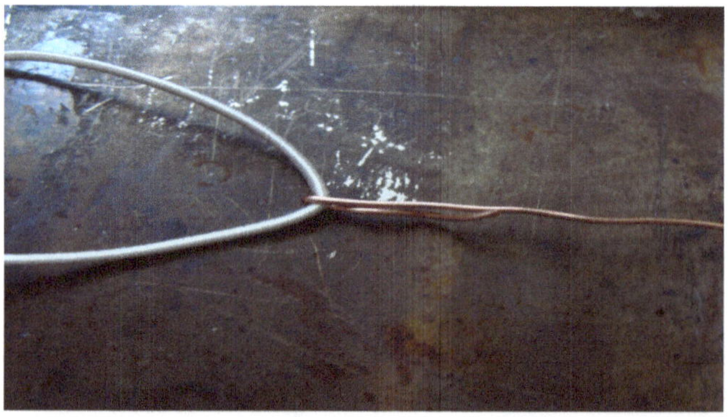

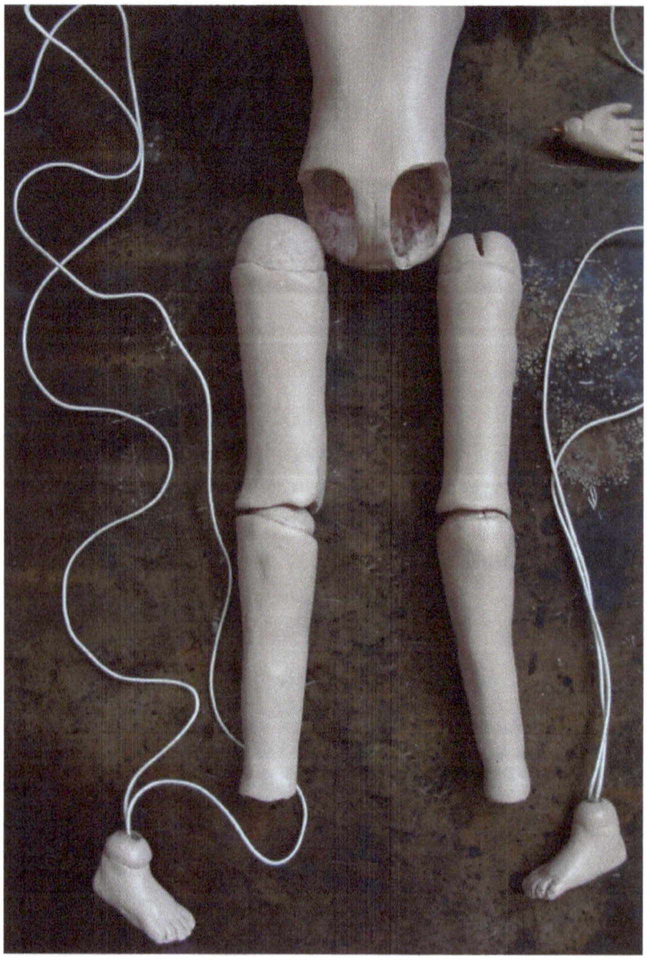

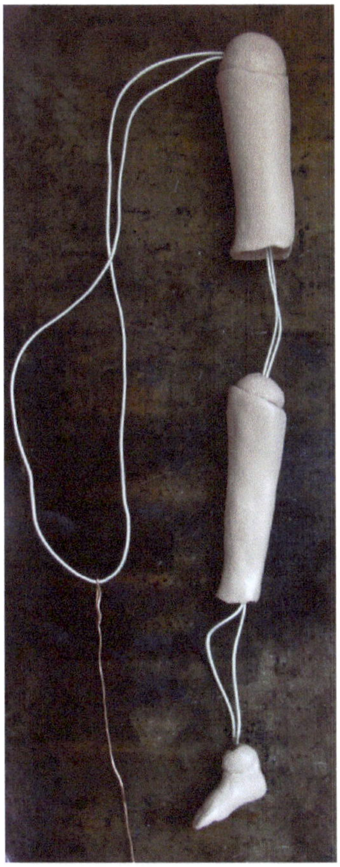

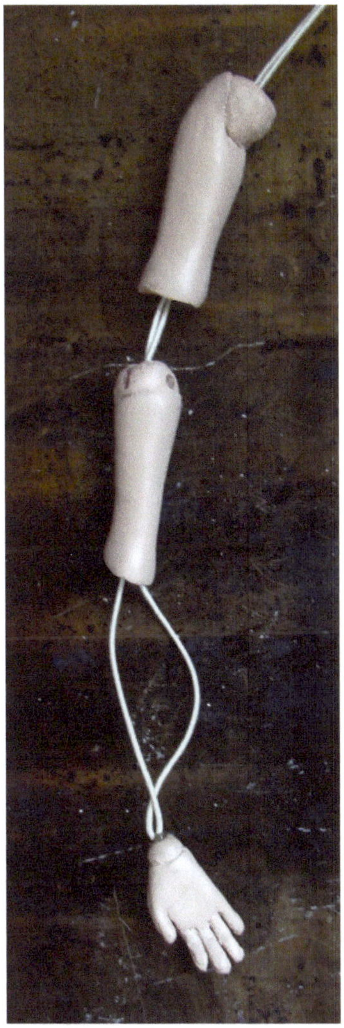

Begin with one ankle, and thread the elastic through the chin, thigh, up into the body, through the neck and into the head. Repeat for the second leg.

Do the same for the arm, securing the second hand in place pulling the elastic taut before knotting securely. The elastic needs to be tight in order for your doll to hold her position and poses.

Double check that everything is in the correct place, then pull the elastics for the legs tight, and secure in place, from inside the head. Place the cap on the back of the head and affix in place with crazy glue or tacky white glue.
Voila, you are ready to attach your chosen wig (or create one yourself) and get your doll all dressed up.

You may have noticed the fickle winds of change blew in and I found myself caught up in them. That is why she no longer has brown eyes, but blue ones instead and funky black hair. She just screamed *Goth doll*, but I haven't had a chance to put together a proper gothic outfit for her yet. Hopefully by the next article. I was planning a cutesy-frilly-girlie outfit, but she'd have none of it…and in the end the dolls *always* get their way!

Congratulations on completing your very own Ball Jointed Doll! Have fun posing and dressing her up!

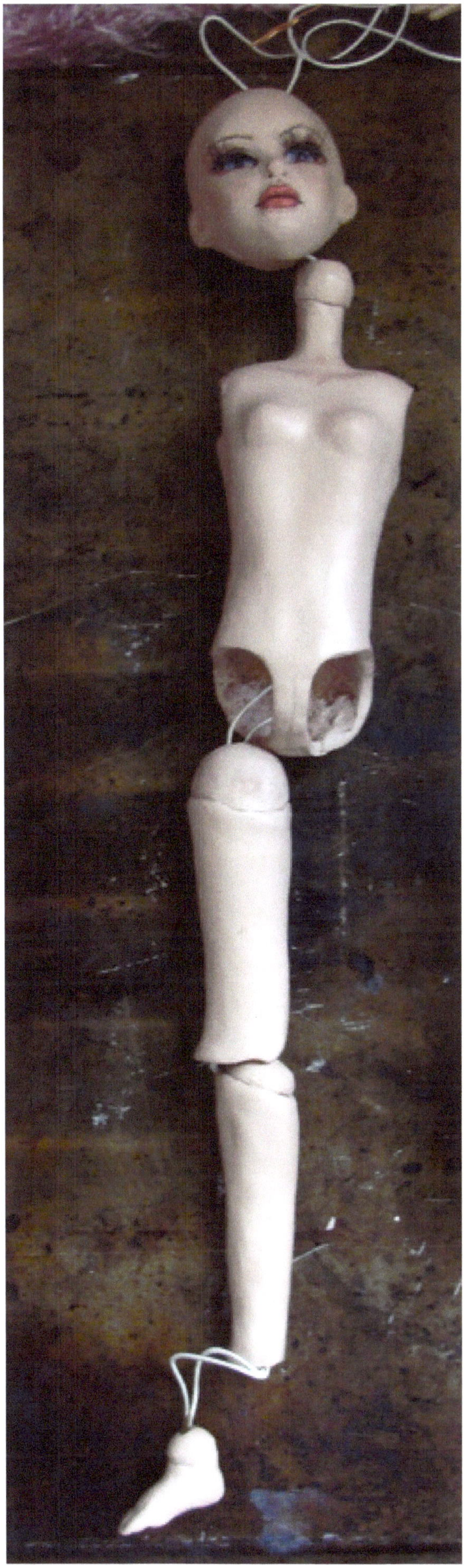

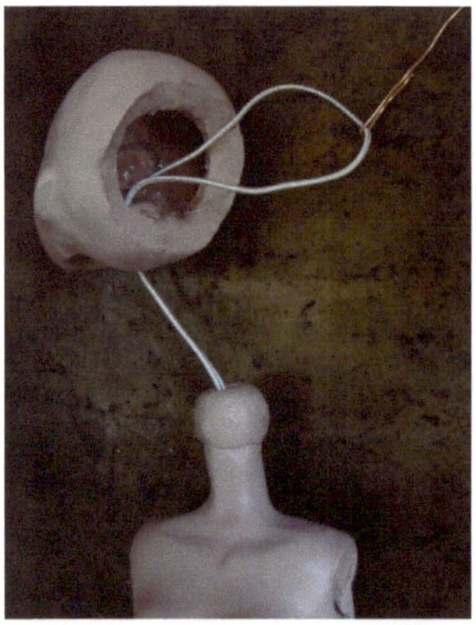
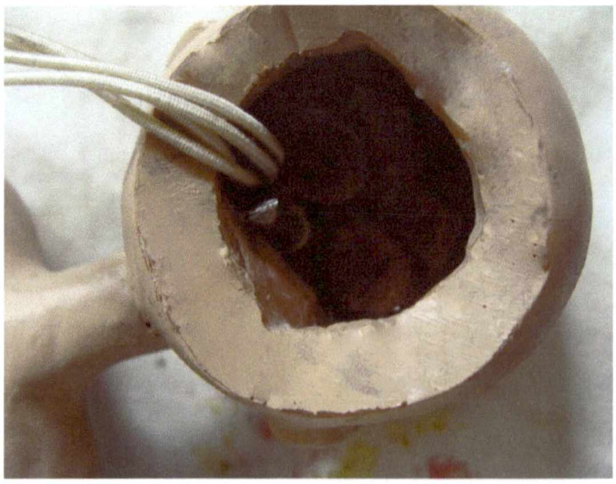
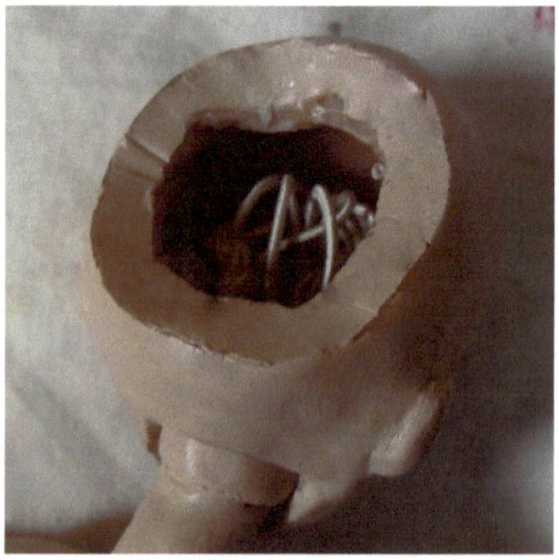
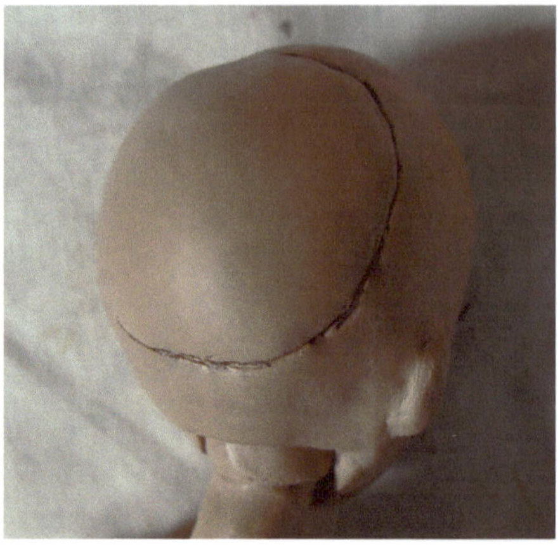
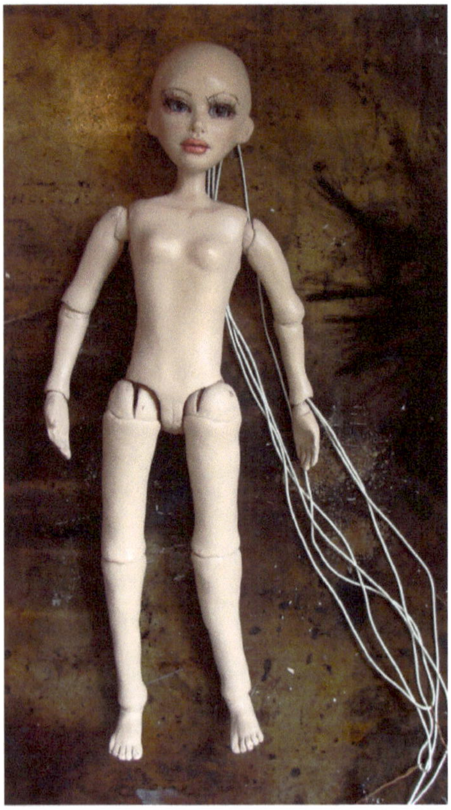

Michele Barrow-Belisle
Masquerade Studio
www.masqueradestudio.com
info@masqueradestudio.com
michelebelisle.blogspot.com

Lorraine's Reborn Babies

By Reborn Artist Lorraine Craill

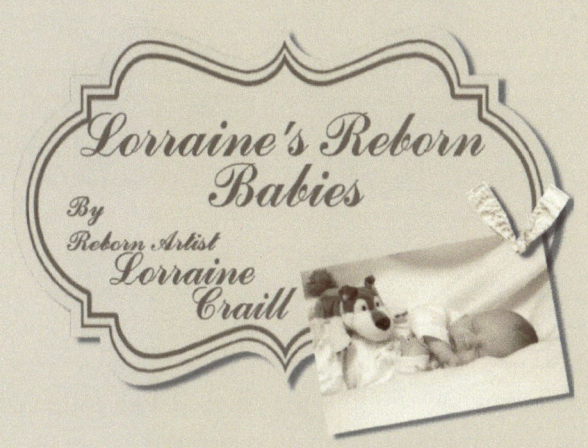

Lifelike Babies by Lorraine Craill

52 Siegfried Kuschke Street
Sasolburg
1947
OFS
South Africa

+27 16 973 3147 telephone
+86 671 5402 fax
+82 855 8563 cell phone

www.lifelikebabies.co.za   craill@mweb.co.za   www.lorrainecraill.co.za

Adrianne Inspired Creations

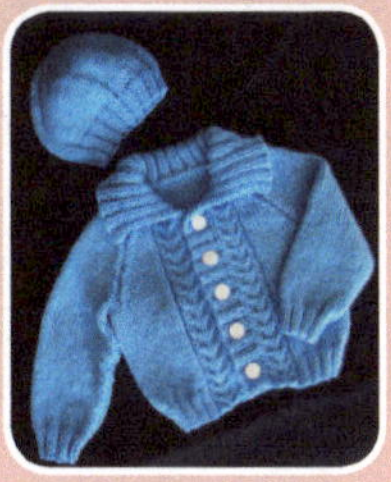

by Artist Cheryl Bage

Handmade Clothing & Assessories
for your Ball Jointed Dolls,
Reborns or OOAKs

Quality Reborn Baby Dolls

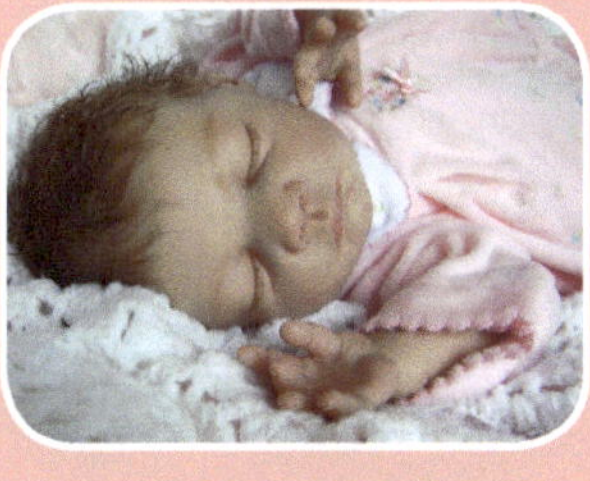

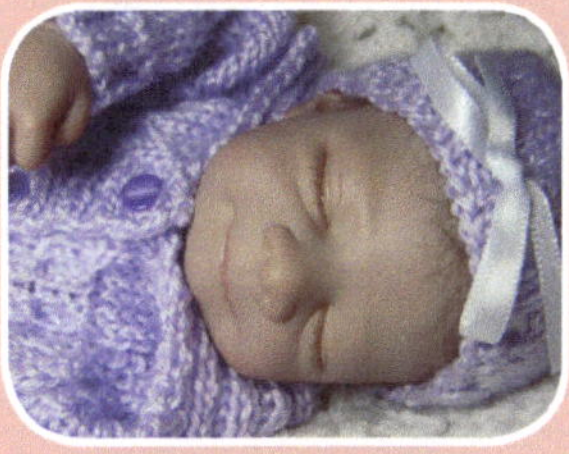

Custom orders welcome

www.AdrianneInspiredCreations.com

Creating a Stunning Faceup

with Cristy Stone
Xtremedolls

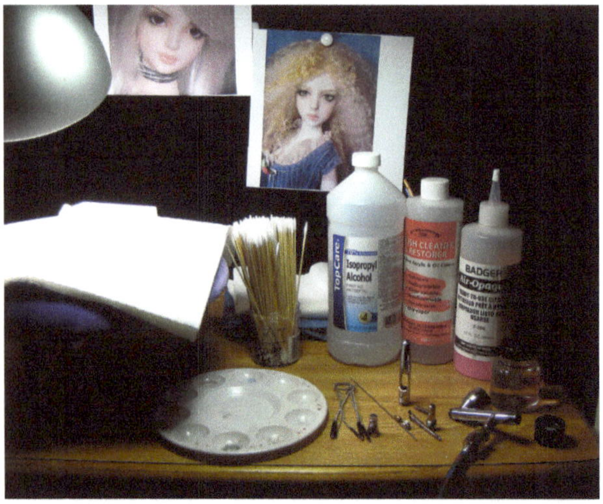

Getting Started

First off , when I accept a commission I request the following from the client: color likes/dislikes, reference any pictures you like which can be from my website or magazine pics of real people. I also ask them to include a list of any special mods/request when sending the head. I like to have time to study the doll and the information before I begin.

For this tutorial I will be painting a Unoa Sist. The client has requested the sculpted eyebrows that come on the head to be removed and has referenced 2 faceups on my website at www.xtremedolls.com

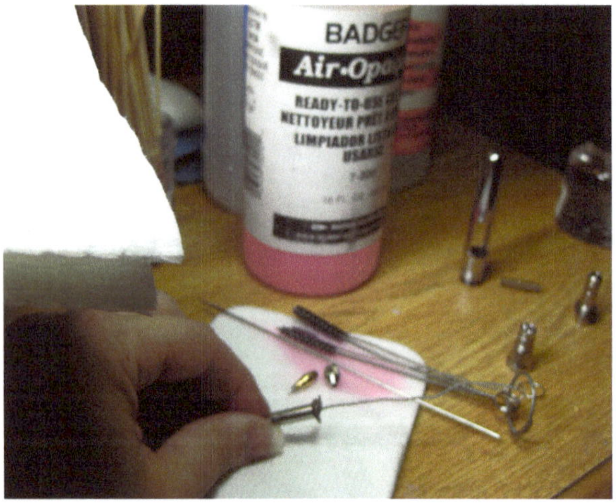

You will need the following supplies which will be used in this airbrush tutorial. Iwata Eclipse Airbrush, or similar, I use Golden and ComArt airbrush paints, Badger Airbrush cleaner, Winsor & Newton Brush Cleaner/Restorer, 70% Alcohol solution, clean water, sanding block, tooth picks, paper towels, and lots of q-tips. In addition to this I always have a resin head cap for testing colors. For sealing your work you will need MSC UV CUT FLAT , a Respirator, Gloss sealer for the lips, Alleenes's Fast Acting Tacky Glue, Liner Brush, and eyelashes. From start to finish it takes me anywhere between 6-9 hours to complete the face.

Now lets get started.

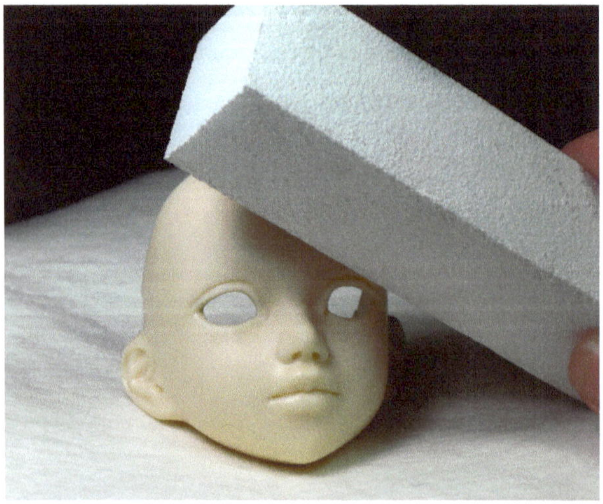

Begin by making sure your airbrush is clean. This will be the most important thing to remember. One tiny bit of dry paint will effect the way your brush works. You will need to run the Badger Airbrush cleaner through the airbrush each time you change a color. If you do not do this the color left in the chamber will mix with your new color.

Sand down the sculpted brow as the client requested. I begin each faceup by cleaning the doll with Winsor & Newton Cleaner and mild dish soap and water. Now it's time to paint.

I begin each faceup with the lips because most likely there will be overspray from the airbrush and you will need to clean up the edges and shape your lips. I will be using ComArt Opaque Maroon mixed with a drop of Golden Transparent White for Unoa's lips. Again, I always test my colors on an old resin head cap.

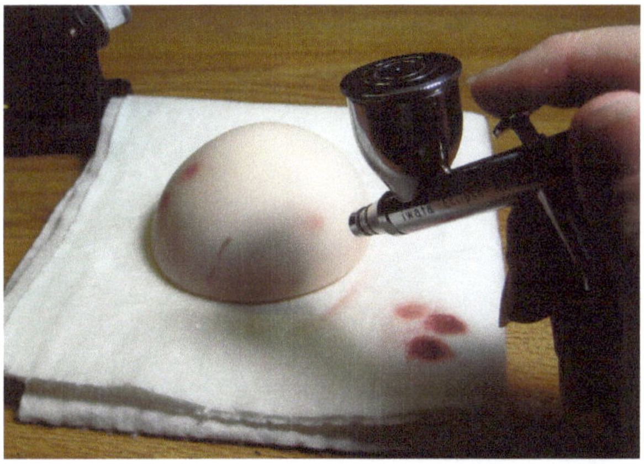

Once I am finished shaping the lips I move outside to apply my first coat of MSC. Be sure to wear your Respirator when spraying. Heat, humidity, and rain can effect the MSC, so make sure your weather conditions are good before spraying.

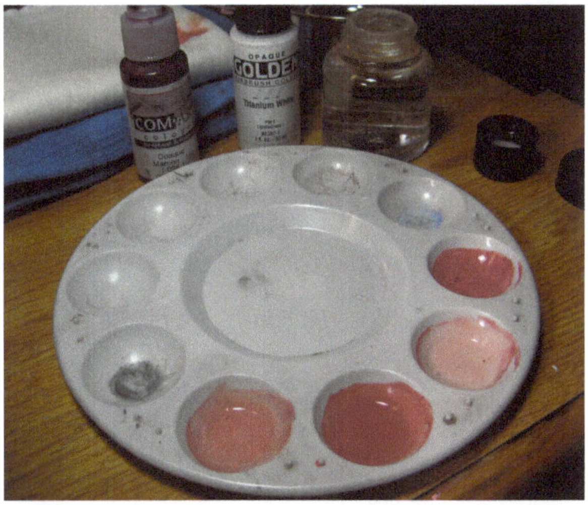

While the doll is drying, I move back inside to mix the remaining paint colors needed to add the details to the lips. I will mix 4 different shades of the Maroon paint to create a realistic look . I use a Loew-Cornell Liner brush for all my details especially for adding the tiny lines to the lips. Once I am happy with them I snap a quick picture to check my work.

Now it's time to move on to the nose. I start by painting the nose holes. Next I use Transparent Warmth in the airbrush to highlight the shape of the nose on the outside corners and the tip.

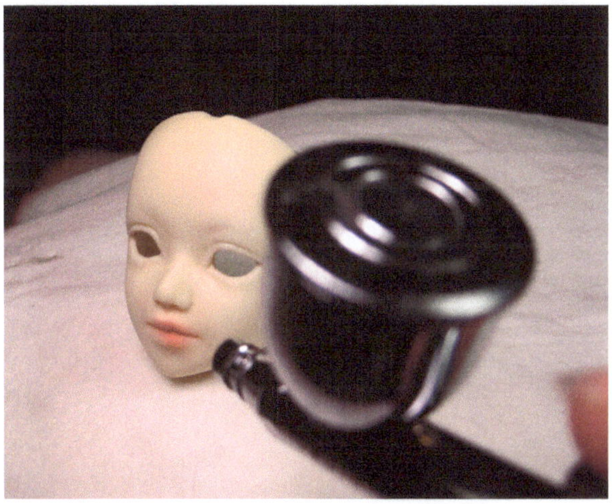

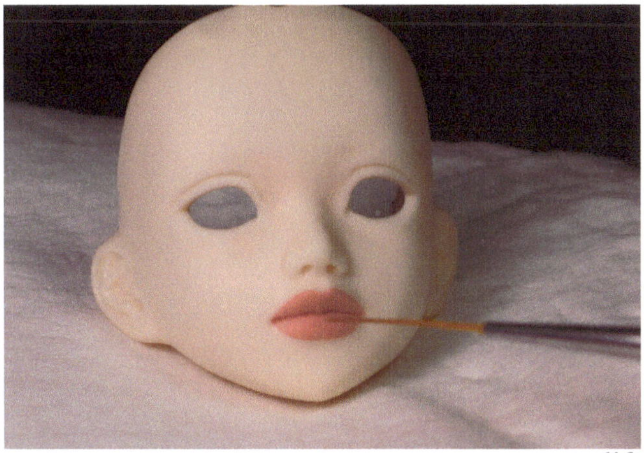

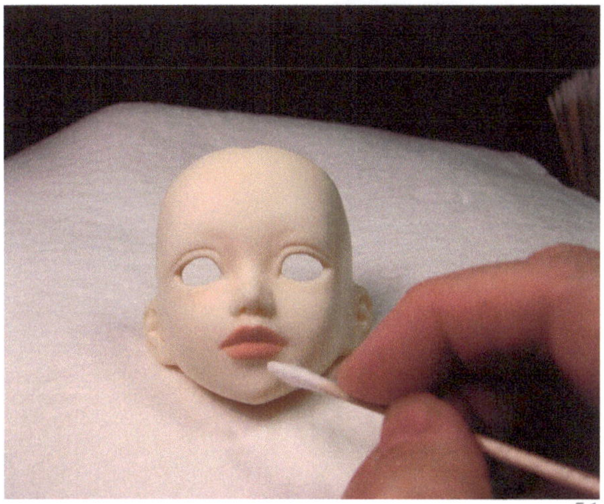

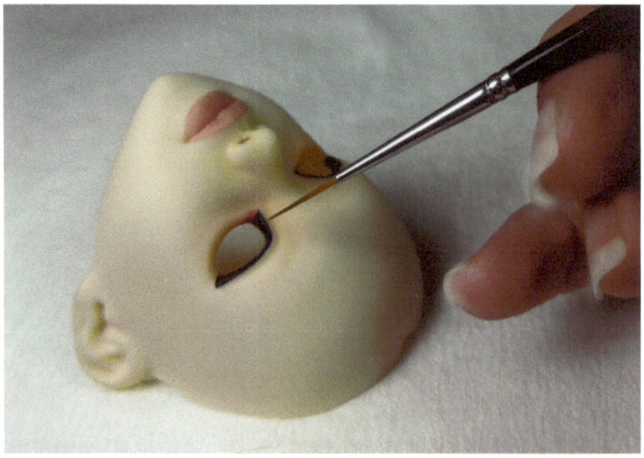

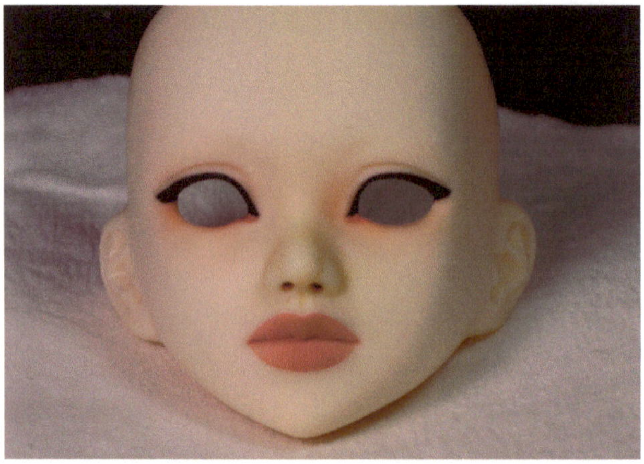

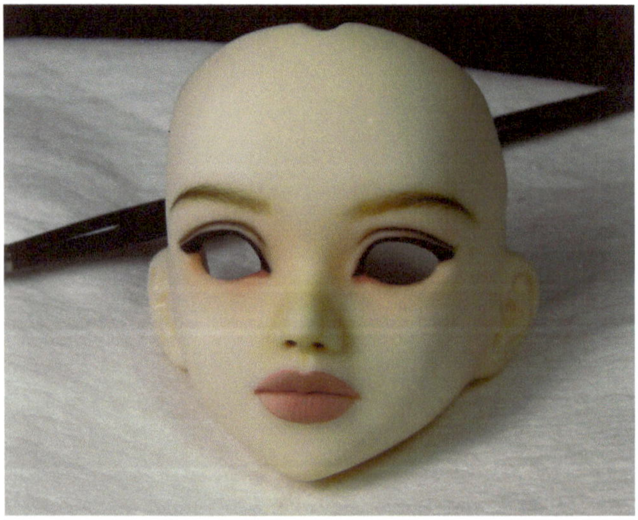

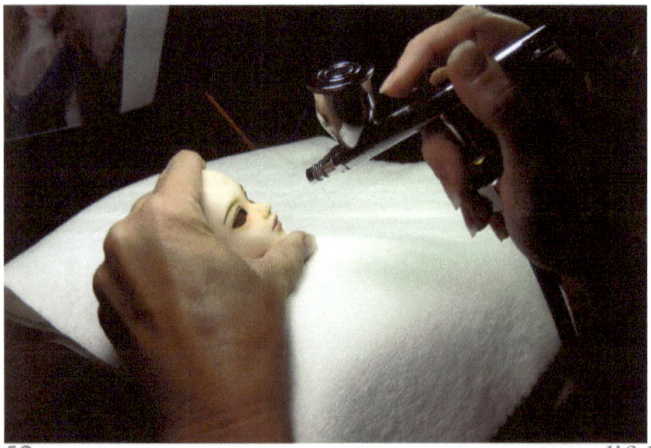

Once you are happy with what you have done it's time to move to the eyes. The first thing I do to the eyes are the tear ducts which I use Opaque Red Oxide in the airbrush. Next I work on the eye liner. If you want to use brown eyelashes then you would use brown liner, in this case the client wants black lashes, so I use black liner. When I am finished with the eyeliner this is the point I want to spray the doll with MSC to preserve the work I have done so far.

Go ahead and paint the crease in your dolls eyelid. I use Raw Umber for this faceup Now it's time to set the stage for the dolls expression. I feel the eyebrows are one of the most important parts of the dolls face. I start by deciding what shape brow I want. In this case the doll is to be a young teenager so I want a slightly arched brow. In this case, I want a light brown brow so I will used 3 colors, Opaque Raw Umber, Opaque Burnt Umber and Transparent Raw Umber. I will start by airbrushing the shape in the lightest color. I also use a q-tip and the 70% alcohol mixed with water to remove unwanted paint. The combination of alcohol and water will not eat through the MSC, but is strong enough to remove the unwanted paint. If you are a beginner, you can use painters tape to mask off your shape. The brows are the most difficult part of the faceup for me. Symmetry is so important and what you do on one side, you have to do on the other. I am right handed, so I paint the left side of the doll right side up, and the right side upside down. You have to figure out what works best for you. Start with your lightest color first and work your way back to the darkest color until your brows are as full as you want them. Once this is finished, it's time to spray with MSC again.

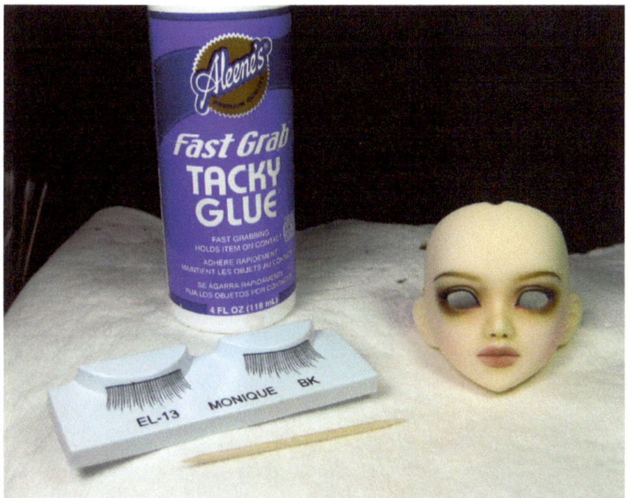

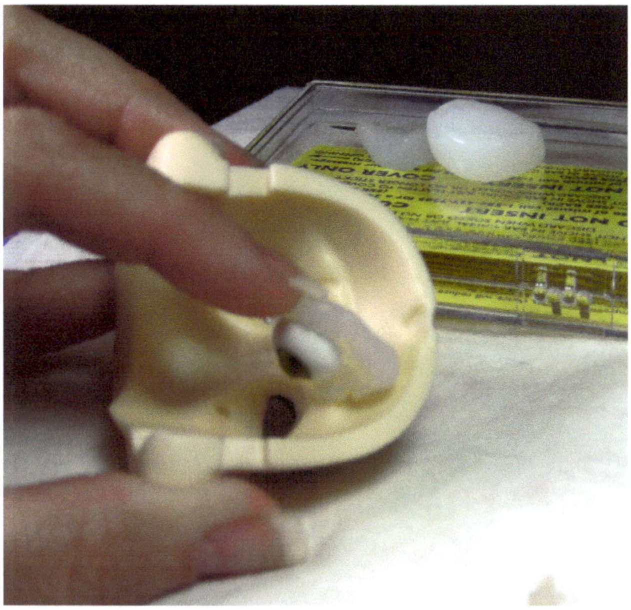

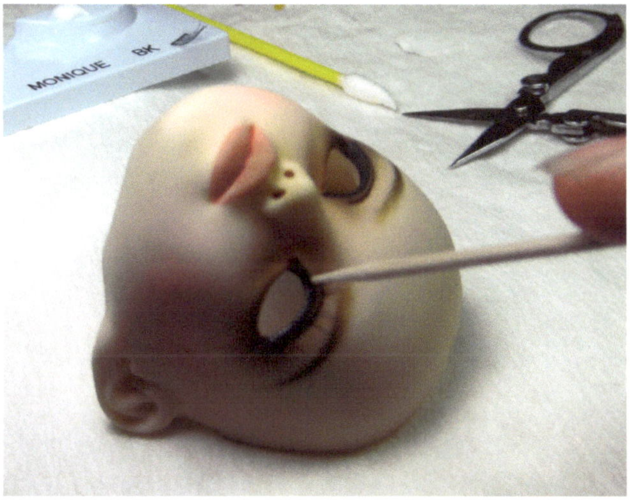

Okay, the hard part is over so get up and walk around. Next I will apply the eyeshadow using Burnt Umber and Transparent White in the airbrush. Once I'm happy, I spray with MSC again. Once the head is dry it's time for lower lashes. I'm using Raw Umber for Unoa's lashes. I stagger the lashes, long, short. Once you are finished with the lashes it's time for blush. Mix Naphthol Red Light, white and a drop of warmth in the airbrush. Spray the blush along the cheek line. When you are finished, check things out and if there are no changes go spray with MSC twice this time with a 30 minute wait in between sprays. While you're waiting, go clean up your airbrush.

Time for lashes. I'm using Monique EL-13 for this faceup. I do a dry fit to the eye before I glue the eyelashes on. Most of the eyelashes have a small tiny band of glue on them which hold them to the packaging, you need to remove this otherwise your toothpick with stick to them and make it hard to attach to the doll. I run a tiny band of glue on the dolls eyelid with a toothpick. Take your lash and just lay it on the lid. Take a clean toothpick and move it around in place until you have it in the position you want. Take your q-tip and wipe off any access glue. Don't worry about it too much because it dries clear.

Now for the finishing touches. Grab your gloss sealer. I paint it over the tear ducks and the bottom lashes. For the lips, I gloss them and wait until they are dry and give them a second coat of gloss. Make sure the gloss does not run into the center of the mouth because when it dries it will look like spit bubbles. If the gloss gets in the crease of the mouth you can take a dry paint brush and remove the

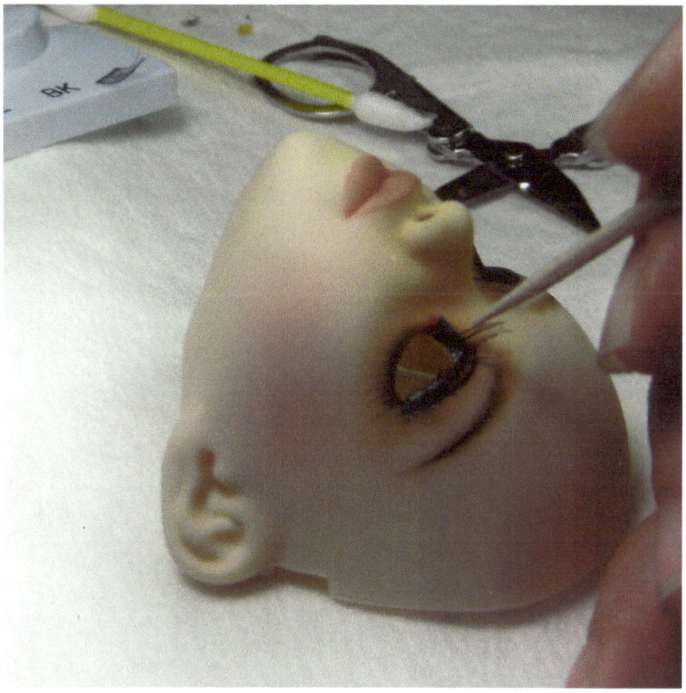

excess. I let everything dry overnight or for at least 8 hours before inserting the eyes for pictures.

I use Mack's Clear Earplugs to hold the eyes in. You can use any kind of putty that works best for you, but I really prefer the Mack's.

The best advice I can offer is to take your time, and take pictures along the way.

Painting Silicone Dolls

by Donna Lee Originals

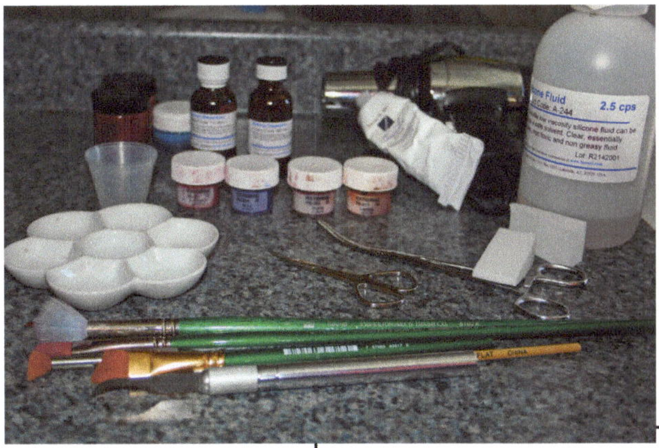

Solid Silicone dolls can only be painted with silicone based products. This is because only silicone sticks to silicone. There is no singular way to paint silicone dolls.
Described below, is the method, products, and techniques that work for me.

I buy almost everything from FACTOR 2 online at www.factor2.com

Supplies Needed:

*Extrinsic Coloration Paints:
- C-Stipple FE-228
- Umber FE-217
- Plum FE-301
- Blue FE-235
- White FE-200

*Silicone fluid A-244
*Matting Agent MD-564
*TS-564 Acetoxy Silicone
*Silicone Sealer TS-564
*Curved Exacto Knife
*Heat Gun
*Silicone Doll Parts
*Porcelain Mixing Tray
*Paint Mixing jars
*Hemostats
*Tiny Scissors
*Assorted Brushes

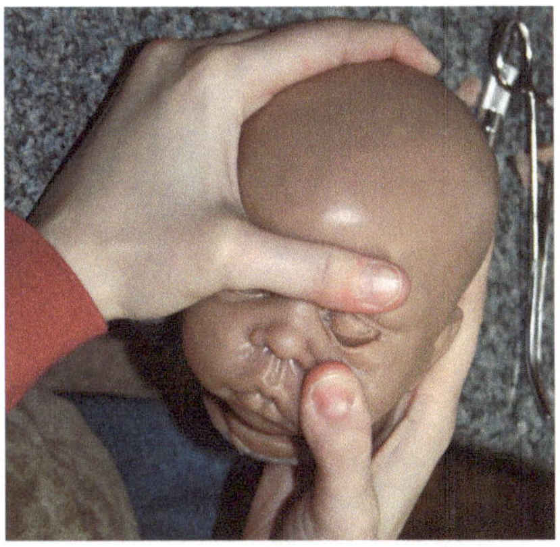

HOW TO DO IT:

The first step is to decide whether you are going to root the head before or after you paint. After rooting, you need to start on the eyes. If the doll's eyes are open, you will need to cut the silicone eyeballs out using a curved blade. You do this by cutting a complete circle all the way around the eye opening.

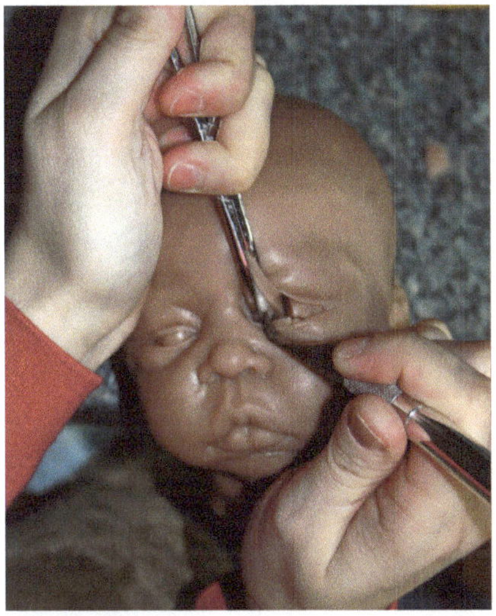

Then make a crisscross cut in each silicone eyeball. Each eye will now be sectioned into 4 pieces.

Pull each piece out one at a time, using hemostats and your blade. This is tricky, but you will get better the more you practice. Sometimes, my husband helps by pulling the eyes open, so I can see better where need to cut.

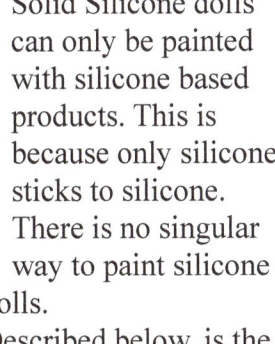

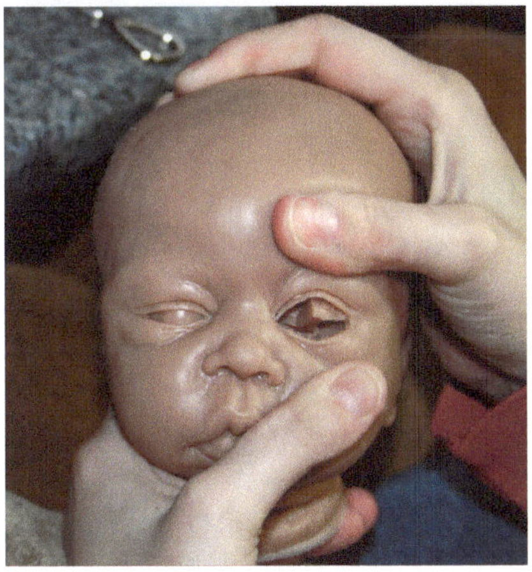

Don't worry if you slightly cut or tear the outer eye, you can re-silicone tears by using a 2 part silicone/activator mixture that you would get from your pourer. Follow your pourer's instructions on how to properly mix the silicone with the activator. Then you have to work very quickly because it hardens into solid silicone within a few minutes.

If any silicone tags remain around the eye opening, you can use your tiny scissors to trim them off the eyelids.

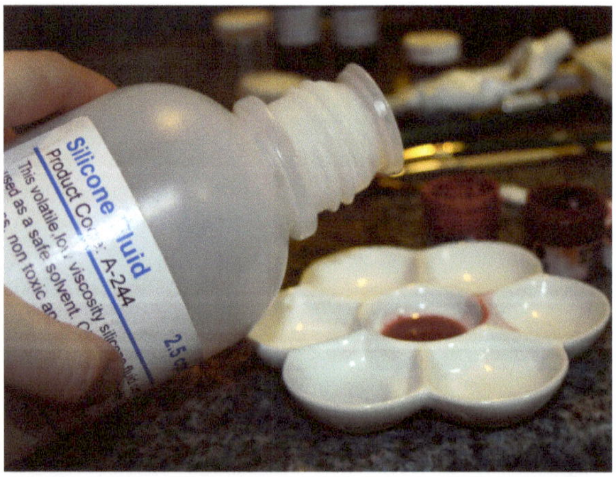

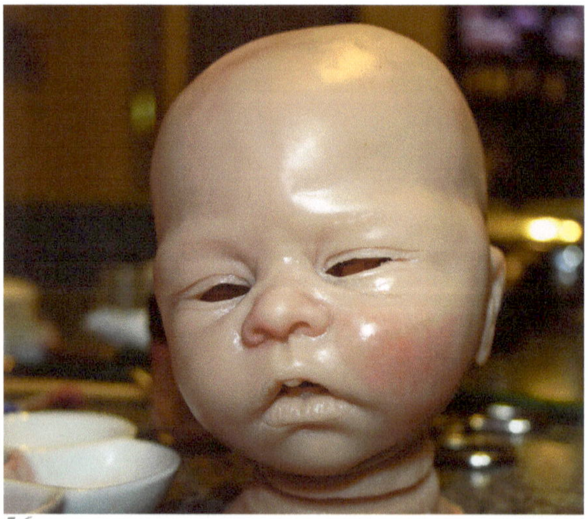

To prepare the silicone parts to receive the paint, you must use acetone on all pieces. Afterwards, wash the pieces in dish soap, and let air-dry overnight.
You are now ready to paint.

You will be using Silicone fluid A-244 to dilute the paint. I can't say enough about this product. It's completely non-toxic, odorless, and colorless. It soaks right into the silicone, and evaporates quickly, leaving only paint behind. It is the consistency of very light oil. I even use it to dilute Genesis paints for vinyl reborn dolls.

You will begin painting process by mixing together in a jar, equal amounts of Umber and C-Stipple and a tiny toothpick dot of blue. Use your Silicone fluid to dilute the paint and make a nice watercolor consistency.

The color you have mixed in the jar will be your *Concentrated Blushing Color.*

Now take your brush and put a few dabs of this concentrated mixture into 3 of the porcelain-mixing compartments. Add silicone fluid to dilute. Keep experimenting to find the exact color you want for the *final blushing color*. Then put the *Concentrated Blushing Color* away to use for another day.

This is how I mix my colors:

For general blushing (cheeks, elbows, knees and feet), I use the *Final blushing color.*

For lips, I dilute plum, umber, and some *Final blushing color* with silicone fluid.

For creases, I add some umber to the *Final blushing color*.
For eyebrows, I dilute umber with silicone fluid, and a tiny drop of *Final blushing color*

For veining, I dilute blue with the silicone fluid.
For blood vessels or stork bites, I use the *lip color mixture* with a tiny amount of blue to give a reddish *(slightly purple)* tone.

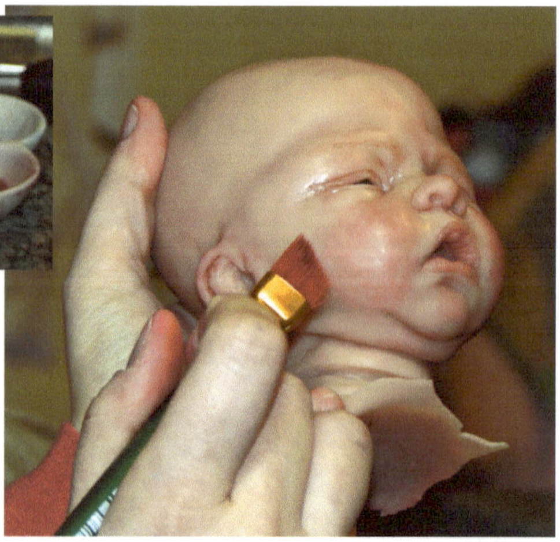

If I am painting an older baby, I paint color on with a cosmetic sponge, and then "blot" the rest off.

This gives a clean flawless look.
For a newborn baby, I paint color on with a brush in, say, 100 tiny dots to give a blotchy look. Then I use an angled brush that is *DRY* to feather the edges of paint, and blend the painted sections into the unpainted sections.

After blushing the doll. I change the color slightly to add depth. And then I use a very thin brush to add color to every single crease on the baby (eye creases, around mouth and nose, under chin etc).

The next part completely depends on your individualized preference. This is where I add the small details such as: delicate veins, tiny blood vessels/ capillaries, realistic blemishes, milk spots, 'stork bites' etc.

After painting the entire doll, I let sit it for at least 48 hours.

Day 1: Apply paint

Day 2: Touch up any spots that need more paint, and paint the nail-tips.

To do the nails you need to mix a tiny pin drop amount of white paint with TS-564 Acetoxy Silicone. This product starts to harden right away, so work as quick as you can. The mixture will be the consistency of warm taffy. You will take the end of a brush, dip it into the mixture, and pull away, thus making a long string of paint. Allow this string of paint to gently fall onto the nail-tip in the exact position you want.
It takes practice and after 1 minute, the stuff thickens too much to make a thin string. So I usually have to mix a few batches in order to do 1 doll.

Day 3: Do nothing

Day 4: Heat gun and apply Silicone Sealer TS-564. I use the heat gun to warm up the silicone; and make it easier for the sealer to adhere to the doll. After heating up, I immediately seal the paint.

The sealer needs to go on thin by "*tapping it on the face*" rather than spreading and smoothing it on. I cannot stress this enough. Let it sit all day. After several hours, I seal one more time a much heavier coat. The parts will be very shiny and slightly tacky after drying.

Day 5: Apply Matting Agent MD-564 liberally with a mop brush. I have taken a photo showing half the face with sealer and half the face with matting agent to show the drastic difference matting agent will make.

After matting the doll, it will feel somewhat sticky. This is normal.

Day 6: Insert the eyes. To do this, tear off a small piece of a cosmetic sponge, and place inside eye socket. Then you gently insert the half round or oval eyes into the socket. Glue eyes and eyelashes in place with the tiniest amount of TS-564 Acetoxy Silicone.

For squinty babies, you may need to trim the eyes with a dremel tool in order for the eyes to fit correctly.

Now all that's left is to root hair (*if you haven't yet*), and put on a body. I usually wait at least a week or two before shipping (or rooting) just to ensure that the paint has completely adhered.

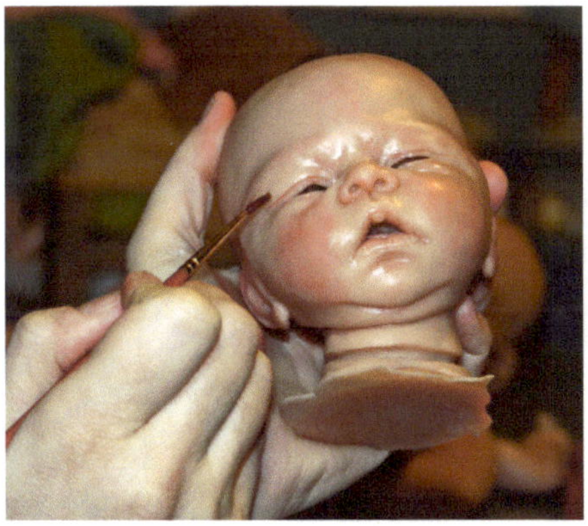

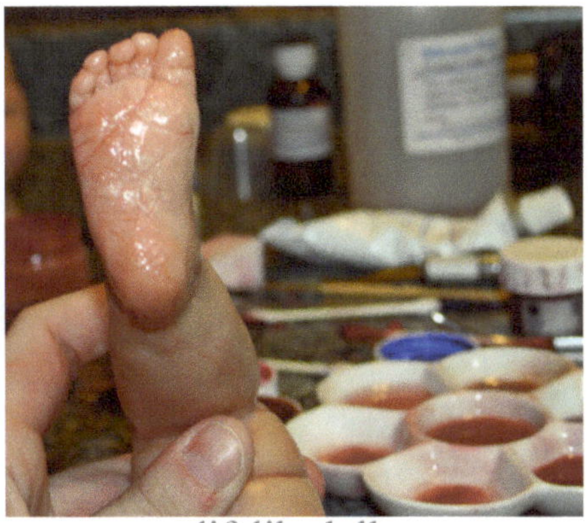

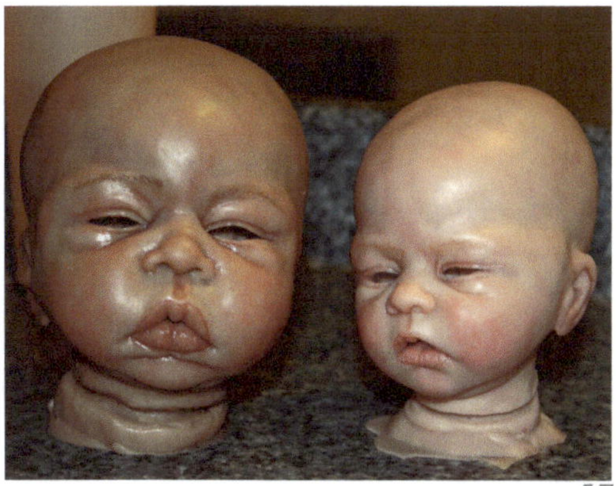

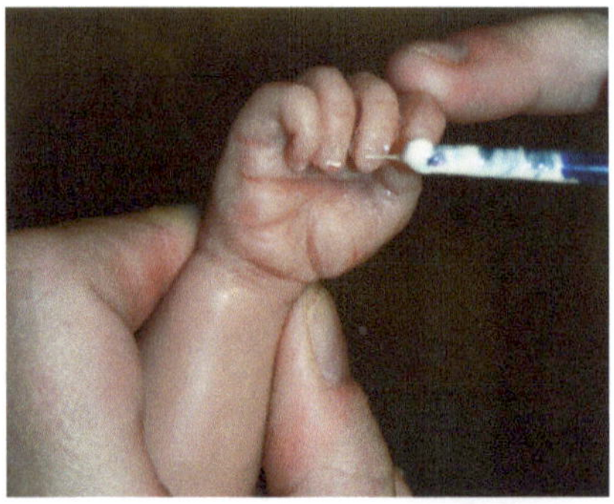

TIPS:
Never paint at night.
Never use sealer that is more than 6 months old, or goes on thicker than usual.
Never use sealer that has PARTIALLY cured in the bottle. Don't do it. It will only APPEAR to stick to your doll, and then a day later will peel off.

Always shake the matting agent before applying.

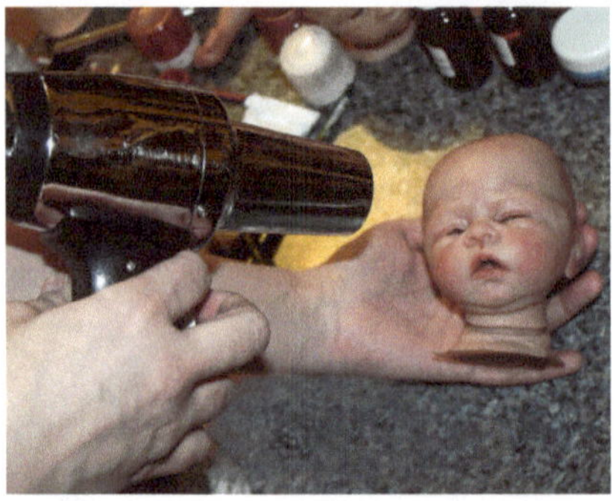

Sometimes, after bushing the matting agent on, you will see a few small white spots. Just tap the spots with your fingers and they will go away.

Always throw the bottle away if the matting agent goes on VERY white all over..

You can use Baby Powder on doll to removes the tackiness after matting. Make sure the powder does not contain talc or it will go on shiny. Brush lightly over silicone with a makeup brush. The baby powder gives a really nice smooth feel to the silicone, and will keep fuzzies off somewhat.

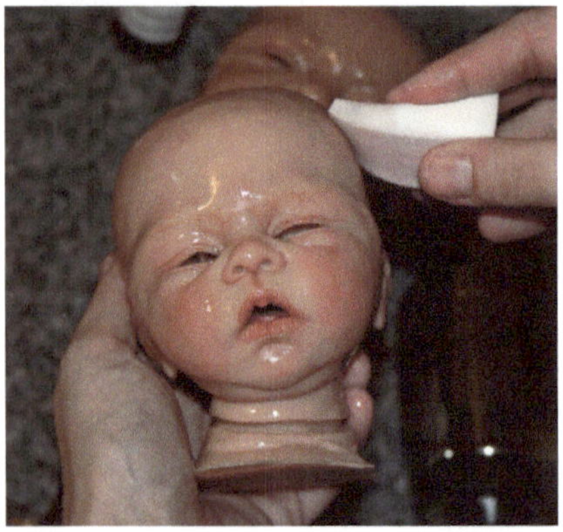

IMPORTANT NOTE: I always ask that my silicone molder/pourer use #15 sure platinum silicone. I know a few artists that use #10 with no problems; however, I have personally painted on both the #10 and #15, and I could not get the paint to adhere on the #10. The #15 is slightly firmer, but by using it, I have had no peeling paint issues.

Donna Lee Originals
www.donnaleeoriginals.com

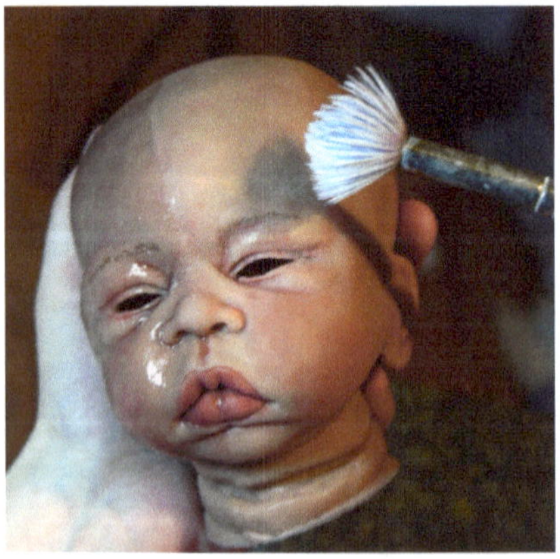

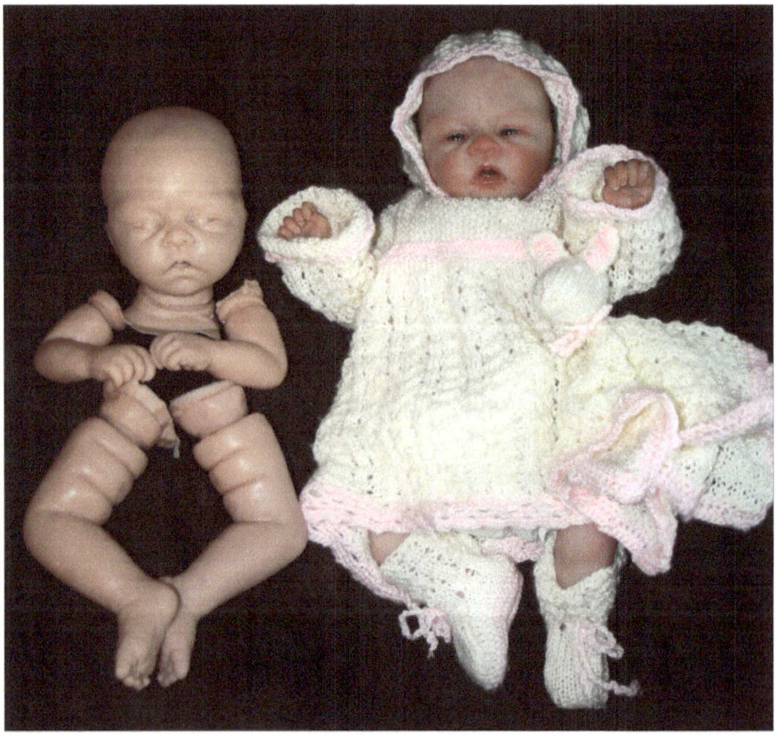

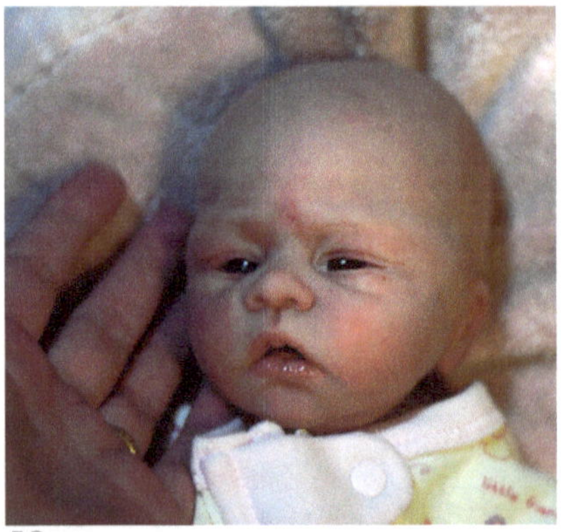

www.suesmadewithlovereborn nursery.com
also available, clothing and accessories from: Willbeth, Sarah Louise, Carters..
Lee Middleton, Ashton Drake and Adora Dolls also available online.
Sues Made With Love Reborn Nursery - Artist Sue Haiser
Beautiful lifelike reborn babies to cherish for a lifetime - NSW Australia

The Doll Collectors Club of NSW
Sydney AUSTRALIA
30TH ANNUAL
DOLL FAIR
incl Toys Bears & Collectables
NEW VENUE
Liverpool Catholic Club
cnr Hoxton Park & Joadja Rds (Look for Mercure Hotel)
30 & 31 July 2011
Sat 10-4pm Sun 10-3pm
Fabulous Traders from all over Australia selling Antique, Vintage & Modern Dolls, Bears, Toys & Collectables. Clothes, fabrics, supplies, hand made Art Dolls & Bears. Furniture, Miniatures, Reborns & kits.
Learn about collecting Dolls & Bears
Fair enquiries: Jan 02 9525 8291
Club enquiries: Connie 02 9389 0324
www.dollclubnsw.com.au dollfairnsw@gmail.com

“Butterfly” Cardigan

for Large Artist Type Dolls

A free sweater pattern by DollsWest Designs sized to fit a 27-inch (69 cm) Artist Doll

Doll Measurements:	Inches	cm
Height	27	69
Chest	14	36
Waist	13.75	35
Hips (fullest part)	16.25	42
Neck:	6.25	15
Arm Length:	10.75	27
Back of neck to Waist:	6	16

Yarn: 100% Merino Fingering weight wool (Palette) from KnitPicks.com or anything similar that will knit to the gauge listed below. Uses approx. 450 yards.

Gauge: 8.5 stitches per inch, 11 rows per inch on size 2 (3 mm) needles

Note: All odd number of rows are the Right side of the work, all even number of rows are the Wrong side of the work.

Colors used:
A: Cotton Candy (dark pink) – Main Color
B: White
C: Celadon heather (green)
D: Bluebell (blue)

Sleeves:
Cast on 60 sts on size 2 (3 mm) needles with main yarn color "A"
Row 1: K all sts
Row 2: K
Row 3: P
Row 4: K
Row 5: K
Row 6: P
Row 7: P
Row 8: K
Row 9: P
Row 10: P
Row 11: K
Row 12: K
Row 13: P
Row 14: K
Row 15: K
Row 16: P
Row 17: Change to yarn color "B" Work stockinette pattern, K all sts
Row 18: P all sts
Rows 19 through row 24: Change to yarn color "C" and continue to work even in stockinette stitch
Rows 25 and 26: Change to yarn color "B". Work stockinette pattern
Rows 27 through row 32: Change to yarn color "D". Work stockinette pattern
Rows 33 and 34: Change to yarn color "B". Work stockinette pattern
Rows 35 and 35: Change to main yarn color "A". Work stockinette pattern
Row 37: (RS) Cast off 3 stitches at beginning of row. K rest of sts. (57 sts)
Row 38: (WS) Cast off 3 stitches at beginning of row. Purl rest of sts. (54 sts)
Row 39: (RS) K1, SSK, Knit to last 3 sts, K2tog, K1. (52 sts)
Cut yarn, leaving at least a 10-inch tail. Leave sleeve on spare needle or stitch holder.

Work second sleeve in the same manner. Steam and block sleeves while they are flat. Block each sleeve 7 inches wide and 3.5 inches long. Let dry thoroughly while you work on the body.

Body: The body will be worked in three parts: Right Front, Back and Left Front. Work in the following order:

Right Front:
Cast on 34 sts on size 2 (3 mm) needles with main yarn color "A"
Row 1: K all sts
Row 2: K
Row 3: P
Row 4: K
Row 5: K
Row 6: P
Row 7: P
Row 8: K
Row 9: P
Row 10: P
Row 11: K
Row 12: K
Row 13: P
Row 14: K
Row 15: K
Row 16: P
Row 17: Change to yarn color "B". Work stockinette pattern. You will be working a seed stitch on the right and left fronts to keep the edges flat. Work as follows: P1, K1, P1, K to end
Row 18: (WS) P to last 3 sts, P1, K1, P1
Rows 19 through row 24: Change to yarn color "C" and repeat rows 17 and 18
Rows 25 and 26: Change to yarn color "B" and repeat rows 17 and 18
Rows 27 through row 32: Change to yarn color "D" and repeat rows 17 and 18
Rows 33 and 34: Change to yarn color "B" and repeat rows 17 and 18
Rows 35 through row 58 Change to main color yarn

"A" and repeat rows 17 and 18
Row 59: (RS) P1, K1, P1, Knit to the last four stitches. Cast them off. Cut yarn, leaving at least a 10-inch tail. Leave sleeve on spare needle or stitch holder. (30 sts)

Back:
Cast on 68 sts on size 2 (3 mm) needles with main color yarn "A"
Row 1: K all sts
Row 2: K
Row 3: P
Row 4: K
Row 5: K
Row 6: P
Row 7: P
Row 8: K
Row 9: P
Row 10: P
Row 11: K
Row 12: K
Row 13: P
Row 14: K
Row 15: K
Row 16: P
Row 17: Change to yarn color "B". Work stockinette pattern. Knit all stitches
Row 18: (WS) Purl all stitches
Rows 19 through row 24: Change to yarn color "C" and repeat rows 17 and 18
Rows 25 and 26: Change to yarn color "B" and repeat rows 17 and 18
Rows 27 through row 32: Change to yarn color "D" and repeat rows 17 and 18
Rows 33 and 34: Change to yarn color "B" and repeat rows 17 and 18
Rows 35 through row 58 Change to main color yarn "A" and repeat rows 17 and 18
Row 59: (RS) Cast off 5 stitches, Knit to last 5 sts and cast them off. Cut yarn, leaving at least an 8-inch tail. Leave sleeve on spare needle or stitch holder. (58 sts)

Left Front:
Cast on 34 sts on size 2 (3 mm) needles with main yarn color "A"
Row 1: K all sts
Row 2: K
Row 3: P
Row 4: K
Row 5: K
Row 6: P
Row 7: P
Row 8: K
Row 9: P
Row 10: P
Row 11: K
Row 12: K
Row 13: P
Row 14: K
Row 15: K
Row 16: P
Row 17: Change to yarn color "B". Work stockinette pattern. You will be working a seed stitch pattern on the right and left fronts to keep the edges flat. Work as follows: Knit to last 3 sts, P1, K1, P1
Row 18: (WS) P1, K1, P1, Purl to end
Rows 19 through row 24: Change to yarn color "C" and repeat rows 17 and 18
Rows 25 and 26: Change to yarn color "B" and repeat rows 17 and 18
Rows 27 through row 32: Change to yarn color "D" and repeat rows 17 and 18
Rows 33 and 34: Change to yarn color "B" and repeat rows 17 and 18
Rows 35 through row 58 Change to main color yarn "A" and repeat rows 17 and 18
Row 59: (RS) Cast off 4 stitches, K to end. (30 sts) DO NOT CUT YARN! LEAVE ALL STITCHES ON WORKING NEEDLE!

While the body pieces are flat, steam and block them. Let dry thoroughly before you proceed with adding in the sleeves. The pieces should be blocked to the following sizes:
Fronts: 4 inches wide, 5.25 inches long. Back: 8 inches wide, 5.25 inches long.

Row 60: (WS) With the Left Front section on working

needle continue as follows:
P1, K1, P1, P to the end, place marker, purl in first sleeve, place marker, pick up the Back section and P to the end, place marker, purl in second sleeve, place marker, pick up the Right Front and P to last 3 sts, P1, K1, P1 (222 sts)

Now you will begin to work decrease for the raglan sleeve section. You will be reducing the stitch count by 8 sts on every odd numbered row (right side). Row count begins again.

Row 1: (RS) Change to yarn color "B". P1, K1, P1, [K to 3 sts before marker, K2tog, K1, slip marker, K1, SSK]* Work four times then K to last 3 sts, P1, K1, P1
Row 2: (WS) P1, K1, P1, Purl to last 3 sts, P1, K1, P1
Rows 3 through row 8: Change to yarn color "C". Repeat rows 1 and 2.
Rows 9 and 10: Change to yarn color "B". Repeat rows 1 and 2
Rows 11 through row 16: Change to yarn color "D". Repeat rows 1 and 2
Rows 17 and 18: Change to yarn color "B". Repeat rows 1 and 2
Rows 19 through row 38: Change to main yarn color "A". Repeat rows 1 and 2
Stitch count on row 38 = 70 stitches.

Neck edge:
Change to needle size 1 (2.25 mm) needles and work as follows, continuing to use main yarn color "A":
Row 1: K
Row 2: K
Row 3: P
Row 4: K
Row 5: P
Row 6: Bind off all stitches in knit pattern. Leave a long enough tail to make a buttonhole loop on the right side. You can either single crochet the loop or work buttonhole stitches over the yarn. Weave in yarn end and make sure it is secured in place.

Sew up sleeve and side seams. Sew up the underarm seam. Weave in all yarn ends. Attach small button on the left front to line up with your buttonhole loop. Once again, steam and block the entire sweater. Let dry thoroughly.

Abbreviations

Beg Beginning
B/O Bind off (cast off sts)
C4F Slip 2 sts onto cn and hold at front of work, K2, K2 from cn
C4B Slip 2 sts onto cn and hold at back of work, K2, K2 from cn
CC Contrast Color
CN Cable needle
C/O Cast on
Cont Continue
Dc Double crochet
Dec Decrease
DPN(s) Double pointed needle(s)
Foll Following
Inc Increase
KFB Knit 1 in front and back of stitch
K2tog Knit 2 together
K3tog Knit 3 together
M1 Make one
M1P Make one Purl
MC Main Color
P Purl
P2tog Purl 2 together
PFB Purl1 in front and back of stitch
PM Place Marker
PSSO Pass slipped stitch over
Rem Remaining
Rep Repeat
RS Right Side
Sc Single crochet
Sl slip
SKP Slip, Knit, Pass
SK2P Slip 1, Knit 2 together, Pass slipped stitch over
SSK Slip, Slip, Knit OR slip 2 stitches one at a time, knit 2 slipped stitches together
St(s) Stitch(es)
St st Stockinette stitch
WS Wrong side
WYIB With yarn in back
WYIF With yarn in front
Yfwd Yarn forward, or to the front, knit next stitch
YO Yarn Over

Knitted Cardigan

Here is a very easy short-sleeved knitted cardigan pattern that will fit a variety of mid range dolls, including, MSD size ball-jointed dolls, Ellowyne, and the Kish Chrysalis series. Done in two coordinating yarn colors, the edge of the sleeves and bottom are finished with a delicate picot edge. Perfect for spring and summer and can be worn with dresses, skirts and tops, or pants and long sleeve tops. Your dolls will want more in several colors!

This short "cardy" was inspired by a woman's sweater pattern by Louisa Harding. I love to replicate designs for dolls. I find it a challenge to be able to chart out a pattern and "dolly-size" it, making it in scale for the particular doll(s) I have chosen to dress.

Although I am relatively a "late-bloomer" when it comes to hand knitting, I have been charting and designing sweaters for my knitting machines for quite some time. It is sort of a backwards way to start out, but the skills I learned while using my knitting machines, have enabled me to design knitwear for dolls.

Although you only need to know how to knit and purl, you must be able to read instructions, and increase and decrease stitches. This sweater uses lace weight yarn on size 3/0 (1.5 mm) needles with a fine gauge. Please make sure you obtain the gauge I specify in the pattern. You do not have to use the yarn I show but do knit up a swatch to make sure what you have selected will knit up in the size for the dolls listed. Also, check your gauge while you are knitting to make sure you are knitting evenly.

If you enjoy knitting for your dolls, I invite you to visit my website, www.dollswestdesigns.com. I have several downloadable free patterns. I offer a new free pattern once a quarter. I have several patterns for sale as well that fit a large variety of modern ball-jointed and fashion dolls. I send the patterns via pdf files so I can ship them worldwide. I occasionally offer some of my sweaters for sale.

Should you have any questions about this pattern or my website, please feel free to email me. My email address is dollswest@centurytel.net.

I hope you enjoy knitting this sweet little cardigan up for your dolls!

Happy Knitting!

Cynthia Berrier
www.dollswestdesigns.com
Kalispell, Montana USA

Abbreviations

Beg	Beginning
B/O	Bind off (cast off sts)
C4F	Slip 2 sts onto cn and hold at front of work, K2, K2 from cn
C4B	Slip 2 sts onto cn and hold at back of work, K2, K2 from cn
CC	Contrast Color
CN	Cable needle
C/O	Cast on
Cont	Continue
Dc	Double crochet
Dec	Decrease
DPN(s)	Double pointed needle(s)
Foll	Following
Inc	Increase
KFB	Knit 1 in front and back of stitch
K2tog	Knit 2 together
K3tog	Knit 3 together
M1	Make one
M1P	Make one Purl
MC	Main Color
P	Purl
P2tog	Purl 2 together
PFB	Purl1 in front and back of stitch
PM	Place Marker
PSSO	Pass slipped stitch over
Rem	Remaining
Rep	Repeat
RS	Right Side
Sc	Single crochet
Sl	slip
SKP	Slip, Knit, Pass
SK2P	Slip 1, Knit 2 together, Pass slipped stitch over
SSK	Slip, Slip, Knit
St(s)	Stitch(es)
St st	Stockinette stitch
WS	Wrong side
WYIB	With yarn in back
WYIF	With yarn in front
Yfwd	Yarn forward, or to the front, knit next stitch
YO	Yarn Over

Short Sleeve Cardy with Picot Edge

Yarn: KnitPicks Lace weight 100% Merino wool yarn or Jagger Spun Zephyr Wool/Silk Lace weight Yarn from www.theknitter.com
Gauge: 14 sts and 18 rows per inch (stockinette stitch) on 3/0 (1.5 mm) needles

Sleeves:
Using 3/0 (1.5 mm) needles, and contrasting color yarn, work picot cast on as follows:
*Cast on 5 sts using the "cable cast on" method. Cast off 2 sts. Slip st on RH needle back onto LH needle. (3 sts now on LH needle) Repeat from * until there are 39 sts on needle, cast on.
Row 1: K all sts
Row 2: K all sts
Change to main color of yarn
Row 3: K all sts
Row 4: K all sts

Start stockinette stitch pattern. Work even in pattern.
Row 5: (RS) K all sts
Row 6: (WS) P all sts
Rows 7 through row 26: Repeat rows 5 and 6, working in an even stockinette stitch pattern.

Shape sleeve cap. Work as follows:
Row 1: (RS) Cast off 3 sts, K to end (36 sts)
Row 2: (WS) Cast off 3 sts, P to end (33 sts)
Row 3: SSK, K to last 2 sts, K2tog (31 sts)
Row 4: P
Repeat Rows 3 and 4 through row 26 (stitch count on row 26 = (9 sts)
Row 27: (RS) Cast off in pattern (K). (9 sts cast off)

Repeat for second sleeve. Steam and block sleeves while they are flat. Let dry while you work on the body.

Body:
Using 3/0 (1.5 mm) needles, and contrasting color yarn, work picot cast on as follows:
*Cast on 5 sts using the "cable cast on" method. Cast off 2 sts. Slip st on RH needle back onto LH needle. (3 sts now on LH needle) Repeat from * until there are 93 sts on needle, cast on.
Row 1: K all sts
Row 2: K all sts
Change to main color of yarn

Row 3: K all sts
Row 4: K all sts
You will now begin stockinette stitch.
You will be using a Double Garter Stitch Edge on the Front edges. I found that if you worked a double garter stitch edge at the beginning and end of each row that the edges laid down flatter and smoother. No other finish is needed. Instructions are given for each row.

Double Garter Stitch Edge: On every row, slip the first stitch knit wise, knit the second stitch, and then work to the end of the row, knitting the last two stitches.

Row 5: (RS) Sl 1 st, K rest of sts
Row 6: (WS) Sl 1 st, K1, P to last 2 sts, K2
Rows 7 through row 32: Repeat rows 5 and 6
Row 33: (RS) Sl 1 st, K21, Cast off 3 sts, K43, Cast off 3 sts, K22
Row 34: (WS) Sl 1 st, K1, P20. Place the 43 sts for the back on a spare needle or stitch holder and place the last 22 sts for the right front on a spare needle or stitch holder
You will now be working on the Left Front
Row 35: (RS) K2tog, K to end (21 sts)
Row 36: (WS) Sl 1, K1, P to end
Row 37: (RS) K2tog, K to end (20 sts)
Row 38: (WS) Sl 1, K1, P to end
Row 39: (RS) K all sts
Row 40: (WS) Sl 1, K1, P to end
Row 41: (RS) K all sts
Row 42: (WS) Sl 1, K1, P to end
Row 43: (RS) K13, Place 7 sts on stitch holder (safety pin works well)
Row 44: (WS) P
Row 45: (RS) K to last 2 sts, SSK (12 sts)
Row 46: (WS) P
Row 47: (RS) K to last 2 sts, SSK (11 sts)
Row 48: (WS) P
Row 49: (RS) K to last 2 sts, SSK (10 sts)
Row 50: (WS) P
Row 51: (RS) K to last 2 sts, SSK (9 sts)
Row 52: (WS) P
Row 53: (RS) K
Row 54: (WS) P
Row 55: (RS) K
Row 56: (WS) P
Row 57: (RS) K
Row 58: (WS) P
Row 59: (RS) K
Row 60: (WS) P
Place the 9 sts on stitch holder (safety pin works well)
You will now be working on the Back
Row 34: (WS) Attach yarn to wrong side and P all sts (43 sts)
Row 35: (RS) K2tog, K to last 2 sts, SSK (41 sts)
Row 36: (WS) P all sts
Row 37: (RS) K2tog, K to last 2 sts, SSK (39 sts)
Row 38: (WS) P all sts
Rows 39 through row 60: work even in stockinette stitch pattern
Place 9 sts on one stitch holder, 21 sts on another stitch holder, and last 9 sts on another stitch holder.
Again, safety pins work well to hold a small amount of these tiny stitches.
You will now be working on the Right Front
Row 34: (WS) Attach yarn to wrong side and P to last 2 sts, K2 (22 sts)
Row 35: (RS) Sl 1, K to last 2 sts, SSK (21 sts)

Row 36: (WS) P to last 2 sts, K2
Row 37: (RS) Sl 1, K to last 2 sts, SSK (20 sts)
Row 38: (WS) P to last 2 sts, K2
Row 39: (RS) Sl 1, K to end
Row 40: (WS) P to last 2 sts, K2
Row 41: RS) Sl 1, K to end
Row 42: (WS) P13, Place last 7 sts on stitch holder
Row 43: (RS) K2tog, K to end (12 sts)
Row 44: (WS) P
Row 45: (RS) K2tog, K to end (11 sts)
Row 46: (WS) P
Row 47: (RS) K2tog, K to end (10 sts)
Row 48: (WS) P
Row 49: (RS) K2tog, K to end (9 sts)
Row 50: (WS) P
Row 51: (RS) K
Row 52: (WS) P
Row 53: (RS) K
Row 54: (WS) P
Row 55: (RS) K
Row 56: (WS) P
Row 57: (RS) K
Row 58: (WS) P
Row 59: (RS) K
Row 60: (WS) P
Place the 9 sts on stitch holder (safety pin works well)

While body is flat, steam and block. Let dry thoroughly.

Graft the shoulder seams together by working the Kitchner stitch. Sew up sleeve seams and attach by hand to armholes.

Work neckline as follows:
Place the 7 sts from the right front onto working needle, pick up 15 sts on right front neck edge, place 21 sts from stitch holder for back neck line on working needle, pick up 15 sts on left front neck edge and finally, place the last 7 sts from the left front onto working needle. (65 sts)
Attach contrasting yarn to the right front and work the following rows:
Row 1: (RS) P all sts
Row 2: (WS) K all sts
Row 3: (RS) P
Row 4: (WS) K all sts
Row 5: (RS) P all sts
Row 6: (WS) Bind off all sts with K st

You should be at the front of the right front edge. Cut yarn leaving about 12 inches. With a small crochet hook, work a chain stitch long enough to form a loop for a small button. Attach loop to neck edge and weave in yarn.
Weave in all yarn ends. Sew on button on left front edge to match the loop.
Steam and block once again. Let dry thoroughly.

Hat & Booties Pattern

to Knit by Paulene Seymour

Materials
Yarn: double knit /baby sport
3. 50 mm needles

Abreviations
rib rows: 1 knit 1 purl starting with a knit ending in a purl st.
St st (stocking stitch): 1 row knit, 1 row purl
k. Knit p. purl
yon. Yarn on needle.
K2tog. knit 2 stitches together
pattern rows mean using pattern below
cast off. bind off.

Pattern
1. (* k 1 yon k 1) all into one stitch, p3 repeat from* to end
2. * p 3tog knit 3 repeat from * to end
3. * p3 (kl yon kl) all into one stitch repeat from * to end
4. * k 3 p3tog repeat from * to end
These 4 rows form the pattern.

Booties
Cast on 28 sts
St st 3 rows
Next row: kl * yon k 2tog repeat from * to end last stitch k 1.
St St 4 rows
work 8 rows of pattern.
Next row: kl * yon k 2 tog repeat from * to end kl
knit 1 row
Divide for top of foot
Next row: k 19 stitches turn plO stitches turn.
On these 10 stitches work 12 rows in st st break off yarn.
Right side facing join yarn and pick up 9 stitches along the side 10 stitches across top and 9 stitches down other side. 48 st.
Purl 1 row.
Work 6 rows off pattern
To shape sole:
Knit 1 row
Next row: K2 k2tog k16 stitches k2tog k 5 stitches k 2tog k 16 stitches k 2 tog kl
knit 1 row.
Next row: K 1 k2tog k15 stitches k 2 tog k4 stitches k2 tog k15 stitches k2 tog kl
Next row: kl k2tog k13 stitches k2 tog k4 stitches k2tog k13 stitches k2tog k1. cast off
Sew picot edge down, sew side seam and sole. Sew in all loose ends. Thread ribbon though holes.
Make second bootie to match.

Hat
Cast on 72 stitches
Work 3 rows in stocking st.
Next row: Knit 1* yon knit 2 tog repeat from * to end knit 1.
Work 4 rows in stocking st
Pattern 8 rows.
Knit 1 row
rib row (knit 1 purl 1) for 10 rows ending with wrong side facing for next row.
Pattern 20 rows
With right side facing and starting with a knit row shape crown:
1. Knit 4 Sts. *knit 2 tog k5 repeat from * to last 3 sts k3
2nd and alternate rows knit.
3. knit 3 *knit 2 tog knit 4 repeat from* to last 3 sts knit 3
5. knit 2 sts * knit 2tog knit 3 repeat from* to last 3 sts knit 3 .
7 . knit 1 * knit 2 tog knit 2 repeat from * to last 3 sts knit 3
9. * knit 2 tog knit 1 repeat from * to last 3 sts 2 tog
11. Knit 1 knit2tog 10 times .break off yarn leaving enough to pull through sts on needle. Pull sts tight and sew down side of hat . Sew picot edge back on rim. Turn right side out, turn up edge and sew on a flower or bow.

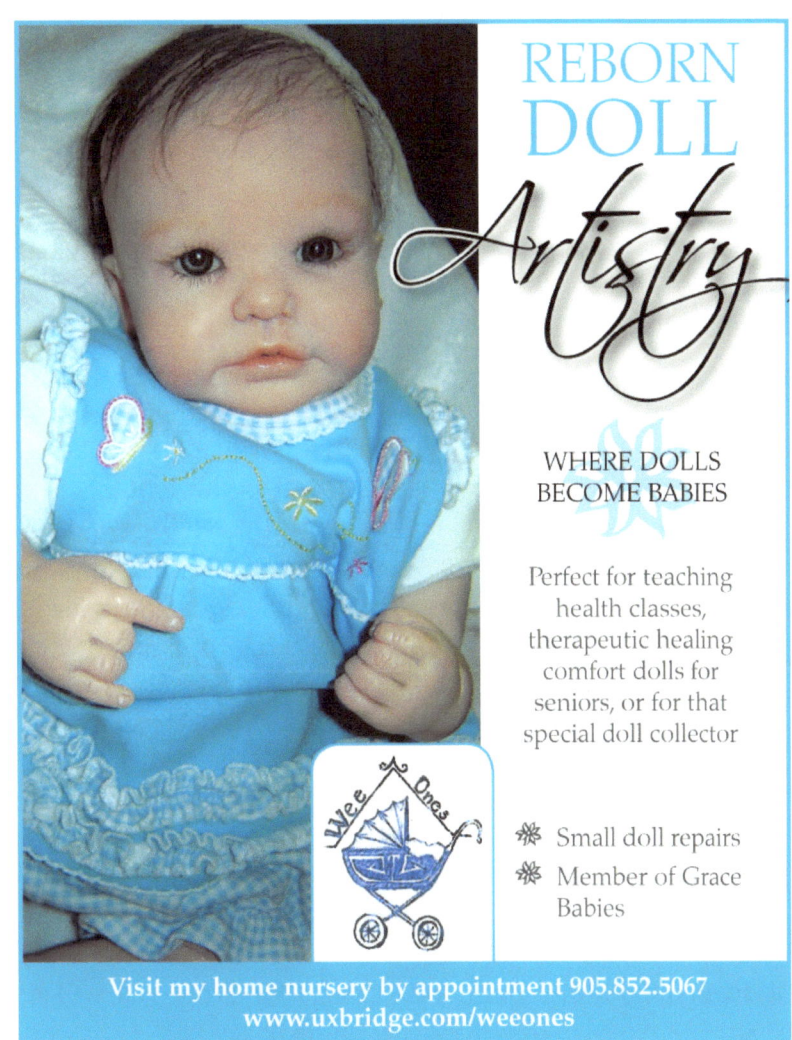

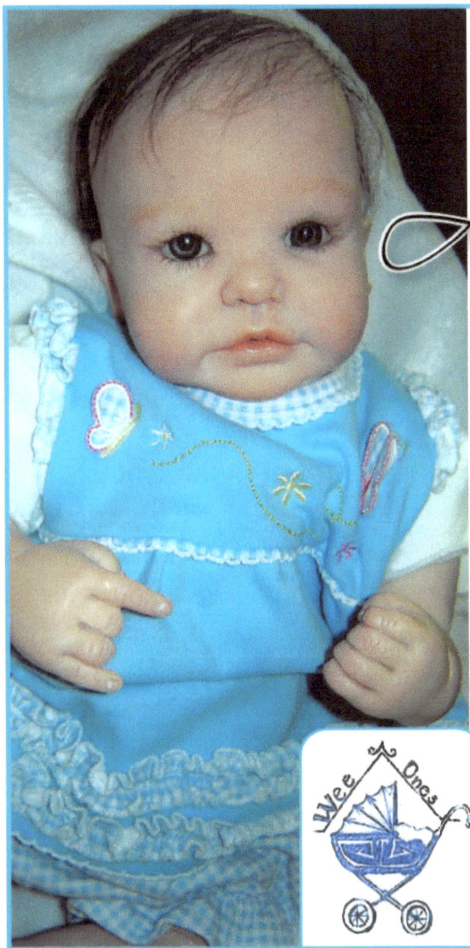

Mouse Outfit

By Carol Anne Carlile

20" mouse – use TLC weight yarn & "F" crochet hook – 1 skein each color
14" mouse – use Bernat baby yarn & "F" hook – 1 skein each color
10" mouse – use a fine fingering baby yarn (#1) and "C or D" hook – 1 skein each color
Hook sizes depend on how tight you crochet.
¼" ribbon in lengths needed for booties, hat & waist of panties. Be sure to leave the ribbon long enough to tie in a pretty bow.

Special instructions: "work corner" (2dc, ch 1, 2dc in next ch or sp) ch 3 at end of row always counts as your first dc of the next row.

sc = single crochet
sl st = slip stitch
ch = chain
dc = double crochet
hdc = half double crochet

ALWAYS REMEMBER -- Your "ch 3" at the end of each row is your first dc's when counting the dc on the next row.

TOP:

Ch 48
Row 1: Dc in 4th ch from hook & in next 5 ch (7dc), work corner (2dc, ch 1, 2dc in next ch or sp) (always work "corner s" like this), dc in next 7 ch, corner, dc in next 14 dc, corner, dc in next 7 ch, corner, dc in last 7 ch, ch 3, turn.

Row 2: 9 dc, corner, 11 dc, corner, 18 dc, corner, 11 dc, corner, 9 dc, ch 3, turn.

Row 3: 11 dc, corner, 15 dc, corner, 22 dc, corner, 15 dc, corner, 11 dc, ch 3, turn.

Row 4: 13 dc, corner, 19 dc, corner, 26 dc, corner, 19 dc, corner, 13 dc, ch 3, turn.

Row 5: 15 dc, corner, 23 dc, corner, 30 dc, corner, 23 dc, corner, 15 dc, ch 3, turn.

Row 6: (Left Back) 18 dc, ending with 1 dc in ch-1 space, end off.

Row 6: (front section) skip to next corner, join yarn in the ch-1 space, ch 3, dc across front to next corner, end with dc in ch-1 space, end off.

Row 6: (right back) skip to next corner, join yarn in the ch-1 sp, ch 3, dc to end of row, ch 3, turn.

Row 7: (you will join all three sections together now) dc across back section, working 2 dc in last st, sk next section (for arm), work 2 dc in first st of front section, dc across, ending with 2 dc in last st, skip next arm section, work 2 dc in first st of left back section, dc across to end, ch 3, turn.

Row 8: (increase row) dc across row, working 2 dc in every 9th stitch, but don't do last increase that is almost at the end of the row. You only want 8 increases across the row. Ch 3, turn.

Row 9: Dc across row, at end of row, join to beginning of row. Now you will be working in rounds. Ch 3, turn.

Rows 10 – 16: dc around, join, ch 3, turn. (at end of row 16, ch 4, turn.)

Row 17: * sk 1 st, sl st in next, ch 4, repeat from * across row, ending with ch 2, dc in first st, ch 4, turn. This will give you your last ch 4 space & put you in the middle of the ch-4 space for the next row.

Rows 18 – 20: ch 4, sl st in next ch-4 loop, repeat around, end off at end of row 20.

SLEEVES:

Row 1: Join yarn to underarm, dc around, join, ch 3, turn. (38 dc)

Rows 2 & 3: dc around, join, ch 3, turn.

Row 4: (decrease row) dc next 2 sts together, dc in next, repeat from * around, join.

Row 5: work ch-4 loops, sk 1 st, sl st in next st. end off.

Back Button Hole Flap:

Row 1: join to left side of back at neck. Sc down to where you started working in rounds. Ch 1, turn

Row 2: sc back up to neck opening.

Row 3: (button hole row) 1 sc, ch 2, sk 2, 5 sc, ch 2, sk 2, 5 sc, ch 2, sk 2, sc to end. Ch 1, turn.

Row 4: sc down row, working 2 sc in each ch-2 space. Ch 1, turn.

Row 5: sc across row, end off, leaving enough length of yarn to stitch the end of the flap to the dress so it will lay flat.

Sew buttons on opposite side of opening, matching the buttons to the button holes.

Neck opening:

Row 1: join to back left opening, ch 3, dec next 2 sts together, dc in next, repeat around neck, ch 4, turn.

Row 2: work in ch-4 loops with sk 1, sl st in next, sk next across row, end off.

PANTIES: (make 2)

Row 1: ch 42, dc in 4th ch from hook and continue across. Ch 3, turn.

Rows 2 – 8: dc across, ch 3, turn.

Row 9: (increase for crotch) work 19 dc, work 2 dc in each of next 2 sts, dc to end of row, ch 3, turn.

Rows 10 – 13: Dc across row, working increase of 2 dc in the center 2 dc of row, ch 3, turn.

Rows 14 & 15: dec at crotch edge, end off at end of row 15. Sew back & front together down sides & across crotch. Then work legs.

Row 1: Join yarn to leg opening, ch 2, *work 2 hdc, dec next 2 as 1 st, rep around opening, join, ch 4, turn.

Row 2: work in the ch-4 loops as for rest of outfit. End off.

Panties waist:

Row 1: join yarn at side seam, ch 4, sk 1, dc in next, * ch 1, sk 1, dc in next, repeat from * around, join to 3rd ch of beginning ch-4. Ch 2, turn.

Row 2: work row of hdc, working 1 st in each dc & 1 st in each ch-1 sp. Join, ch 4, turn.

Row 3: work row of ch-4 loops around as previous.

Mouse tail:

Join yarn to center back of panties, ch 25, work 3 sc in each chain back up to panties. This makes for the curly curl tail. If you want a straight tail, work 1 sc in each ch. If you want a curl only on the end of the tail, work 3 sc only as far as you want curl, then finish with sc the rest of the row. End off yarn, hide inside panties. Add a pretty ribbon bow to the tail.

BOOTIES:

Sole: (in contrast color yarn)

Row 1: Ch 12, 4 dc in 4th ch from hook, dc in next 7 ch, 5 dc in last ch. Working on opposite side of ch, dc in 7 sts, join, ch 3, turn.

Row 2: dc in same st, dc in next 7 dc, 2 c in each of next 5 dc, dc in next 7 dc, 2 dc in each of next 4 dc, join. End off.

Side:

Row 1: join white yarn at back of sole, ch 3, work dc around sole, join, ch 3, turn.

Rows 2 & 3: dc around, join. End off at end of row 3.

Toe/Top):

Row 1: With either white or contrast color, ch 7, dc in 4th from hook & in next 2 ch, 5 dc in end ch, dc on opposite side of beg ch, ch 3, turn. (13 dc)

Row 2: dc across 4, 2 dc in each of next 5 dc, dc to end of row. Don't end off. (18 dc)
Join toe/top to bootie:
Fold the top in half lengthwise to find the middle, then fold the bootie in half lengthwise to find the middle stitch. Match the two stitches together, hold & go along side to end of the top where your yarn loop is. Working thru both sections, sc around the toe/top piece to opposite side of bootie top, end off.

Cuff:

Row 1: Join yarn to back of bootie, ch 4, sk 1 st, dc in next, ch 1, sk 1, dc in next around bootie opening. This creates the row you weave the ribbon thru. Ch 3, turn.

Row 2: Dc around working in each dc & each ch-1 space. Join, ch 4, turn.

Row 3: work the ch-4 loops around, end off.

HAT

Ch 4, join. Ch 3, turn.

Row 1: work 12 dc in loop, join, ch 3, turn.
(remember, your ch-3 at end of row is your first dc of

next row)

Row 2: work 2 dc in each dc of previous row. Join, ch 3, turn. (24 dc)

Row 3: dc in same st as beg ch-3, *dc in next st, 2 dc in next st, rep around, join, ch 3, turn (36 dc)

Row 4: inc, 2 dc, inc across row, join, ch 3, turn. (48 dc)

Row 5: inc, 3 dc, rep around row, join, ch 3, turn. (60 dc)

Rows 6-9: work even in dc around hat, join, ch 3, turn. (ch 4 at end of row 9)

Row 10. Work ribbon row of ch 1, sk 1, dc in next. Join, ch 2, turn.

Row 11: work hdc around working 1 hdc in each dc & 1 hdc in each ch-1 sp, join, ch 4, turn.

Row 12: work in ch-4 loops as in rest of outfit. End off.

Ears: make 2 circles of each color

Row 1: Ch 4, join to form ring. Ch 3, work 12 dc in ring, join, ch 3, turn.

Row 2: work 2 dc in each dc of previous round, join, end off.

Lay the contrasting colored circle on top of the white circle & sc around outside, join, end off.

Sew one ear to each side of hat in position you think looks best.

Crochet Mary Janes

for 20" Berenguer or similar size doll.
by Cheryl Bage

You will need:
1 ball baby/fingering weight yarn (50g)
3mm crochet hook
2 buttons

Beginning: Ch 15

1st rnd: 3dc in 4th ch from hook. 1 dc in next ch. 1 hdc in next ch. 1 sc in each of the next 2 ch. 1 hdc in the next ch. 1 dc in each of the next 2 ch. 1 tr in each of the next 3 ch. 9 tr in last ch. Working along opposite side of ch, 1 tr in each of next 3 ch. 1 dc in each of next 2 ch. 1 hdc in next ch. 1 sc in each of next 2 ch. 1 hdc in next ch. 1 dc in next ch. 4 dc in same ch as first 3 dc. Ss to top of ch 3. (37 sts.)

2nd rnd: Ch 3. 2 dc in next st. 1 dc in next st. 2 dc in nest st. 1 dc in each of the next 10 sts. (2 dc in next st. 1 dc in next st) 4 times. 2 dc in next st. 1 dc in each of next 10 sts. (2 dc in next st. 1 dc in next st.) twice. Ss to top of ch 3. (46 sts.)

3rd rnd: Ch 3. Miss first dc. 1 dc in back loop only of each dc to end of round. Ss in top of ch 3.

4th rnd: Ch 3. Miss first dc. 1 dc in each dc around. Ss in top of ch 3.

5th rnd: Ch 2. Hdc in the next 13 dc. (dc 2 tog) 2 times. (tr 2 tog) 5 times. (dc 2 tog) 2 times. Hdc to end of round. Ss in top of ch 2. (37 sts.)

Continue each shoe to correspond:

Right Shoe:
Ch 2. Hdc in next 8 sts. Ch 15. Hdc in back loop of 3rd ch from hook. Hdc in back loop of next 11 ch. Sc in next unworked hdc and in next 17 hdc. Hdc in each st to end of round. Ss in top of ch 2. Finish off.

Left Shoe:
Ch 2. Hdc in next 8 sts. Sc in next 18 sts. Ch 15. Hdc in back loop of 3rd ch from hook. Hdc in back loop of next 11 ch. Hdc in next unworked hdc and in each st to end of round. Ss in top of ch 2. Fasten off.

To finish sew buttons on opposite side of shoe from strap. Use the space between sts at the end of the strap for the buttonhole.
Optionally, you can sew a small bow or flower to the top of the instep. You could also crochet a border around the sole in the remaining loops on round 3. I do this using size 10 crochet cotton and a 1.6mm hook crocheting (sc, ch 2, sc) in each loop around.

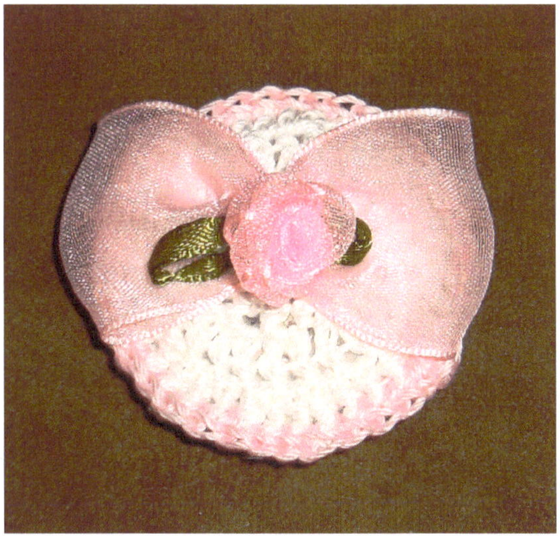

Pretty Pacifiers

by Carol Carlile

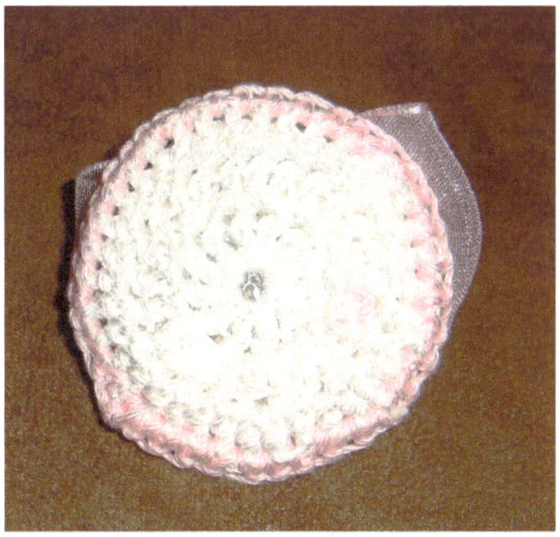

Round paci

Materials : few yards of #10 crochet thread
small piece of plastic
one earth magnet

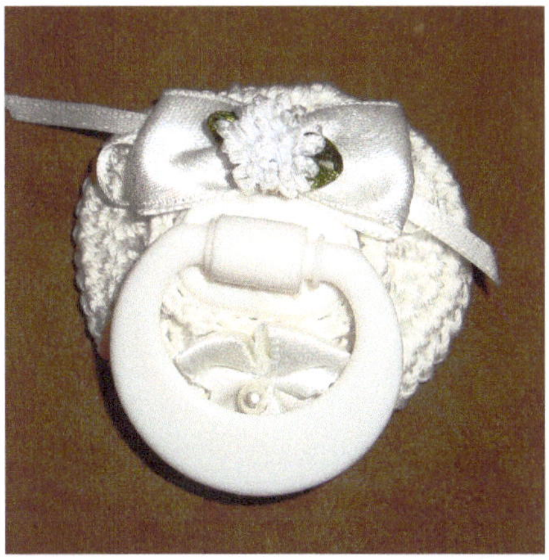

Directions: (make 2 of these circles)
Round 1: Chain 4, work 11 dc in first ch, join, ch 3, turn (12 dc)
Round 2: Work 2 dc in each dc of previous row, join, ch 3, turn (24 dc)
Round 3: dc in bottom of turning ch, * dc in next dc, 2 dc in next dc, repeat from *
around, join, end off. (36 dc)

Cut the plastic in a circle that will fit just inside the crocheted circles, glue one magnet in the center of the plastic circle. Join thread to any stitch, work one round of sc around outside of circle, working thru both crocheted circles to join them together with the piece of plastic inside. join, end off. Decorate as desired.

Cover for regular Pacifier

Materials: 1 white pacifier with nipple cut off
1 earth magnet
few yards of #10 white crochet thread

Rounds 1 thru 3: work as for round pacifier, do not end off.
Round 4: work even in dc around, join, ch 3, turn. (36 dc)
Round 5: repeat round 4.
Round 6: work decrease st over next 2 dc, * dc in next st, dec over next two, repeat from * around, join, ch 3, turn.
Round 7: repeat round 6, end off.

Weave a piece of crochet thread thru the top loops of round 7, then draw the crocheted cover around the pacifier & tighten the thread up around the base of the handle. Tie ends & hide inside the cover. Decorate as desired.

Ribbons-a-plenty!

by Carol Carlile, Crochet Haven Presents

Finished Size: 0-3 Months

Materials for entire set:
7 oz Pink Bernat Baby yarn
1 oz White Bernat Baby yarn
2 strips of ¼" elastic 15 inches long
31 white clover flowers with pink roses in center
¼" white ribbon –
2 strips 18" for booties
2 strips 20" for pantaloon legs
2 strips 18" for sleeves
2 strips 20" for waist
22 strips 6 ½" for skirt
Hook: Size 2 (2.75 mm) steel crochet hook or size to meet gauge

Gauge: 3 dc rows = 1" 6 dc = 1"

Directions -- DRESS

Beginning at neck with pink, ch 64
Row 1: Dc in 4th ch from hook, and in each of next 8 ch, in next ch work corner (2 dc, ch 1, 2 dc), dc in each of next 9 ch, work corner, dc in each of next 20 ch, work corner, dc in each of last 10 ch. Ch 3, turn.
Rows 2-8: *Dc in each dc across to first ch-1 sp, work corner in ch-1 sp; rep from * across row, end with dc in each remaining dc, ch 3 turn.
Note: You will work RS Back, LS back and Front Sections separately until Row 14 where you will join all threes sections.

Back – Right Side
Row 9: Dc in each dc across to ch-1 corner sp, ch 3 turn.
Rows 10-11: Dc in each dc across, ch 3 turn.
Row 12: Dc in bottom of turning ch (increase made) dc in each dc across, ch 3 turn.
Row 13: Dc in each dc across to last st, 2 dc in last dc. (increase made) Fasten off.
Skip next 41 dc of Row 8. (The skipped stitches will be worked later for the sleeve.)

Front
Join yarn in next ch-1 sp, sl st to next dc, ch 3.
Row 9: Dc in each dc across to next ch-1 sp, ch 3 turn.
Row 10-11: Dc in each dc across, ch 3 turn.
Rows 12-13: Dc in bottom of turning ch (increase made) dc in each dc across, 2 dc in last st (increase made), ch 3 turn.
Skip next 41 dc of Row 8 for sleeve.
Back- Left Side
Join yarn in next ch-1 sp, sl st in next dc, ch 3.
Row 9: Dc in each dc across to next ch-1 sp, ch 3 turn.
Row 10-11: Dc in each dc across, ch 3 turn.
Row 12: Dc in each dc across, 2 dc in last st (increase), ch 3 turn.
Row 13: dc in bottom of turn ch, dc in each dc across. DO NOT END OFF, ch 1 turn.

Skirt
Row 14: Sc in each dc across, back and front sections, ch 3 turn.
Rows 15-16: Dc in each of next 4 dc * ch 2, dc in each of next 5 dc, rep from * across, ch 3 turn
Row 17: Dc in each of next 4 dc, *ch 2, skip next ch-2 sp, dc in each of next 5 dc; rep from * across, sl st in top of beg ch to join, ch 5 turn. (joined skirt at back opening)
Row 18: *Dc in each of next 5 dc, ch 2, skip next ch-2 sp; rep from * around, end with dc in each of last 4 dc; sl st in 3rd ch of beg ch, ch 3 turn.
Row 19: Rep Row 17, end with ch 2, sl st in top of beg ch, ch 5 turn.
Row 20: Increase row - *2 dc in next dc, dc in each dc across to last dc, 2 dc in next dc, ch 2; rep from *

around, end with dc in bottom of beg ch, sl st in 3rd ch of beg ch, ch 3 turn. Increase every 6th row on skirt.
Row 21: Dc in each dc of group * ch 2, dc in each of dc of next group, rep from * around, end with ch 2, sl st in top of beg ch, ch 5 turn.
Row 22: Dc in each dc of group *ch 2, dc in each dc of next group; rep from * around, sl st in 3rd ch of beg ch, ch 3 turn.
Row 23-24: Rep Row 21 & 22
Row 25: Rep Row 21.
Rows 26-31: Rep last 6 rows.
Rows 32: *Dc in each dc across group, 2 dc in next ch-2 sp, rep from * around, sl st in top of beg ch.
Fasten off. DO NOT TURN.
Row 33: With white (shell row) Beg sc, * sk 2 dc, 9 tr in next dc, sk 2 dc, sc in next dc; rep from * around.
Fasten Off.

Back Opening
Row 1: Join pink yarn to left neck edge. Work 32 sc down one side and another 32 sc up the other side to neck edge, ch 1 turn. (64 sc)
Row 2: Sc in each sc across, ch 1 turn.
Row 3: (buttonhole row). Sc in each of next 2 sc, sk 2, sc in each of next 7 sc, ch 2, sk 2, sc in each of next 7 sc, ch 2, sk 2 (3 button holes created) sc in each remaining sc across, ch 1 turn.
Row 4: Sc in each sc across working 2 sc in each ch-2 sps of previous row, ch 1 turn.
Row 5: Sc in each sc across. Fasten off.

Neck & Collar
Row 1: Join white with sl st in last st made on back opening, ch 3, dc in each dc across, ch 4 turn.

(Ribbon Row)
Row 2: *Sk 1 dc, sc in next dc, ch 3; rep from * across, end with sc in last dc, ch 4 turn.
Rows 3-5: Sc in next ch-3 sp, ch 3; rep from * across end with sc in last ch-3 sp, ch 1 turn.
Row 6: *3 sc in next ch-3 sp; rep from * across. Fasten off

Sleeves Join pink yarn at underarm
Row 1: Ch 3, work 65 dc evenly around, ch 3, turn.
Rows 2-10: Dc in each dc around, ch 3 turn.
Row 11: Dc in each dc around, ch 4 turn.
Row 12: Sk 1 dc, dc in next dc, *ch 1, sk 1, dc in next dc; rep from * around, join with sl st in 3rd ch of beg ch. Fasten off.
Row 13: Join white, ch 3 in same st, 1 dc, ch 1, 2 dc, * in next dc (2 dc, ch 1, 2 dc); rep from * around, join with sl st. Fasten off.

Weave ribbon through the ch-2 spaces down the dress skirt. Fold end of ribbon over and attach to the dress with a flower.

Weave ribbon through Row 12 on sleeves, tie in bow. Weave ribbon through Row 1 on neck; sew under ends at back opening.

Sew 4 buttons on back opening of dress.

Finished Size: 0-3 Months

Materials for entire set: (continued from last issue)
7 oz Pink Bernat Baby yarn
1 oz White Bernat Baby yarn
1 strips of ¼" elastic 15 inches long
2 white clover flowers with pink roses in center.
¼" white ribbon –
2 strips 20" for pantaloon legs

Hook: Size 2 (2.75 mm) steel crochet hook or size to meet gauge
Gauge: 3 dc rows = 1" 6 dc = 1"

Pantaloons

With pink, Ch 120, join to form circle, ch 3.
Row 1: Work dc in each ch around, join, ch 3, turn
Rows 2–4: Work dc in each dc around, ch 1, turn. (120 dc)
Row 5: Fold down first two rows, lay ring of elastic in the fold and sc around joining row 1 to row 5, join, ch 3, turn.
Row 6: *Work dc in each of next 39 dc, work 2 dc in next dc, (increase made). Rep from * around row. ch 3, turn. (123 dc)
Rows 7–14: Work dc in each of next 123 dc, join, ch 3 turn.
Row 15: Dc in top of ch 3, work dc in each of next 60 dc, work 2 dc in each of next 2 dc [increase made] work dc in each of next 60 dc, work 2 dc in each of next 2 dc, [increase made] join, turn.
Row 16: Sl st in first dc, ch 3, dc in same dc, work dc in each of next 62 dc, work 2 dc in each of next 2 dc (increases made), work dc in each of next 62 dc, work 2 dc in next dc, (increase made) join, turn.
Row 17: Sl st in first dc, ch 3, dc in same dc, work dc in each of next 64 dc, 2 dc in each of next 2 dc (increases made), work dc in each of next 64 dc, end with last two dc being dc together (decrease made.) Join, turn.
Row 18: Sl st in first dc, ch 3, dc in same dc, work dc in each of next 66 dc, 2 dc in each of next 2 dc, (increases made), work dc in each of next 66 dc, work 2 dc in each of next 2 dc, (increases made) join, turn.
Row 19: Sl st in first dc, ch 3, dc in same dc, work dc in each of next 68 dc, work 2 dc in each of next 2 dc (increases made), work dc in each of next 68 dc, work 2 dc in next dc (increase made) join, turn.
Row 20: Sl st in first dc, ch 3, dc in same dc, work dc in each of next 70 dc, work 2 dc in each of next 2 dc (increase made), work dc in each of next 70 dc, work 2 dc in next dc, join, turn.
Row 21: Sl st in first dc, ch 3, dc in same dc, work dc in each of next 72 dc, work 2 dc in each of next 2 dc (increase made), work dc in each of next 72 dc, work 2 dc in next dc, join, turn.
Row 22: Sl st in first dc, ch 3, dc in same dc, work dc in each of next 74 dc, work 2 dc in each of next 2 dc (increases made), work dc in each of next 74 dc, work 2 dc in next dc (increase made), join, turn.

Legs
Row 23: Sl st in next dc, ch 2, work dc in each of next 75 dc, dc next 2 dc together (decrease made) join to first dc, turn.
Row 24: Sl st in next dc, ch 2, work dc in each of next 73 dc, dc next 2 dc together (decrease made), join to first dc, turn.
Rows 25–28: Rep as for previous 2 rows twice more, decreasing at the beginning and end of each row.
Row 29–35: Sl st to next dc, ch 3, dc in each dc across row, join, ch 3, turn. At end of Row 35, join, ch 4, turn.

Ribbon Row
Row 36: *Sk 1 dc, dc in next dc, ch 1, rep from * across row. Join, do not turn.
Rows 37 & 38: Work as for the last 2 rows on the sleeves of the dress.

Ruffles for the Back (Optional)
1st Ruffle
Lay pantaloons flat and find the sides
Row 1: With the waistband facing towards you, attach

yarn with a sc around the post of the side st on row 12 of the pantaloons, *ch 3, sk next 2 dc, sc around the post of the next dc, rep from * across to the other side of the pantaloons, ch 1, turn.

Row 2: Sl st to loop, ch 4 [counts as tr], work 9 tr in same loop, *sc in next loop, work 10 tr in next loop, rep from * across, ch 1 turn.

Row 3: Sl st to first tr, ch 1, sc in same tr, * (ch 2, sc in next tr) 9 times, sk next sc, sc in next tr, Rep from * around, end off, weave in end.

2nd and 3rd Ruffle

Attach yarn in the 15th (18th) row of pantaloons and Rep as for first ruffle.

Ribbon Row

Row 36: * Sk 1 st, dc in next st, ch 1, rep from * across. join, do not turn.

Rows 37-38: Work as for the last 2 rows on the sleeves of the dress.

Bottom Ruffles

First Ruffle

Lay pantaloons flat and find the sides.

Row 1: With the waistband facing towards you, attach white with an sc around the post of the side st on row 12 of the pantaloons. *Ch 3, sk 2 dc, sc around the post of the next st, rep from * across to the other side of the pantaloons. (21 ch-3 loops.) Ch 1, turn.

Row 2: Sl st to loop, ch 4 [counts as tr], 9 tr in same loop, *sc in next loop, 10 tr in next loop, rep from * across, ch 1 turn.

Row 3: Sl st to 1st tr, ch 1, sc in same st, * (ch 2, sc in next tr) 9 times, sk next sc, sc in next tr, rep from * around, end off, weave in end.

Second and Third Ruffles

Attach white in the 15th (18th) row of pantaloons and rep as for first ruffle.

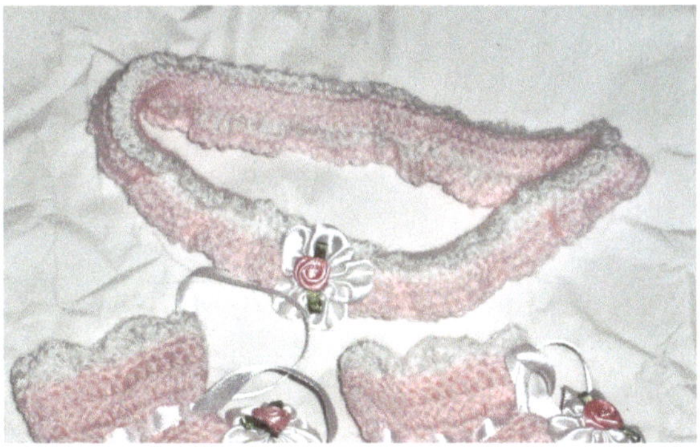

Finished Size: 0-3 Months

Materials for entire set: (continued from last issue)
1 oz Pink Bernat Baby yarn
1 strips of ¼" elastic 15 inches long
1 white clover flowers with pink roses in center.

Hook: Size 2 (2.75 mm) steel crochet hook or size to meet gauge
Gauge: 3 dc rows = 1" 6 dc = 1"

Headband

With pink yarn,

Row 1: ch 120, join to form circle. Ch 3, turn.

Rows 2-3: Work dc in each ch around. Join, ch 3, turn.

Row 4: Work in back loops only, dc in each dc around, ch 3, turn.

Row 5: Work dc in each dc around, join.

Row 6: Fold over the elastic and working through rows 1 and 5, (sc, ch 2) in each st around, making sure the elastic is inside. End off

Row 7: On opposite side of headband, join yarn, in unworked loops of row 3, Rep row 6, end off.

Sew rosette bow on center of headband.

Finished Size: 0-3 Months

Materials:
1 oz Pink Bernat Baby yarn
2 white clover flowers with pink roses in center
¼" white ribbon –2 strips 18" for booties

Hook: Size 2 (2.75 mm) steel crochet hook or size to meet gauge

Gauge: 3 dc rows = 1" 6 dc = 1"

Sole
With pink, ch 14
Row 1: Sc in 2nd ch from hook, 2 sc in next ch, sc in next 9 sts, 2 sc in next ch, 4 sc in last ch. Working in free loops of beg ch, work 2 sc in next ch, sc in each of next 9 ch, 2 sc in each of next 2 ch, join with sl st to 1st sc, ch 1, turn.
Row 2: Sc in same sp, 2 sc in each of next 2 sc, sc in each of next 11 sc, 2 sc in each of next 5 sc, 11 sc, 2 sc in each of last 2 sc, join with sl st, ch 1, turn.
Row 3: Work sc in same sp and 2 sc in each of next 2 sc, 1 sc in next st, 2 sc in next st, sc in each of next 11 sts, 2 sc in each of the next 7 sts, sc in each of next 11 sts, 2 sc in next st, 1 sc in next st, 2 sc in last 4 sts, join with sl st, ch 1, turn.
Row 4: Sc in each st around, end off.

Side and Top
Row 1: Sc in BLO of each st around, join, ch 1, turn.
Rows 2-4: Sc in each st around, join, ch 1, turn.
Row 5: Work 21 sc, (sc in next st, sk next st) 7 times, work 21 sc to end of round, join, ch 1, turn. (49 sts)
Row 6: Sc around, join, ch 1, turn. (49 sts)
Row 7: Work 22 sc, sk next sc (sc in next sc, sk next sc) twice, 22 sc to end, join, ch 1, turn. (46 sts)
Row 8: Sc around, join, ch 1, turn. (46 sts)
Row 9: Work 18 sc, sk next sc (sc in next sc, sk next sc) 4 times, 18 sc, sk last sc, join, ch 1, turn. (40 st)
Row 10: Sc around, join, ch 1, turn. 40 sts)
Row 11: Work 16 sc, (sk 1 sc, sc in next sc) 4 times, 16 sc to end, join, ch 1, turn.(36 sts)
Row 12: Work 13 sc, ch 6, sk 10 sc, sc to end, join, ch 4, turn.
Row 13: *Sk 1 sc, dc in next sc, ch 1, rep from * around row, join, ch 1, turn.
Row 14: Sc around, join, ch 1, turn. (32 dc)
Row 15: Sc in joining, * ch 2, sc in next, Rep from * around, join, end off.

For a ridge around the sole, go back to the un-worked loops on row 4. Work a row of sc, join, end off.

Note:Pattern not exactly as shown in picture. Booties are worked in a solid colour.

BABY BOTTLE COVER

to Crochet
For 4 ounce bottle

Round 1: Ch 4, work 11 DC in first ch loop, join to 3rd loop of beginning ch. Ch 3, turn.
Round 2: Work 2 DC in each dc around, join, ch 3, turn.
Round 3: 2 DC in next st, *(dc in next st, 2 dc in next st), rep from *around, join with sl st in top of turning ch, ch 3, turn.
Round 4: Rep row 3. Ch 4, turn.
Round 5: Dc in bottom of turning ch, *sk 2 sts, work open shell of (dc, ch 1, dc) in next st, rep from * around, join to 3rd ch of turning ch, sl st into space. Ch 4, turn.
Round 6 – 17: Rep round 5 (for larger bottle, add more rows)
Round 18: ch 4, (dc, ch 1) in each ch-1 sp and between each shell, join to 3rd loop of beg ch-4, ch 3, turn. (ribbon row)
Round 19: Dc in same space as turning ch, work 2 dc in each st & sp around, join, ch 6, turn.
Round 20: sl st in 3rd loop of beg ch (picot made), dc in same st. *DC in next st, ch 3, sl st in 1st ch, dc in same st. Repeat from * around, join in beg ch, end off.

Weave ribbon thru stitches of round 18, tie in a bow.

Beaded Dress Doll's Set

Materials: Any fine yarn to gauge.
Model crocheted using:
Patons Astra Yarn—50 g(1 ¾ oz) ball
White - 9 balls
¼" white polyester satin ribbon:
1 – 44" length for waist
2 – 18" lengths for booties
2 – 20" length for sleeves
2—18" lengths for bottom of pantaloons
2—15" lengths of ¼" elastic sewn
3 3/8" buttons (9mm)
591 small "Pony Beads"
Gauge: 8 dc = 1" 4 dc rows = 1"
Hook: Size 2 (2.75 mm) Steel Crochet Hook (or size needed for gauge)

Directions

Work Corner means working (2 dc, ch 2, 2 dc) in the next ch-2 space throughout the bodice. Beginning at neck edge, Ch 87

Row 1: Dc in 4th ch from hook and in each of next 11 sts, (2 dc, ch 2, 2 dc) in next ch, dc in each of next 14 sts, (2 dc, ch 2, 2 dc) in next ch, dc in each of next 26 sts, (2 dc, ch 2, 2 dc) in next ch, dc in each of next 14 sts, (2 dc, ch 2, 2 dc) in next ch, dc in each next 13 sts, ch 3, turn. (Your first double crochet of the next row.)

Rows 2-10: Dc to corner, work corner, dc to next corner, work corner, dc to next corner, work corner, dc to next corner, work corner, dc to end. Ch 3, turn.

Row 11: Dc in each of the next 33 dc, 2 dc in next ch-2 space, ch 14, sk next 54 dc, 2 dc in next ch-2 sp, dc in each of next 66 dc, 2 dc in next ch-2 sp, sk next 54 dc, ch 16, 2 dc in next ch-2 sp, dc in last 34 dc. Ch 3, turn.

Row 12: Work dc in each dc and in each ch across (180 dc), ch 3, turn.

Row 13: Work dc, ch-1 in each dc across row, ch 3, turn.

Row 14: Work dc in each dc and each ch-1 sp across, ch 3, turn.

Row 15: Work dc in each of next 5 dc, *ch 3, add bead (drop thread from hook and insert hook in opposite end of bead, pull through the dropped loop), work dc in each of next 8 dc, Rep from * across, ending with 5 dc. Ch 3, turn.

Row 16: Dc in each dc across row, increasing 1 dc on each side of the bead. DO NOT INCREASE BEFORE 1ST BEAD OR AFTER LAST BEAD. This will make 10 dc on each side of bead and will increase your stitches. Ch 3, turn.

Rows 17 & 18: Work dc in each dc across row. Ch 3, turn.

Row 19: *Add bead, work dc in each of next 10 dc, rep from * across row, ending with add bead, join to beginning ch 3 of row (you will now be working in rounds). Ch 3, turn.

Row 20 (increase row): Work dc in each dc across, increasing 1 st before and after each bead [12 dc between each bead], join, Ch 3, turn.

Rows 21 & 22: Work dc in each dc across row. Ch 3, turn.

Row 23: Work dc in each of next 6 dc, *bead, work dc in each of next 12 dc, rep from * around. Join. Ch 3, turn.

Row 24 (increase row): Work dc in each dc across, increasing 1 st before and after each bead. [14 dc between each bead], join. Ch 3, turn.

Rows 25-26: Work dc in each dc across row. Ch 3, turn.

Row 27: Work dc in next 14 dc,* bead, work dc in each of next 14 dc, rep from * across row. Join, ch 3, turn.

Row 28 (increase row): Work dc in each dc across, increasing 1 st before and after each bead. [16 dc between each bead], join. Ch 3, turn.

Rows 29 & 30: Work dc in each dc across row, ch 3, turn.

Row 31. Work dc in each of next 8 dc, *bead, work dc in each of next 16 dc. Rep from * across ending with dc in each of next 8 dc. Join, ch 3, turn.

Row 32 (increase row): Work dc in each dc across, increasing 1 st before and after each bead. [18 dc between each bead], join. Ch 3, turn

Rows 33-35: Work dc in each dc across row, ch 3, turn. [At end of Row 35, ch 1, turn]

Row 36: Sc in same st as joining, sk 2 dc, work 6 dc in next dc, sk 2 dc, sc in next dc. Rep around bottom of dress, join. Slip stitch into next stitch, ch 3, turn.
Row 37: Work in open shells as follows: *sl st to 2nd dc of next shell, sk next 2 dc, (ch 3, 2 dc, bead, 3 dc) in same st, (3 dc, bead, 3 dc) in next dc, sk next 3 dc, (3 dc, bead, 3 dc) in next dc, sk 2 dc, Rep from * around bottom of dress, join & end off.

Sleeves
Row 1: Join thread to center bottom of armhole. Ch 3, work dc in each st around arm opening, join. Ch 3, turn.
Rows 2-6: Work dc in each dc around, join. Ch 3, turn after each row except after row 6, ch 4, turn.

Ribbon Row
Row 7: *Sk next dc, dc in next dc, ch 1. Rep from * around row. Join in 3rd st of ch-4. Ch 1, turn.
Row 8: Work open shell as follows: sl st to ch-1 space, work (3 dc, bead, 3 dc) in ch-1 space, sk next ch-1 space, work open shell in next ch-1 space. Rep around row, join and end off.

Back Opening
Row 1: Beg on left side, join thread in top of last dc and work 2 sc in end of each row down the back opening. Continue up other side and ch 1, turn.
Row 2: Sc in each sc across row, ch 1, turn.
Row 3 Buttonhole row (left side): Work sc in next 2 sc, ch 2, sk 2 sc, work sc in each of next 8 sc, ch 2, sk 2 sc, work sc in each of next 8 sc, ch 2, sk 2 sc, work sc in each of next 14 sc down left side. Ch 1, turn. (3 button holes)
Row 4: Work sc in each sc across row, working 2 sc in each ch-2 space. Ch 1, turn.
Row 5: Work sc in each of next sc to bottom of opening.
End off, leaving a small length of thread to tack down the left side over the right side.

Neck
Row 1: Join thread to one edge of neck opening and work sc in each sc across neck. Ch 1, turn.
Row 2: Sc in each sc across row. Ch 4, turn.
Row 3: *Sk next sc, dc in next sc, ch 1. Rep from * across row, [you should end up with an odd number of ch-1 sp.] ch 1, turn.
Row 4: Sl st to ch-1 sp, (ch 3, work dc in each of next 2 dc, bead, work dc in each of next 3 dc) in same sp, * sk next ch-1 sp, (work dc in each of next 3 dc, bead, work dc in each of next 3 dc) in next ch-1 sp, rep from *across row. End off. (23 beads)

Booties
Make two (15 beads for each bootie)

Top of foot
Ch 12
Row 1: Dc in 4th ch from hk and dc in each ch across, ch 3, turn.
Rows 2-5: Dc in each dc across row. End off after Row 5.

Foot
Row 1: Ch 10, join with a sc in last dc of Row 5, continue to work sc in each of next sc around three sides of piece, ch 10, join to 1st ch, ch 3, turn. (30 sc around the bootie top)
Rows 2: Dc in each ch and dc around, join to top of ch-3, ch 3, turn.
Rows 3 & 4: Work dc in each dc across row, ch 3, turn.
Row 5: *In next 2 dc, work 1 dc, (decrease made), dc in each of next 2 dc, rep from * around row. Join, ch 3, turn.
Row 6: In next 2 dc work 1 dc (decrease made) twice, work dc in next 10 dc, in next 2 dc work 1 dc fives times (5 decreases made), work dc in next 10 dc, in next 2 dc work 1 dc twice, (2 decreases made), join. Do not end off. Turn bootie inside out and fold together lengthwise. Loosely sl st through the outside loops of each side, end off, weave in end and turn right side out.

Cuff (15 beads for each cuff)
Row 1: Join in center back (at the joining). Work in each of of next 30 sc, join, do not turn.

Ribbon Row
Row 2: Ch 4, *sk 1 sc, dc in next sc. Rep from * around, ch 1, join. Do not turn, ch 3.
Row 3: Work dc in each dc and ch-1 space across. Ch 3, turn.
Row 4: Work dc in each dc across, end with ch 1. (do not turn.)
Row 5: Work dc in first dc, *bead, work dc in each of next 2 dc, rep from * around row. Join. Ch 1, do not turn. (15 beads)
Row 6: Work sc in each sc around, join. Ch 1, do not turn.

Row 7: *Work sc in next sc, sk next 2 sc, work dc in next 3 sc, ch 2, work dc in next 3 sc, sk nest 2 sc, rep from * around, join, end off.

Pantaloons

Ch 120, join to form circle, ch 3.
Row 1: Work dc in each ch around, join, ch 3, turn
Rows 2–4: Work dc in each dc around, ch 1, turn. (120 dc)
Row 5: Fold down first two rows, lay ring of elastic in the fold and sc around joining row 1 to row 5, join, ch 3, turn.
Row 6: *Work dc in each of next 39 dc, work 2 dc in next dc, (increase made). Rep from * around row. ch 3, turn. (123 dc)
Rows 7–14: Work dc in each of next 123 dc, join, ch 3 , turn.
Row 15: Dc in top of ch 3, work dc in each of next 60 dc, work 2 dc in each of next 2 dc [increase made] work dc in each of next 60 dc, work 2 dc in each of next 2 dc, [increase made] join, turn.
Row 16: Sl st in first dc, ch 3, dc in same dc, work dc in each of next 62 dc, work 2 dc in each of next 2 dc (increases made), work dc in each of next 62 dc, work 2 dc in next dc, (increase made) join, turn.
Row 17: Sl st in first dc, ch 3, dc in same dc, work dc in each of next 64 dc, 2 dc in each of next 2 dc (increases made), work dc in each of next 64 dc, end with last two dc being dc together (decrease made.) Join, turn.
Row 18: Sl st in first dc, ch 3, dc in same dc, work dc in each of next 66 dc, 2 dc in each of next 2 dc, (increases made), work dc in each of next 66 dc, work 2 dc in each of next 2 dc, (increases made) join, turn.
Row 19: Sl st in first dc, ch 3, dc in same dc, work dc in each of next 68 dc, work 2 dc in each of next 2 dc (increases made), work dc in each of next 68 dc, work 2 dc in next dc (increase made) join, turn.
Row 20: Sl st in first dc, ch 3, dc in same dc, work dc in each of next 70 dc, work 2 dc in each of next 2 dc (increase made), work dc in each of next 70 dc, work 2 dc in next dc, join, turn.
Row 21: Sl st in first dc, ch 3, dc in same dc, work dc in each of next 72 dc, work 2 dc in each of next 2 dc (increase made), work dc in each of next 72 dc, work 2 dc in next dc, join, turn.
Row 22: Sl st in first dc, ch 3, dc in same dc, work dc in each of next 74 dc, work 2 dc in each of next 2 dc (increases made), work dc in each of next 74 dc, work 2 dc in next dc (increase made), join, turn.

Legs

Row 23: Sl st in next dc, ch 2, work dc in each of next 75 dc, dc next 2 dc together (decrease made) join to first dc, turn.
Row 24: Sl st in next dc, ch 2, work dc in each of next 73 dc, dc next 2 dc together (decrease made), join to first dc, turn.
Rows 25–28: Rep as for previous 2 rows twice more, decreasing at the beginning and end of each row.
Row 29–35: Sl st to next dc, ch 3, dc in each dc across row, join, ch 3, turn. At end of Row 35, join, ch 4, turn.

Ribbon Row

Row 36: *Sk 1 dc, dc in next dc, ch 1, rep from * across row. Join, do not turn.
Rows 37 & 38: Work as for the last 2 rows on the sleeves of the dress. (30 beads on bottom of each leg)

Ruffles for the Back (Optional)

1st Ruffle
Lay pantaloons flat and find the sides
Row 1: With the waistband facing towards you, attach yarn with a sc around the post of the side st on row 12 of the pantaloons, *ch 3, sk next 2 dc, sc around the post of the next dc, rep from * across to the other side of the pantaloons, ch 1, turn.
Row 2: Sl st to loop, ch 4 [counts as tr], work 9 tr in same loop, *sc in next loop, work 10 tr in next loop, rep from * across, ch 1 turn.
Row 3: Sl st to first tr, ch 1, sc in same tr, * (ch 2, sc in next tr) 9 times, sk next sc, sc in next tr, Rep from * around, end off, weave in end.
2nd and 3rd Ruffle
Attach yarn in the 15th (18th) row of pantaloons and Rep as for first ruffle.

Headband

Row 1: With white, ch 120, join to form circle. Ch 3, turn.
Rows 2-3: Work dc in each ch around. Join, ch 3, turn.
Row 4: Work in back loops only, dc in each dc around, ch 3, turn.
Row 5: Work dc in each dc around, join.
Row 6: Fold over the elastic and working through rows 1 and 5, (sc, ch 2) in each st around, making sure the elastic is inside. End off
Row 7: On opposite side of headband, join yarn, in unworked loops of row 3, Rep row 6, end off.
Sew rosette bow on center of headband.

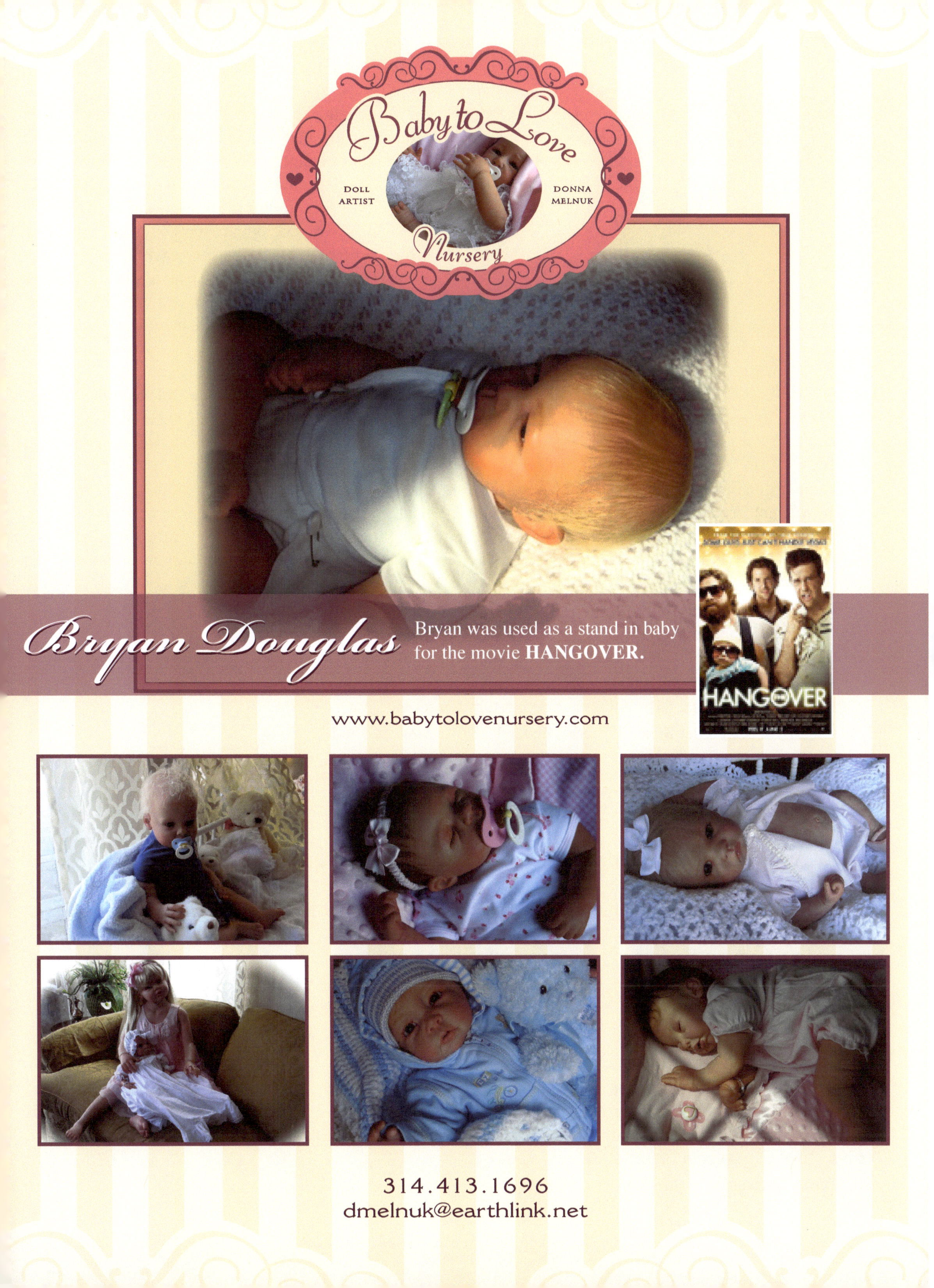

Baby to Love
Doll Artist
Donna Melnuk
Nursery
Bryan Douglas
Bryan was used as a stand in baby for the movie HANGOVER.
HANGOVER
www.babytolovenursery.com
314.413.1696
dmelnuk@earthlink.net

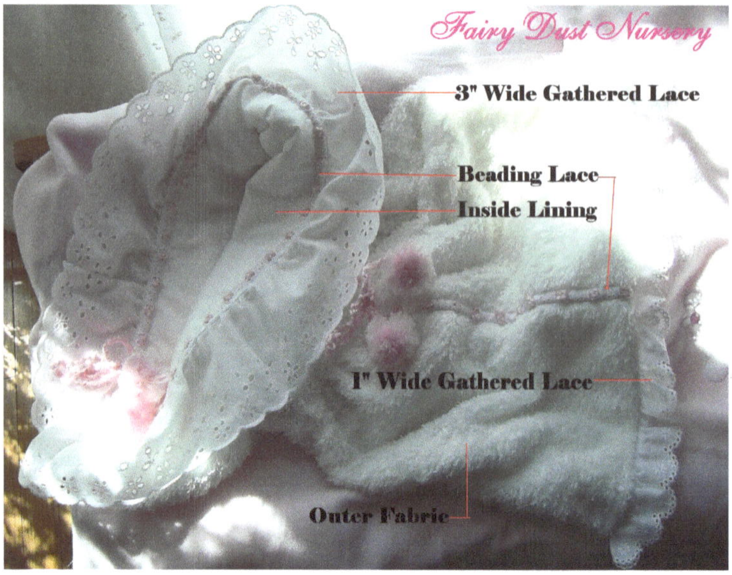

Reborn Bunting Bag (fits up to 20" baby)

I've had many requests for the pattern for my beautiful bunting bag that swaddles my Baby Bella (Sarah Lyn) for her flight to her new mommy in England. I thought I'd share the pattern with everyone since it's the perfect solution to transport baby to her new mommy, while keeping her cozy and protected during her journey. It's very easy for anyone that can thread a bobbin!! Please read through ALL steps prior to beginning this pattern and with the pictures, you'll be able to visualize the method.

Materials Required:
2 pieces 22" long X 19" wide Outer Fabric (heavier fabric: fuzzy, fake fur, velour, chenille, fleece)
2 pieces 22" long X 19" wide Inside Fabric (matching lighter fabric: 100% cotton, flannel, cotton/polyester blend)
1 piece of Inside Fabric 36" long X 1-1/2" wide
3-inch wide gathered lace: 1 metre long (for around the top edge - eyelet is recommended)
1/2 " wide flat Beading Lace to insert ribbon: 1-1/2 metres long (used up the front & around the top edge)
1-inch wide gathered lace for the bottom: 20 inches long (to match 3" wide gathered lace is recommended but not necessary)
1/4 " coordinating colour ribbon to insert through Beading Lace: 3 metres long
1/2" white elastic: approximately 22 inches in length

1. Outer Fabric: With right sides facing and 3/8" seam, sew sides and bottom, leaving the top open. i.e. looks like a pillowcase. Turn right side out.

2. Lining Fabric: Repeat as for Outer Fabric but turn wrong-side-out.

3. Turn top on both outer & lining fabrics under 1/2" to wrong side and iron.

4. Place Lining Fabric 'pillowcase' inside Outer Fabric 'pillowcase', i.e. wrong sides facing each other.

You'll see the inside looks as beautiful as the outside & you should be very happy with your progress so far! Now, isn't this easy??

5. With your 3" gathered lace, choose a starting spot at the back, top edge, and baste the lace onto your 1/2" turned in edge on the Outer Fabric with the bound edge of the lace placed just below the folded over edge, i.e. your lace extends above the edge.

6. Sew the two raw end edges of the lace together to give it a nice finish, with the seam facing out at the back at your starting spot.

Place the Lining Fabric ironed edge over the bound edge of the lace and matching up with the Outer Fabric edge. Sew the top edges together close to the edge, enclosing the bound edge of the lace.

7. Sew the 1/2" wide flat Beading Lace around the top edge, (both edges of the lace, securing the lace).

8. With the 36" X 1-1/2" long piece of Inside Fabric, iron under 1/4" on each of the long edges and 1/4" under each little side. This is your casing for the elastic.

9. Turn your bag inside-out and on the inside of the bag, measure down 8" from the top of the Beading Lace and mark all the way around. Choose a starting spot near the side seam and place and pin the casing edge on this mark. Sew both edges of casing through the two layers around the inside of your bunting bag, leaving ends open to insert elastic. Do not insert elastic at this point.

10. Turn your bag right-side-out.

11. Beginning at the bottom edge of the casing seam line, on the outside -- front & middle, place and sew a piece of Beading Lace through both layers of front side only, ending at the bottom (with top and bottom edges folded over for neatness). Sewing through all layers of front will keep the lining stable inside the bag and also allow you to "gather" up the front for cuteness!!

12. To further stabilize the inside lining, ensure the lining is right down at the bottom on the inside and pin through all layers (front and back) from side to side on the outside.

13. Now that you're confident the lining is in place at the bottom, sew the 1-inch wide gathered lace along the bottom edge, through all layers, folding over end edges for neatness.

14. Thread a piece of 1/4" coordinating ribbon through the Beaded Lace around the circumference of the top edge, long enough to tie in a bow. The top edge can now be slightly gathered if you wish, but not necessary.

15. Fold a piece of 1/4" coordinating ribbon in half and thread the doubled ribbon from bottom to top of the Beaded Lace on the front. (you will have two 'tails' at the top of the lace) Secure at the bottom of the bag by sewing a few stitches of the folded edge of the ribbon at the bottom. Tie the two 'tails' in a bow. If you wish, you can form slight gathers up the front with these ribbons, however, it's not necessary.

Note: In place of the 1/4" coordinating colour ribbon, I crochet-chained the ties and made pom-poms.

16. Insert the 1/2" elastic in the casing, sew it securely and sew casing ends closed.

As always, I'm available by email if you have any questions at all regarding the above pattern and am usually readily available during the day: fairydust@cogeco.ca Don't hesitate to ask the 'silliest' question if it's important to you. I can't wait to see your creations!!!

Happy Sewing!!!

Jan Czuba, Reborn Artist & Seamstress
Fairy Dust Nursery – Home of Zooby Designs--Haute Couture For The Discerning Reborn Baby Doll
www.fairydustbabies.com

Heirloom Sampler Pillow

1/2 Metre White Batiste fabric
1/2 Metre Lace Beading
1 Metre Entredeux
1-1/2 Metres Gathered Lace Edging
1/2 Metre Flat Lace Insertion
Decorative Ribbon (to fit Lace Beading)

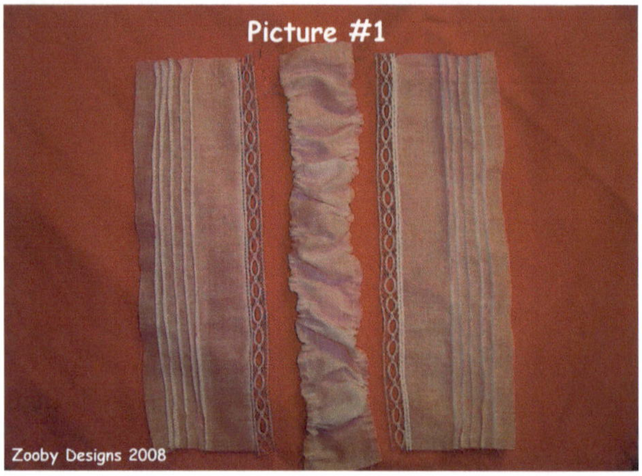

PILLOW TOP

Batiste Strips: Cut TWO - 3-1/2" X 9" strips.
Tucked Strips: On each strip, measure 5/8" from one long side, fold the length of the strip at this point and stitch down the length as close to the fold as possible.
Measure 5/16" from the previous stitching line, fold the length and sew as before.
Continue until you have five tucks in each strip. The tucks should measure ¼" from the stitching line of one tuck to the stitching line of the next. Press all tucks in each strip, the same way.
Sew Entredeux along the length of both sides of each strip.

Lace Beading: Sew lace beading on right edge of left tucked strip and on left side of right tucked strip. Set tucked strips aside.

Batiste Strip: Cut ONE strip of fabric 1-3/4" X 18"
Centre Puffing Strip: Sew a gathering line of stitches on each long side. Pull each gathering thread equally until the puffing strip is 9" long. Sew (zig-zag) puffing stripto lace beading, in between both tucked strips.
(See Picture #1)

Flat Lace Insertion: On left tucked strip, sew flat lace insertion to entredeux. Repeat for right tucked strip.

Batiste Strips: Cut TWO – 1-1/2" X 9" strips.
Sew one strip, lengthwise, on left flat lace insertion and one strip on right flat lace insertion.
(See Picture #2)

Insert ribbon through centre left and right lace beading. I used pink grosgrain ribbon for my pillow.

The pillow top is now complete. **(See Picture #3)**

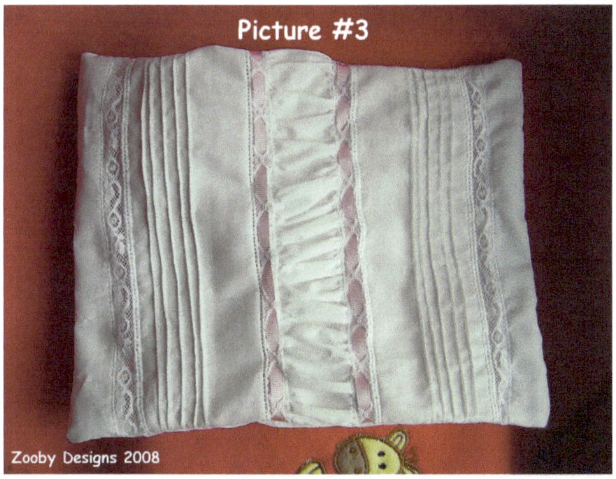

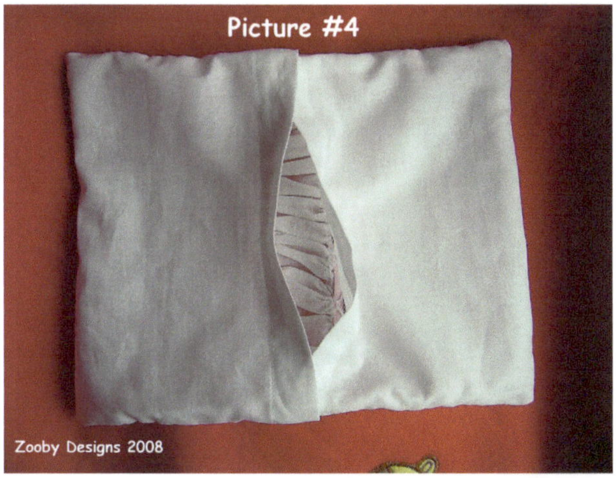

PILLOW BOTTOM

Batiste Strip: Cut TWO – 8-1/2 X 7" strips (NOTE: as your lace insertions & beading may be a different width than what I used in this project, you may have to increase/decrease the length and/or width of these 2 pillow bottom strips).

The two strips will be overlapped in the middle of the pillow bottom for ease of insertion of polyfil or a pillow form.
Fold in one side of each length 1/4" and fold in again approximately 3/4" – to allow one side to overlap the other. Stitch each length to hold in place.
Overlap the backs until they fit the pillow top and baste in place.

The pillow bottom is now complete.

With right sides together, stitch the front to the back. Turn right-side-out and remove the basting stitch in the pillow bottom. **(See Picture #4)**

To Complete: Sew decorative 1-1/4" gathered lace (or width of your choice) around the edge of the pillow. I also added a vintage blue pearl button. Stuff with polyfil or a pillow form.

Happy Sewing!
Jan Czuba, Reborn Artist & Seamstress
Fairy Dust Nursery – Home of Zooby Designs-- Baby Couture For The Discerning Reborn Baby Doll
My website: www.fairydustbabies.com
Email: fairydust@cogeco.ca

Baby Pink TuTu

Materials Required For TuTu
One 6 Inch Wide Roll of Tulle or Tulle Fabric
1/4-Inch Elastic
Organza Ribbon For Bow (optional)
Fabric scissors, ruler

I believe that in the heart of every little girl, rests the dream of becoming a ballerina! So why not start your reborn fashionista off early with her very own Zooby Designs TuTu and help her on her way to making her dreams come true!!! Pair it up, as I have done, with a glam onesie and chic lacey leggings. This quick and easy outfit is 'no sew' and is the perfect designer addition for your little 'twinkle toes'!!

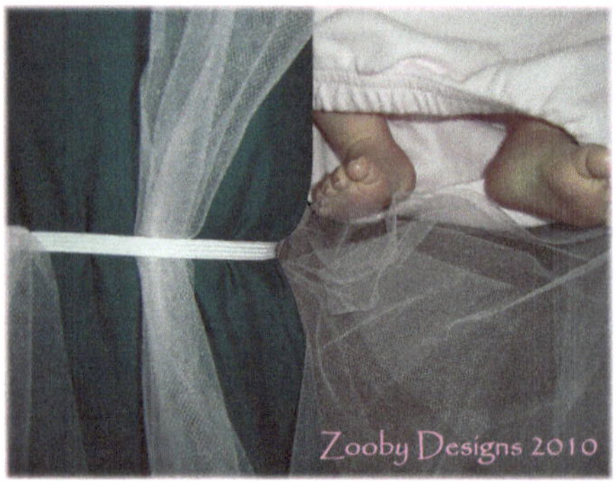

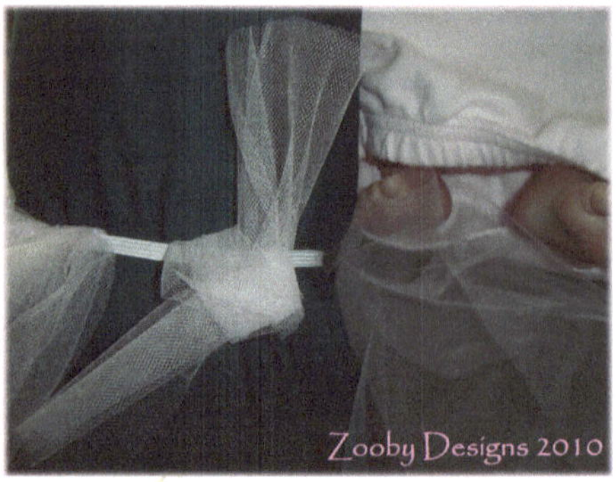

Directions For Creating TuTu for 20-Inch Reborn:

1. Measure your baby from the waist, down to where you want the TuTu hemline and double this measurement. My TuTu is 6 inches long for Baby Madisyn so my tulle pieces will be 6 Inches wide by 12" long (my doubled length). If using a 6 Inch Roll, just cut your lengths from that. If using Tulle Fabric, cut 6 Inch widths of tulle and then cut your lengths from these strips. I have drawers full of Tulle Fabric which I cut in widths and then lengths.

2. Cut 1/4-Inch elastic the circumference of baby's waist. Overlap 1/2 inch on the ends and stitch together, either by machine or by hand. This will ensure a nice comfy, secure fit.

3. You will now begin tying your pieces onto the elastic, with either a single or a double knot. Fold the 12-Inch length evenly over the elastic (6 inches on each side) and tie securely but do not "squeeze" the elastic. Have knot facing down so the inside is flat against baby's tummy. TIP: For ease in tying, slip the elastic onto your leg like a garter.

I use a long pillow form which I slip the elastic over… it makes tying the knot much easier.

4. You can make the TuTu as poufy as you want. Another option, which I have done here, is to use 2 different colours of tulle -- light pink and hot pink. You can even use three colours if you like!!! It's up to you!!

5. If you wish, add a tulle bow made with a few 6 Inch pieces & tie them together with organza ribbon. Tie the organza ribbon onto the front of the TuTu, onto the elastic, between 2 pieces of tied tulle strips. Your little ballerina's TuTu is all ready for her!!

Happy Sewing!
Jan Czuba, Professional Reborn Artist & Seamstress
Fairy Dust Nursery – Home of Zooby Designs -- Baby Couture For The Discerning Reborn Baby Doll
My NEW Website: www.fairydustbabies.com
Email: fairydust@cogeco.ca

Heirloom Baby Bonnet

"Heirloom Sewing" refers to the elegant hand sewing techniques of the late 1800's and early 1900's. Although machine made dresses were prevalent during the Civil War period, later years found women once again lavishing lace and hand embroidery on their children's clothing. These fine garments became heirlooms – treasures to be used by succeeding generations – much like our reborn babies – keepsake treasures to be handed down and loved for our children and grandchildren, for years to come.

While the following Heirloom Baby Bonnet pattern can be hand sewn, the same effect can be nicely achieved with the sewing machine and is much quicker.

Let's make a treasure and create another memory!!

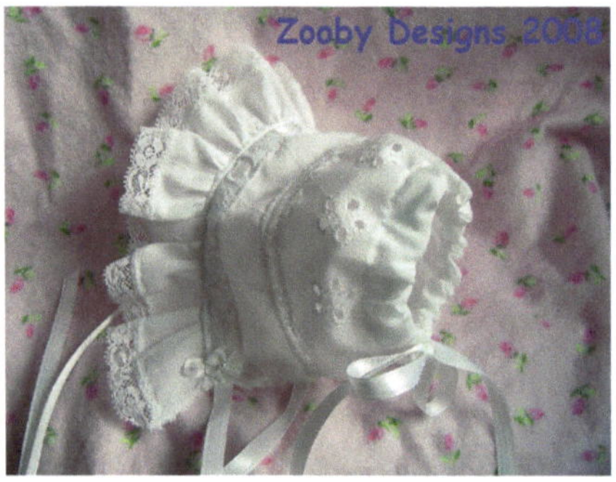

Instructions are based on a 12" circumference head. You can adjust to the size you require with the length and width of the rectangle by "trying the rectangle" on your baby's head first for 'fit'.

1. Cut rectangle of fabric (batiste or poly/cotton is recommended) 9-1/2" X 5-1/4".

2. Cut ruffle of matching fabric 1-1/4" wide by approximately 27" (ie. 2-1/2 to 3 times width).

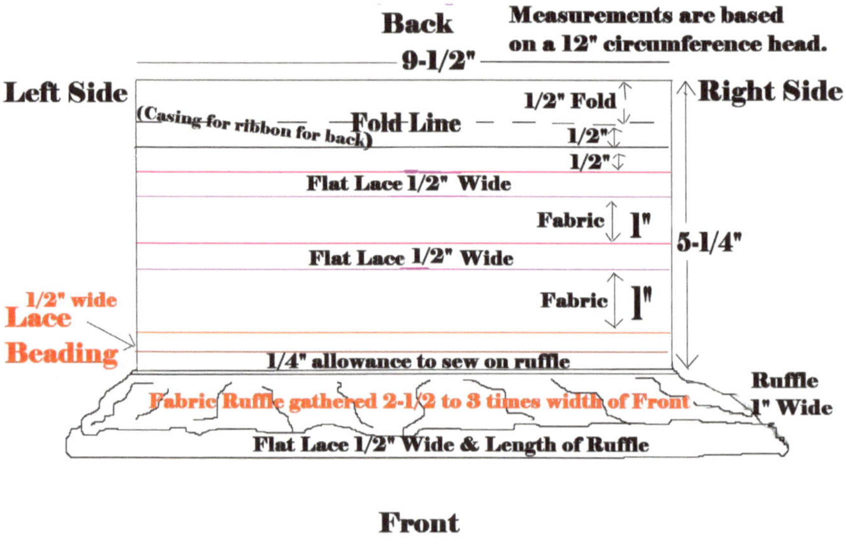

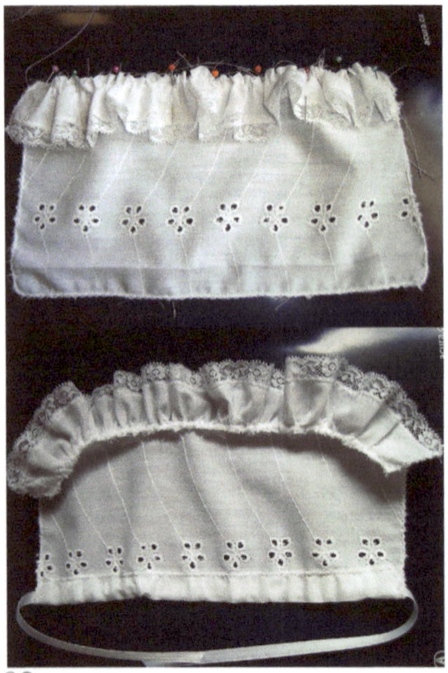

3. Cut one piece of flat lace the length of the Ruffle, for the Ruffle edge.

4. Cut 9-1/2" length(s), one or two pieces, of Flat Lace for inserts, depending on one or two inserts. Because the baby I made this one for has such a small head and that I used eyelet fabric with the pretty back, I just used one insert.

5. Cut 9-1/2" length of Beading Lace.

6. Serge or zig-zag Back and both Sides.

8. Serge or zig-zag flat lace onto Ruffle.

9. Gather Ruffle.

10. With right sides together, serge or zig-zag Ruffle onto Front edge.

11. Fold over Back edge 1/2 " to inside, iron flat.
12. Straight stitch.

13. Place Flat Lace on right side of fabric and serge or zig-zag across the length of both sides. Zig-zag short end of lace on each side of bonnet side to secure. (Repeat for other piece of Flat Lace if you're using 2 pieces)

14. On inside of bonnet, cut away fabric close to each edge. I carefully open the fabric with my 'stitch ripper', cut the fabric straight down the middle & then trim close to edge. (Repeat for other piece of Flat Lace if you're using 2 pieces)

15. Straight stitch both sides of Beaded Lace along length next to Ruffle/Bonnet seam.

16. Insert satin 1/4" satin ribbon through Beaded Lace, leaving lengths on each end for ties.

17. Insert 1/4" satin ribbon through back casing & tie in a bow, as tight/loose as you prefer.

18. Attach little ribbon/pearl bows at front edge on Beaded Lace/Satin Ribbon.

Happy Sewing!
Jan Czuba, Reborn Artist & Seamstress
Fairy Dust Nursery – Home of Zooby Designs-- Baby Couture For The Discerning Reborn Baby Doll
My website: www.fairydustbabies.com
Email: fairydust@cogeco.ca

Sweet Bonnet for Mini OOAK

by Dorothy Steven

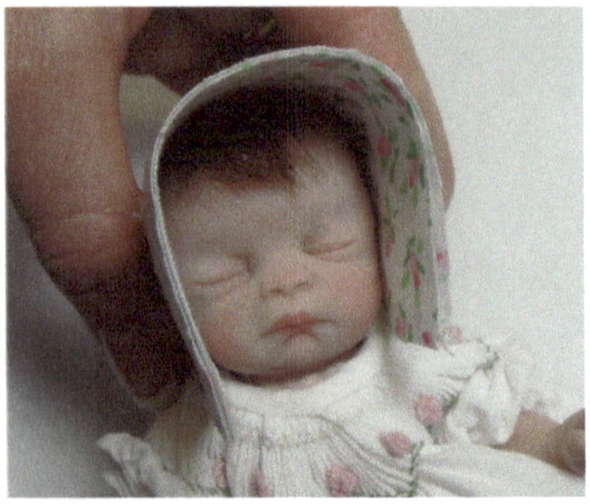

First cut a rectangle piece of fabric, it can be be any type or pattern you choose. I don't use a pattern because every baby I make all have different shape heads.

I then take the piece and measure it to the dolls head like in the photo, make sure the fabric comes almost to her shoulders, for seam allowance.

Fold the rectangle in 1/2 and trim rounded one end like above.

It will look like this opened.

Turn inside out so good sides are on the inside.

Sew along the dotted line and turn inside right and iron flat.

Once the bonnet is ironed flat fold in 1/2 and sew along this dotted line.

Once opened sew along the dotted line at the tip and trim off.
You then turn inside right and mark where you will stitch on the ribbon ties.

You can add lace to the brim as you made the bonnet or even after with fabric glue.

It is a simple vintage looking bonnet.

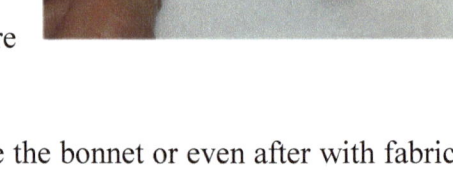

Frilly Hair Band
(with 3-In-One Option)

Materials Required (Pattern based on 15" Circumference - adjust pattern to fit your baby's head)

1 inch width pretty soft ribbon – Length: 19 Inches
1/8 inch Elastic – Length: 13 Inches
Tiny frilly Lace – Length: 38 Inches
32 Inches of matching 1/4 Inch ribbon for hair band bow
Thread to match and needle

Directions for Hair Band & Bow (with 3-In-One Option):

1. Stitch frilly lace on each long side of ribbon. (Picture #1)
2. Stretch and stitch elastic down the middle of the wrong side of ribbon.
3. Bring ends of ribbon together, pin and ensure it nicely fits baby's head. Securely stitch.
4. Mark 1/4 Inch matching ribbon at 2 Inch intervals. (Picture #2) Double thread needle and knot.
5. Beginning at one end, take needle up through one mark and down into the next mark. Continue in this manner until you come to the end of the marked 2-inch intervals. (Picture #3)

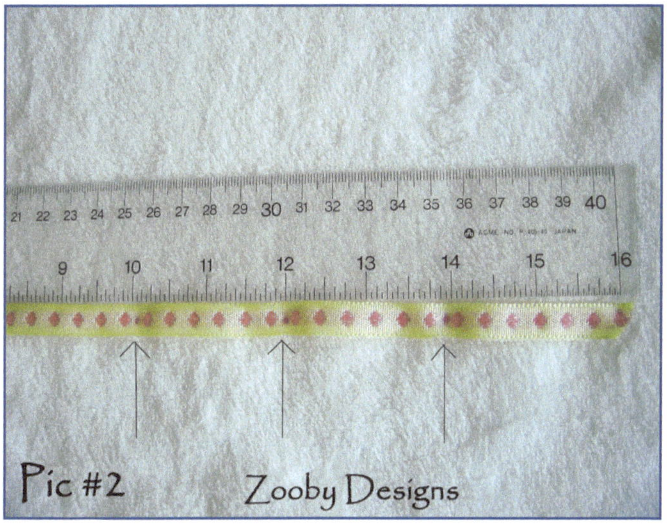

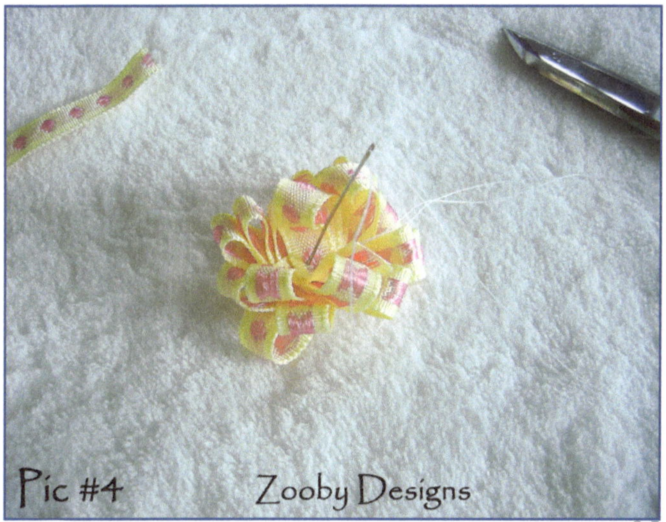

6. Pull thread securely & arrange loops nicely. When you're happy with the loops, take needle down through the middle of bow and back up. Do this 3 or 4 times to secure. (Picture #4) Knot tightly and stitch bow to hair band. (Picture #5) Glue or sew on a faux flower with pearls. (Picture #6)

As an alternative to stitching the bow on the hair band, you can place a magnet on the bow. You then can have the pretty magnetic bow on it's own, or the frilly hair band on it's own, or place the magnetic bow on the hair band on the area of the inside magnet – 3 Hair Decorations In One!!

Happy Sewing!
Jan Czuba, Professional Reborn Artist & Seamstress
Fairy Dust Nursery – Home of Zooby Designs --
Baby Couture For The Discerning Reborn Baby Doll
My website: www.fairydustbabies.com
Email: fairydust@cogeco.ca

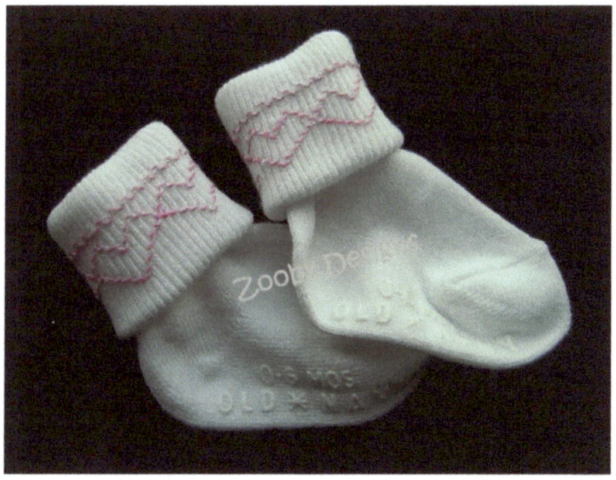

Smocked 'Hearts' Infant Socks

Supply List

1 Pair of Infant Socks – I've used Old Navy 0–6 month size
Standard Size 8 Crewel Embroidery Needle
Good quality 6-strand embroidery floss – any colour
Ruler marked with 1/8 inches
Erasable fabric marker

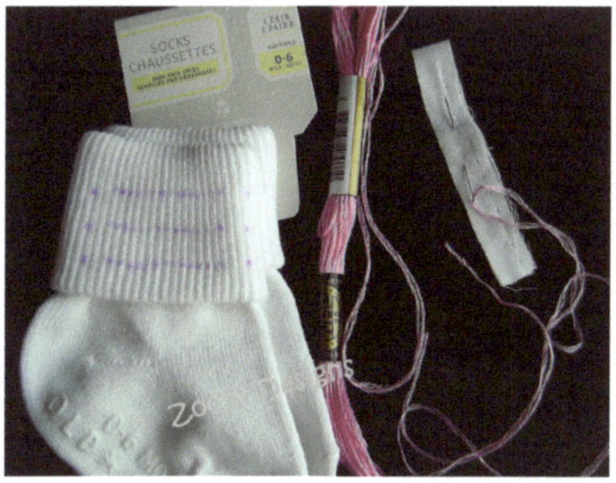

General 'Rules' For This Project

1. Stitches are worked from left to right, picking up the top third of each 'rib'.
2. While smocking your design, bring needle into 'rib' horizontally & parallel, from right to left, using your erasable line marks as a guide (normally, with pleated fabric, you would use threaded gathering lines as a guide, but for this project, we will just mark the socks with an erasable fabric marker).
3. Valley: area between the 'ribs'.
4. When working 'down' your design, floss should be above needle. When working 'up' your design, thread should be below the needle.
5. Your THREE marked lines around the top of the sock will be 3/8" apart.

Basic Stitches For This Project

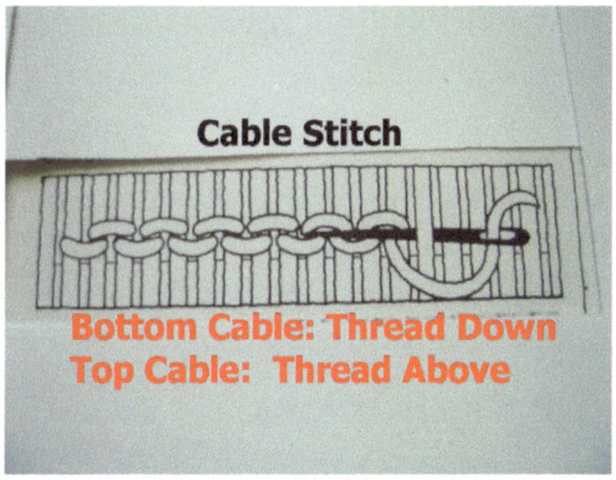

The Cable Stitch:

Bring needle & knotted thread up, from underneath, on the left side of the first rib to be stitched, approximately 1/3 of the way down from the top of the rib. With thread BELOW needle, take floss over this rib & pick up the top of the next rib on the right. Take needle back through to left side of this rib, as shown in picture. This is a Down/Bottom Cable.

With thread ABOVE needle, pick up top 1/3 of the NEXT rib, horizontally, from right to left. Pull the 2 ribs gently together. This stitch is referred to as an Up/Top Cable.

Stitches should be pulled firm, but not too tight. Keep the needle level and parallel to your marked line.

Continue across row, alternating thread position (up or down), on each stitch, ie. Thread UP/above needle to work a Top/Up Cable and Thread DOWN/below needle, to work a Down/Bottom Cable.

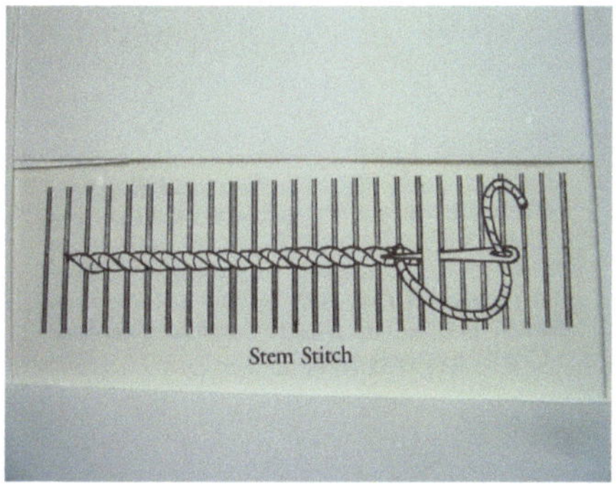

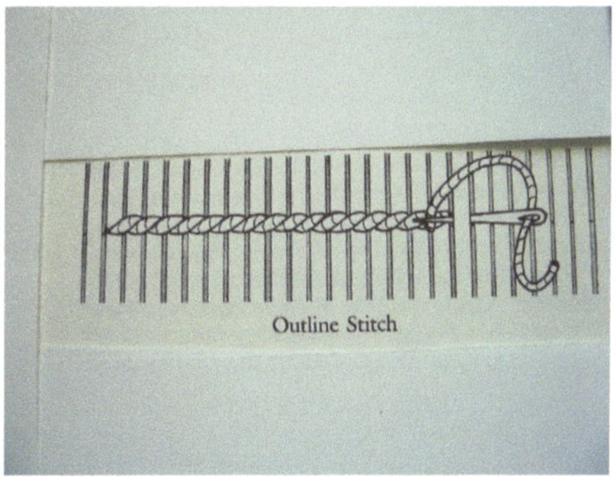

The Outline and Stem Stitch:

These stitches are worked similarly to the Cable Stitch, parallel to the marked line/gathering thread, except all stitches in a row are worked holding the thread in the same position. The thread is kept ABOVE the needle for the Outline Stitch & BELOW the needle for the Stem Stitch.

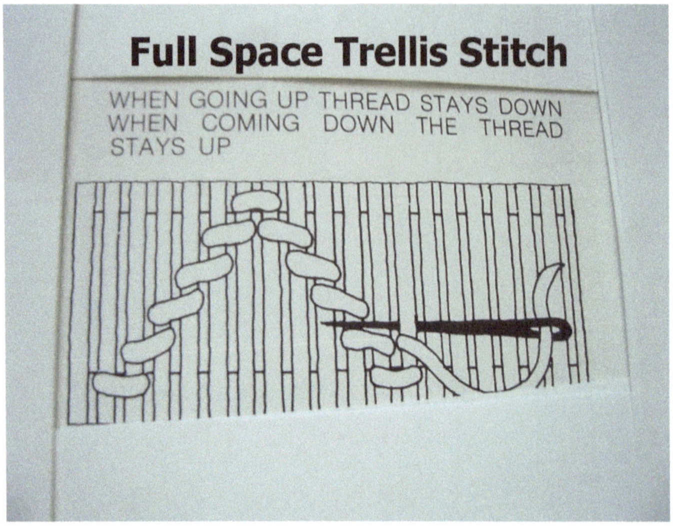

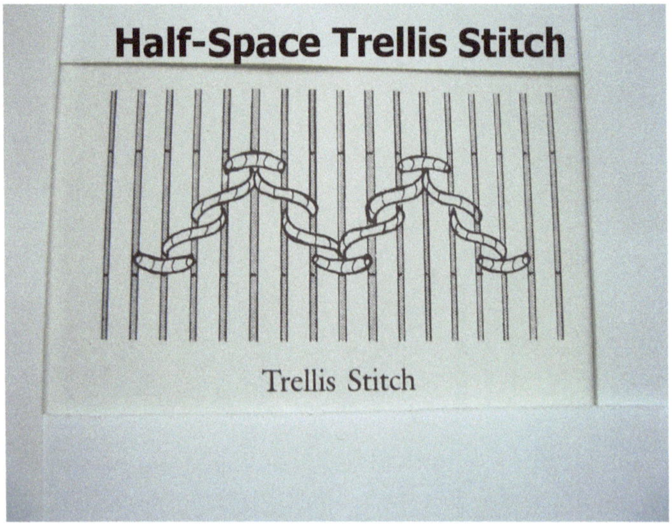

Trellis Stitch

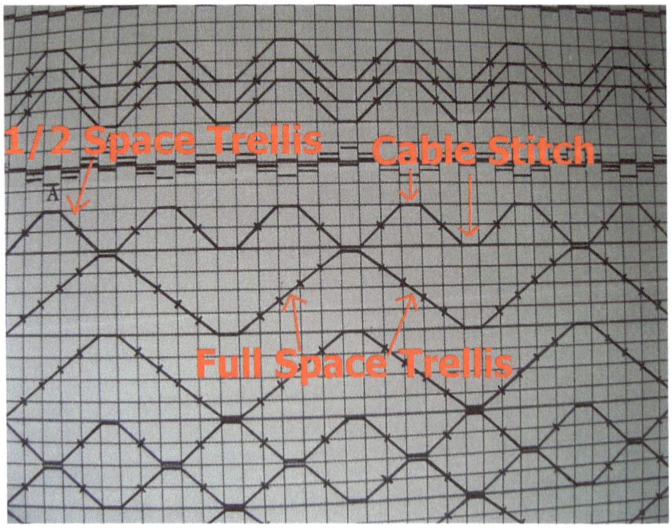

The Trellis Stitch:

The Trellis Stitch is a combination of the Cable Stitch and the Outline & Stem Stitches.
Work a Bottom Cable stitch at the marked line.
Next stitches: For a FULL SPACE Trellis Stitch, Stem Stitch is worked 1/4th of the way up the next rib, then 1/2 the way up the next rib, then 1/3 the way up the next rib and then a Stem Stitch just below the marked line in the next rib.
Next stitch: Make a Top Cable in the next rib.
Next Stitches: Work Outline Stitches coming down (the same way you went up with the Stem Stitch).
A HALF-SPACE Trellis Stitch is worked in the same manner but in only HALF the space, hence, half the stitches, ie. Two stitches as opposed to 4 stitches in the Full Space Trellis Stitch.
And remember, when going up, the thread stays below the needle and when coming down, the thread stays above the needle.

Thread UP for Up/Top Cable & Outline Stitch and Thread DOWN for Down/Bottom Cable & Stem Stitch.

ALSO: Thread DOWN when working upward on your design & thread UP when working downward on your design.

Smocked Hearts Pattern

Now that you're an expert in some of the basic smocking stitches, these little heart socks will be a breeze! Please Note: The socks I use our double cuffed. Mark them first on the double cuff, also placing a mark at the top area of your design, just for reference. (NB: To enable you to smock this area, you must uncuff them, turn them inside out & then you're able to see & work on your markings).

Cut a 15 inch piece of 6–strand floss. Separate each strand to uncurl and thread 3 single strands in your crewel needle & knot end.

From the bottom of the double cuff, measure up 3/8 inch with your erasable marker, all the way around the sock. Measure up 3/8 inch a second time from your first line and a third time. You now have 3 erasable lines around your sock. We will use these guide lines as our "gathering" lines. Now that your lines are marked, undo double cuff & turn inside out. You can see your top reference mark & your 3 guide lines.

First Row: Beginning at the back of the sock (heel area), on the top line (Line 1), with a Bottom Cable, stitch Cable Stitches all the way around the sock, meeting back at your beginning stitch.
Take needle down into a 'valley', between ribs, to the back of your work & knot off & cut floss.

Second Row: Begin at same rib as First Row, but one row (3/8") down, with a HALF TRELLIS Stitch. Continue around sock to your beginning stitch, take needle down into a valley to the back of your work & knot off & cut floss. Remember to only use HALF the width of the space.

Third Row: Begin at same rib as First and Second Rows, but one row (3/8") down with a FULL SPACE TRELLIS Stitch. Continue around sock to your beginning stitch, using the full width of the space. You will now see your hearts 'appear'!!
If your last 'heart' does not join perfectly at the back, due to insufficient 'ribs', just end your work by coming as close to the next heart as possible and take your needle down into a 'valley' to the back of your work, knot off & cut floss.

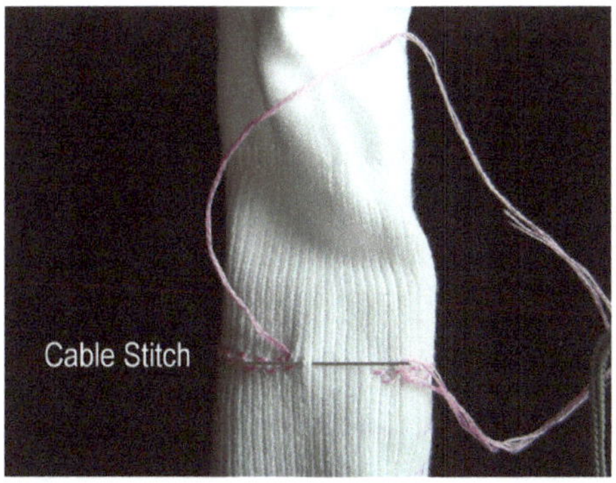

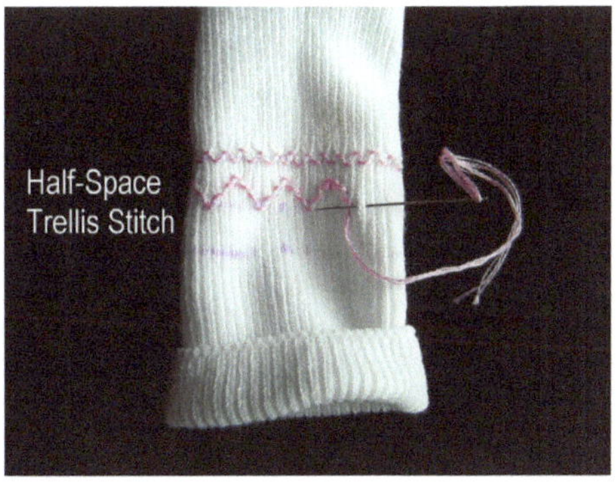

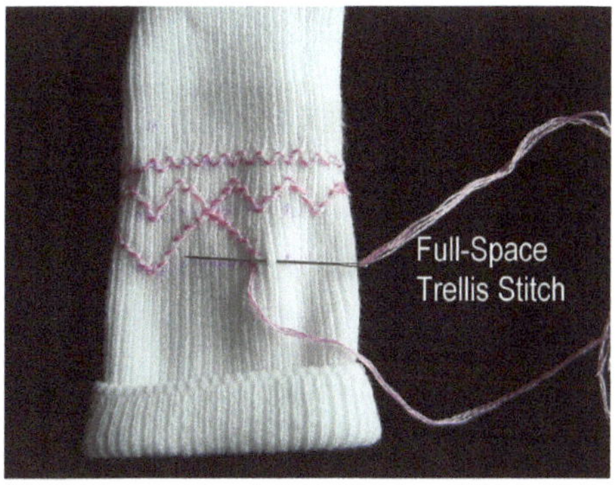

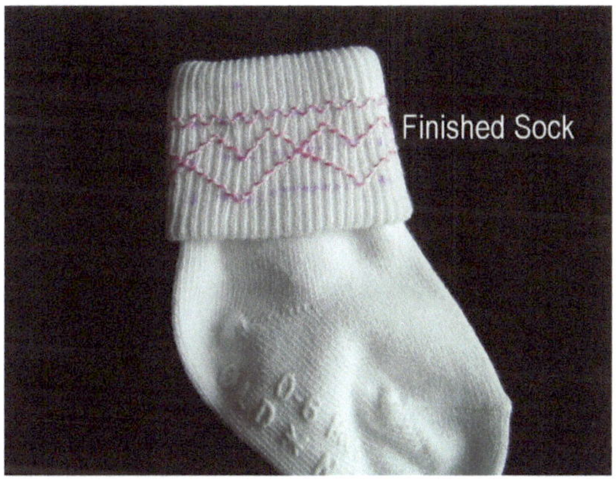

You will now turn your sock right-side-out & re-cuff, to see your beautiful smocked heart design!!

Happy Smocking!
Jan Czuba, Professional Reborn Artist & Seamstress
Fairy Dust Nursery – Home of Zooby Designs -- Baby Couture
For The Discerning Reborn Baby Doll
My website: www.fairydustbabies.com
Email: fairydust@cogeco.ca

Frilly Crib Shoes

Materials Required

(shoe length will fit a 3-inch foot – adjust pattern to fit larger or smaller)
1/4 Yard of 45" Fabric (will yield 3 pairs of shoes) (i.e. poly/cotton, light-weight denim, corduroy, velveteen, fake fur)
3/8 Yard of 1/4" Elastic
3/8 Yard of bias tape in matching colour – or make your own from same fabric
Double-Edged Frilly Lace (or preferred trim as desired)
Thread to match
Seam Allowance: 1/4 Inch

Sewing The Shoes

1. Trace pattern onto tissue paper (to keep your magazine intact). Cut out the pattern from fabric and with right sides together, pin bias tape around inside edge of SHOE TOP, with one edge along the seam line. Press bias tape to wrong side. (Picture #1)

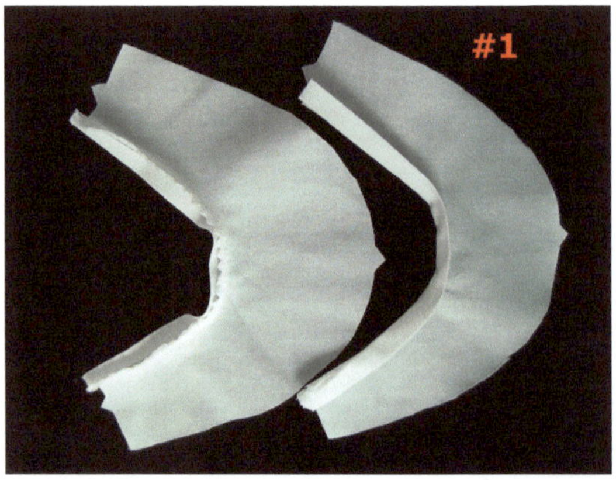

2. With bias tape pressed down, sew around the bottom edge of the bias tape to form the casing for elastic. Insert the elastic (approx. 6" in length) through the casing & stitch each end to secure elastic.

3. With right sides together, sew heel seam, matching notches, on Shoe Top. Press this seam open. On the outside, Top-stitch 1/8" from heal seam, on both sides, for a neater fit. (Picture #2)
NOTE: If you wish to sew a little appliqué, bow or button on the Shoe Top, sew it on prior to sewing the heal seam.

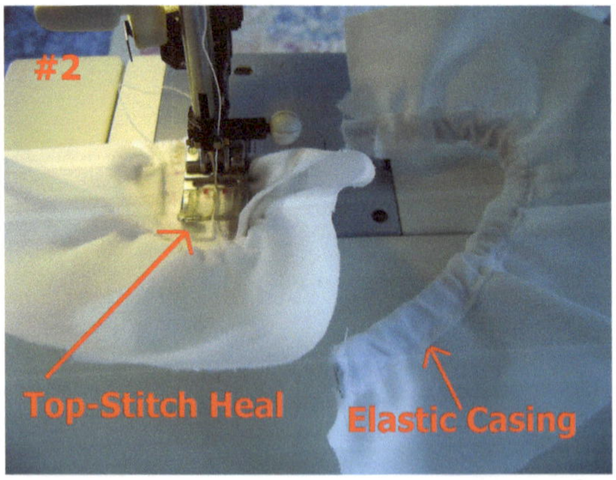

4. With right sides together, pin the Shoe Top and Sole together, matching notches and the dot on Sole, to the heal seam of the Shoe Top. Sew. For reinforcement, you can re-stitch, zig-zag or serge. (Picture #3)

5. Turn Crib Shoes to right side & gently press lower edge seam.

6. Beginning at back of heel, sew double-edged frilly lace to lower edge of shoe, ending at heel back.

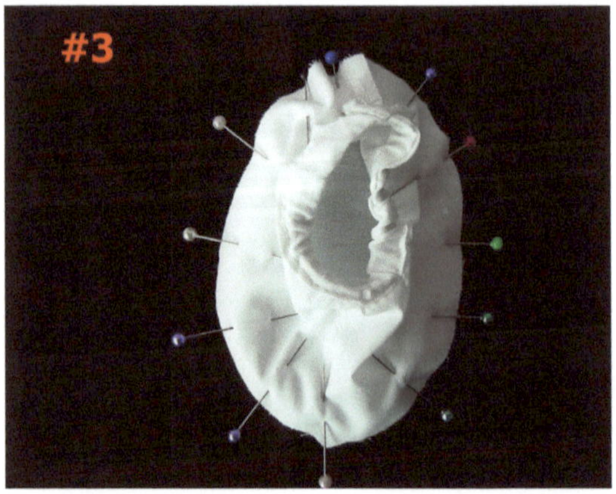

Happy Sewing!

Jan Czuba, Professional Reborn Artist & Seamstress
Fairy Dust Nursery – Home of Zooby Designs -- Baby Couture
For The Discerning Reborn Baby Doll
My website: www.fairydustbabies.com
Email: fairydust@cogeco.ca

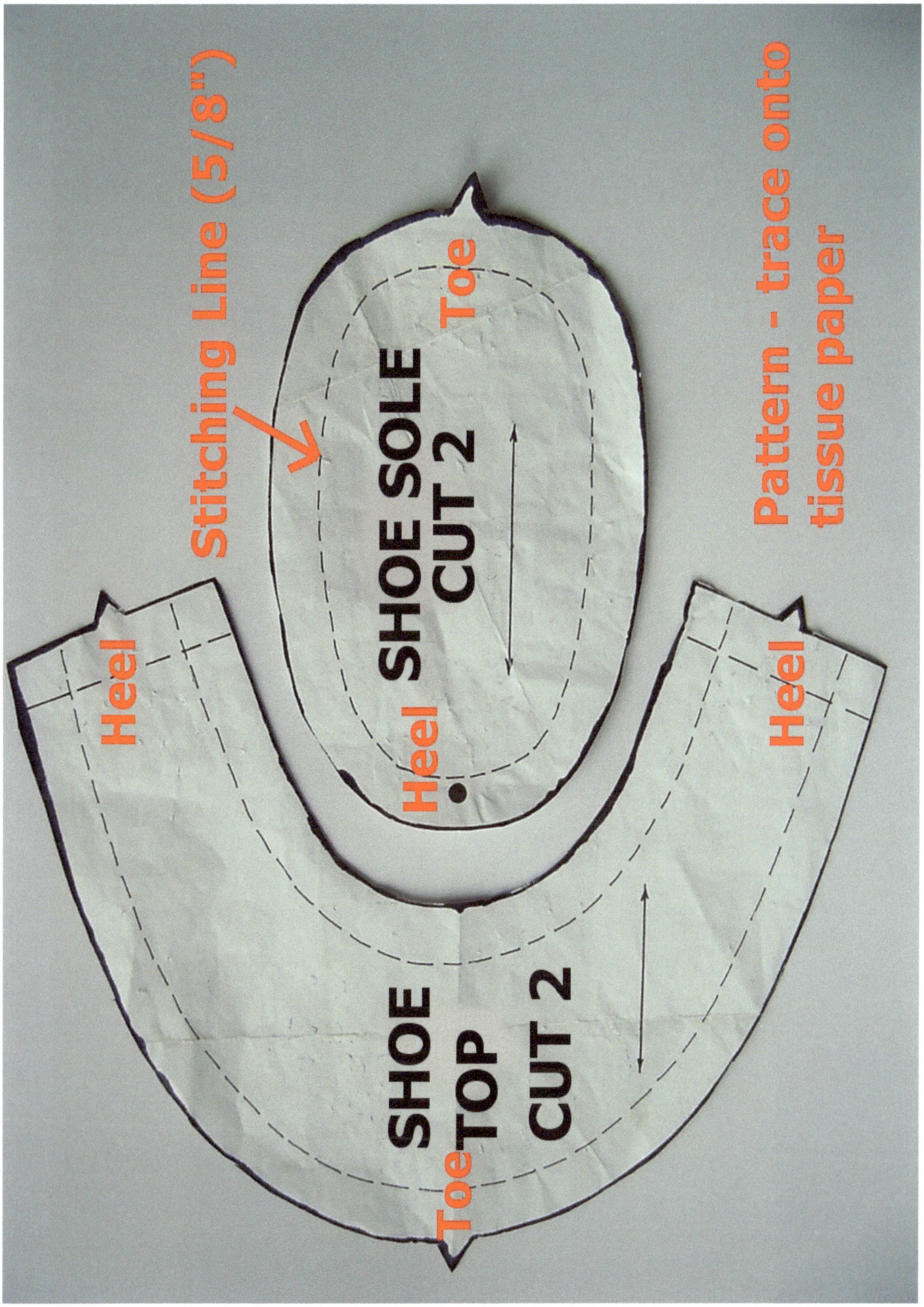
Stitching Line (5/8")
Pattern - trace onto
tissue paper
Toe
SHOE SOLE
CUT 2
Heel
Heel
Heel
Heel
SHOE
TOP
CUT 2
Toe

A Very Special Thank You to these Contributing Artists...

Cheryl Bage
www.adrianneinspiredcreations.com

Michele Barrow-Belisle
www.MasqueradeStudio.com

Cynthia Berrier
www.dollswestdesigns.com

Carol Carlile
www.crochethavenpresents.com/

Jan Czuba
www.fairydustbabies.com

Debbie Henshaw
www.theynevergrowupnursery.com

Donna Lee
www.donnaleeoriginals.com

Daria Makarenkova
ebay ID emwohl

Rachel Maynard
www.preciouslittlebabies.co.uk

Sheri McDonald
www.weewrapbabies.com

Ruth Seyffert
www.blessedbabycreations.com

Paulene Seymour
paulene@sasktel.net

Dorothy Steven
dotstinytots.blogspot.com/

Cristy Stone
www.xtremedolls.com/

Stephanie Sullivan
hunnybunsnursery.com/

www.LifelikeDollsMag.com

Visit us online to...

- Purchase back issues
- Order subscriptions
- Get affordable advertising
- Read interesting articles
- Enter contests
- Read the blog
- Check the event calendar
- Learn about upcoming classes
- Read the call for submissions
- Exchange links
- Become an affiliate